Savoring New Eng

Volume _

Daytrips from Boston by Public Transportation

By
Irene V. Schensted

With Illustrations by Nancy Chalmers and Susan Krohn

NEO Press, Box 32, Peaks Island, Maine 04108

For Marsha, from whose Brookline house many of these expeditions began, and in memory of my mother, Rose Verona

Library of Congress Catalog Card Number 96-92810

Cover drawing, Sailboats on the Charles, by Susan Krohn. Complete Art Credits on page XII.

ISBN 0-911014-26-8

NEO Press, Box 32, Peaks Island, Maine 04108

PREFACE

The Reason Why. I embarked on the series *Savoring New England Car Free* because I was tired of reading guidebooks that began with "take highway such and such" or "walk" books that assumed that you would drive to the trail head, or "bicycling" books that had you loading your bike onto your car to go to a bike trail.

Some Description with Emphasis on Differences. This book and others of the series describe visiting attractions start-to-finish by a combination of public transportation and walking or perhaps renting a bicycle near a public transit terminal in places where traffic is not too aggressive. You get off the bus, or train, or trolley, or boat, and spring along car free and carefree to explore. It's a way of travel that I love, and I hope to reach many kindred souls. The description of a walk begins typically at a train or bus station or a street car stop or a boat dock. What does the situation look like near the station? What are the support services that you encounter -- food, restrooms -- on the way to an attraction? From our view, superhighways are obstacles, and our concern is where can you cross safely. By "a few minutes away" we mean a comfortable *walk* of a few minutes. And if a highlight is some distance away from the intercity transit terminal then we supply information about how you might use the local transit system to assist you, or, if the distance is such that walking might still appeal to you, what the car traffic situation is like, and whether there are sidewalks or a safe place to walk. Often walks of a few miles to an attraction could be ideal -- exhilarating exercise, lovely views -- if only the cars weren't in the way. I usually give the locations of libraries and town halls because they make good information and rest stops.

A Hope. By standing up and being counted as being among those who love trains, trolleys, boats, and buses for actual transport (not visiting them in museums located in remote highway places), I hope that my readers and I can contribute to balancing a transportation system which at present is almost entirely designed for expediting car travel. I believe that everyone (car drivers included) would benefit from government effort devoted to fostering public transport between recreation centers and population centers, and to building separate, pleasant, and safe lanes for walking and bicycling beside roads and on bridges, or, when necessary, to slowing car traffic to allow those traveling by other modes to share the road safely.

Outline of Series. As planned, the *Savoring New England Car-Free* series will contain three Volumes. This book, *Daytrips from Boston by Public Transportation* (PT), the first of the series, includes highlights in Boston, Cambridge, and Brookline, along with a description of the Boston Rapid Transit and Commuter Rail system (the MBTA), then PT daytrips from Boston to attractions in Concord, Lexington, Plymouth, Quincy, and Lowell, and then Marblehead, Salem, Gloucester, Rockport, and Manchester on Boston's North Shore, and then in Providence and Newport, Rhode Island, and other sites on Narragansett Bay, and finally trips to Portsmouth, New Hampshire. The PT times from Boston are usually less than an hour, and not more than 1 1/2 hours. In Volume 2, we describe public transit trips to attractions further from Boston: to Provincetown and other places in Cape Cod, to Martha's Vineyard, Nantucket, and Block Island, and to Portland, Maine and other places along the Maine coast. In each case we follow up with descriptions of attractions that you can reach -- by walking or bicycling or by local PT -- from lodgings in these other bases. In Volume 3 we shall go inland to western New England, and travel from bases there.

More Description. Throughout the series there is a great deal of historical narrative -- about early explorers and Native Americans, the Puritans and their influence on our Nation's institutions, how and why New England spearheaded the American Revolution, its almost mythical maritime past, its role in the Industrial Revolution, the anti-slavery and women's suffrage movements, and so on -- because these subjects fascinate nearly everyone, myself included, who lives in or visits New England. On every walk, whether urban, or to outdoor recreation by cliffs and beaches or along mountain trails, the buildings and landscape remind one constantly of the region's early history. And the many historic parks and outstanding museums, and venerable but thriving educational institutions, contain so much that illuminates the Nation's beginnings and growth. But I like to think that I haven't neglected present day New England, which intertwines with the old -- its new enterprises, its lively shops, parks, and art galleries, vibrant music and theatre, its terrific restaurants, and its ethnically diverse neighborhoods.

A Caution and Invitation. The series was begun some years ago when I explored all the places described starting either from my sister's house in Brookline, Massachusetts or from my own on Peaks Island, Maine. But I had to set the work aside for some years. The past year was spent in updating the material for this first volume. But even as I updated, I noted that by the end of the year some of the remarks were already outdated!! And by the time you read this more may have changed. So I hope my readers will be forgiving (and will check PT schedules, especially the last evening return times), and that they will inform me of errors that they've found, and give their descriptions of highlights of their own start-to-finish car-free adventures, and become my co-authors in future volumes of the series.

ACKNOWLEDGEMENTS

I am grateful to friends and relatives for helping me in many ways in readying this book for press: proof-reading and criticism, information and suggestions, companionship on car free trips, explaining the mysteries of my Claris Works, encouragement and inspiration, and forbearance and patience during the long preparation period. It is a pleasure to thank Mary Verona, Rose and Gene Wilson, Robin Kowel-Kern, Jennifer Gordon, Sally Walker, Craige Schensted, Elizabeth Ryan, Lynn Heinemann, Joan Larkin, Gus, Carolyn, and Mimi Rabson, Deena and Maurice Gordon, Maurice O'Reilly, Norm Rasulis, Annie Romanychyn, Mary Lavendier, Barabara King, Mary Lou Kelley, Marianna Rowe, Shirley Harrison, Sarah Gold, and last but not least, Susan Scandlen, who invented the slogan *Car-free is Carefree.*

Of course, I take full responsibility for all errors and deficiencies.

I am also very grateful to Nancy Chalmers and the late Susan Krohn for their fine illustrations, which so enhance the appearance of the book. Their enthusiasm for the work often inspirited me. See page XII for more on art credits.

During the course of preparing this book, I made extensive use of the excellent collections of the Portland and Boston public libraries, and benefited from the prompt response to my inquiries of several New England tourist bureaus, chambers of commerce, and public agencies, including: Greater Boston Visitors and Convention Bureau; Rhode Island Bureau of Tourism; Rhode Island Transit Authority (RIPTA); Massachusetts Bay Transit Authority (MBTA); and the chambers of commerce and tourist bureaus of: Marblehead; Salem; Plymouth; Rockport; Gloucester; and Newport County. (Addresses and phone numbers are given in the information sections of the text.) The books etc. that I used while preparing this guidebook are listed in the bibliography.

IV   A Miscellany of Updates
(Written in fall 1996, as we go to press)

World Wide Web Addresses.   This past year (1995-1996), as this book of the series was being prepared for the press, the World Wide Web (www) has emerged as a major method for accessing the Internet. Many organizations and institutions -- libraries, museums, transit authorities, etc. etc. -- have constructed World Wide Web sites for dispensing information. For the many who now have access to the World Wide Web, either through their own computers, schools or workplaces, or at public libraries, www addresses can be excellent supplements to the telephone numbers listed in the text. **On page 242**, along with a collection of useful telephone numbers, we give some www addresses. At the **MBTA web address** given there, you'll find maps as well as schedule and fare information.

By the time you read this book, the **Boston Harbor Islands** (see pages 57, 58), may be adopted as part of the National Historic Park system.

Poetry Lovers Rejoice! A program sponsored jointly by the MBTA, the Poetry Association of America, and the American Institute of Graphic Arts will soon bring stanzas to T trains, trolleys, and buses, to supplement the great variety of publications T travelers now bring with them.   Poem selections (to be replaced each month) will be made from the works of local poets including Nobel Prize winners Seamus Heaney, who spends four months a year away from his home in Ireland teaching at Harvard, and native son Derek Walcott. In addition, there will be poetry laden posters and bill boards at various T stops. (This information was garnered mostly from the *Boston Globe,* Sept. 1996.)

At a corner of School and Washington Streets, near the Old Corner Bookstore and the Old South Meeting House on the Freedom Trail (see pages 21, 22), is the **future site of the Irish Famine Memorial**, a reminder of the potato famine that brought to Boston the immigrants whose descendants now form 25% of Greater Boston's population and contribute so much to its political and cultural life. On a recent visit, Irish President Mary Robinson referred to her arrival in Boston as a "homecoming".

A map at the MBTA's web site shows **projected plans to extend the T to South Shore towns** (like Plymouth). Hooray! (More updates on page 108.)

Lament for the A Green Line. Do the tracks have to go? No!! No!! This line should be restored with a center strip capacious enough for passenger safety.

CONTENTS

Chapter 5
TO PORTSMOUTH, NH CAR FREE, 205-224

VIII   Contents

Bibliography, 225-227

Index, 229-240

Updates and Additional Remarks. These are strewn throughout as follows.

LIST OF MAPS

Chapter 4
To Rhode Island Car Free

Chapter 5
TO PORTSMOUTH, NH CAR FREE

List of Abbreviations and Explanation of Symbols

AIA, American Institute of Architects
AMC, Appalachian Mountain Club
Ave., Avenue (Av. is also used.)
CATA, Cape Ann Transit Authority
CC, Convention Center (as in Hynes CC)
Coop (also the Harvard Coop), Harvard Cooperative Society Department Store
Ctr., Center
Gov. Ctr, Government Center
ICA, Institute for Contemporary Art
LRTA, Lowell Region Transit Authority
Mass., Massachusetts
MBTA, Massachusetts Bay Transit Authority
MDC, Metropolitan District Commission
MFA, Museum of Fine Arts
MGH, Massachusetts General Hospital
MIT, Massachusetts Institute of Technology
NE, New England
PSNC, Preservation Society of Newport County
PT, Public Transportation
RI, Rhode Island
RIPTA, Rhode Island Public Transit Authority
RISD, Rhode Island School of Design
SPNEA, Society for the Preservation of New England Antiquities
Sq., Square
St., Street
T (usually *the* T), MBTA (see above). Ⓣ is used to mark subway or commuter train stations on maps.
Tech Coop, MIT branch of the Coop (see above)
U., University (as in Suffolk U.)
UMass., University of Massachusetts
URI, University of Rhode Island
On maps rooted arrows are used to indicate the type of activity in a district. The root word gives the clue. Thus bank ⤙ indicates financial activities; and theatre ⤙ indicates a theatre district, etc.

Art Credits

The drawing of Sailboats on the Charles on the outer covers is by Susan Krohn. All the drawings on the following pages are by Susan Krohn: 1, 4, 17, 18, 20, 22, 23, 41, 42, 47, 48, 50, 51, 53, 55, 57, 62, 64, 65, 66, 68, 71, 83, 84, 85, 86, 100, 109, 111, 113, 122, 127, 130, 131, 133, 134, 135, 136, 137, 138, 139, 140, 148, 174, 179, 180, 184, 187, 192, 193, 204. In addition the following are by Susan Krohn: the horseman on 28, the children at the Aquarium on 40, and Abbot Hall on 115.

All the drawings on the following pages are by Nancy Chalmers: 2, 6, 7, 12, 14, 19, 24, 25, 27, 30, 36, 37, 44, 45, 56, 59, 61, 63, 95, 96, 102, 103, 106, 107, 117, 149, 183, 186, 188, 198, 203, 205, 207, 211, 213, 214, 215, 220, 222, 223. In addition the following are by Nancy Chalmers: the USS Constitution on 28, Rowe's Wharf on 40, the Spirit of '76 on 115, the Union Congregational Church Entrance on 182.

All the drawings on the following pages are by Irene Schensted: 5, 13, 16, 31, 35, 39, 72, 79, 90, 91, 92, 94, 101, 110, 114, 116, 119, 120, 123, 124, 126, 128, 143, 145, 146, 147, 150, 154, 155, 156, 157, 159, 160, 162, 168, 169, 170, 171, 172, 173, 175, 181, 189, 191, 194, 217, 228. In addition, the church pulpit on 182 is by Irene Schensted.

The drawings on pages 81, 82, 88, and 89 are by Nancy Hansen and appeared originally in the *Songbook of the American Revolution*, edited by Carolyn Rabson.

CHAPTER 1
BOSTON,
CAMBRIDGE,
BROOKLINE

    Here we write of the history and highlights of the three towns and the public transportation system-- intercity transport and the MBTA streetcars, trains, and buses-- that will take us on all the trips in later chapters of this book.

BOSTON, CAMBRIDGE, BROOKLINE

ORGANIZATION OF THIS CHAPTER

Boston, Cambridge, and Brookline are so closely intertwined historically and so closely integrated by public transportation, that it seems natural to include them all in our first chapter. After a brief introduction to Boston, we shall describe the area's public transportation system, which you'll use in the trips we describe in Volume 1, and then we shall go on to Boston highlights, then Cambridge, and then Brookline. **Lodgings for all three will be included at the end of the chapter.**

BOSTON FOUNDED A.D. 1630

The Puritans Arrive. Picture Inspired by a Relief in Boston Common

BOSTON, AN INTRODUCTION

Boston is the great city at the center of New England and **the site of many of the country's leading educational and cultural institutions.** It is the capital of the Commonwealth of Massachusetts, the seat of Suffolk County, and the New England regional center for several Federal agencies. Boston proper has only about 600,000 residents, but the Greater Boston area, comprised of about 100 tightly interwoven communities, has a population of over 3 million, or about one fourth that of all New England. **For the public traveler, Boston is the best *here* from which to get *there* by public transportation.**

Like all great cities, Boston is a place of opportunity and excitement. Young people arrive from all over the world to study at the more than sixty schools of higher learning in the area, including some of the world's most prestigious. Its many medical centers, and research and consulting institutes are also of global repute. It's a place where books and learning are important. of intellectual and artistic ferment, and also **a generally delightful place to be, with a rich variety of urban attractions set amidst three centuries of history**.

Boston had its beginnings in the Great Puritan Migration of the 1630's, when successive waves of Puritans, organized as the **Massachusetts Bay Company**, and seeking to live according to their own religious values, **founded Boston, Cambridge, and a string of North Shore settlements.** Unlike the Pilgrims, who had settled in Plymouth ten years earlier, and who had arrived impoverished and few in number (about 100 souls), the Puritans were numerous (in the thousands), and many were wealthy and well educated. They came with considerable possessions, servants, and livestock, and among them were artisans proficient in the skills necessary for building cities in the "Wildernesse." **The Puritan migration was the largest English New World colonization until that time**. The most precious possession that they carried with them was their charter, obtained, no one knows how, from Charles I, which, unlike Royal charters previously granted to settlers, **allowed them to elect their own Governor and make their own laws. Their first elected Governor was John Winthrop**, who chose to settle on the beautiful Shawmut peninsula, overlooking a wide harbor sheltered by many islands. **It was named Boston, after the town in Lincolnshire, England** from which many leading Puritans had come. It was to remain always the seat of government of the Massachusetts Bay Colony and Province. **By the mid-eighteenth century, it had grown into the *Metropolis of North America*, the greatest English seaport outside of the British Isles,** from which thousands of ships sailed annually.

In Boston today, the 17th, 18th, 19th, and 20th centuries all mingle in a tightly woven tapestry. The City is crammed with historic sites, and the Greater Boston area has more of them. For visitors who want to understand how this nation began and grew, they are the area's greatest attraction.

Boston is a walking city, with business, government, and theater districts closely knotted about its historical central parks, the **Common and Public Garden**. The best way to experience it is the way that we shall -- by a combination of walking and public transportation. To auto drivers, Boston is continuous frustration, but to those afoot it is unceasing delight.

INFORMATION

For an excellent guidebook write to **GREATER BOSTON CONVENTION AND VISITORS BUREAU, P.O. Box 990468, Prudential Tower, Suite 400, Boston, MA 02199-0468. Call (617) 536-4100 or (800) 888-5515.** In Boston there are information centers at the following locations: on **Boston Common** near the Park St. T stop on the Green and Red Lines; at **Boston City Hall** near the Government Center T stop on the Green and Blue Lines; at the **National Park Service Visitors Center, 15 State St.**, on the **Freedom Trail** and near the Park St. T stop (Green and Red Lines) and also near the State St. T stop (Orange and Blue Lines), **call (617) 242-5643**; at the **Visitors Kiosk** at the **Prudential Center**, near the Copley and Hynes/ICA stops on the Green Line. The literature that you receive from the Visitors Bureau will undoubtedly have a list of events. Every Thursday, the *BOSTON GLOBE* publishes its *CALENDAR*, a magazine supplement devoted to events and attractions in the Boston area. For events in Cambridge get the *HARVARD GAZETTE* at the **Holyoke Information Center** near the **Harvard Square T Station** on the Red Line. **Boston By Phone, call (800) 374-7400**, offers 24 hour toll free information on lodgings, attractions, transportation, performing arts and nightlife, and various visitor services. For **World Wide Web surfers**, an address for Boston arts events is http://www.boston.com/home.htm **For T information, see our next section.**

My favorite Boston events are the **Boston Marathon**, held every Patriot's Day (April 19th) to celebrate the "shot heard around the world," and the summer **Esplanade Concerts**, all free.

Near South Station, Financial District high rises overlook traditional Waterfront pursuits. Scene on Northern Ave. near Atlantic.

BOSTON'S PUBLIC TRANSIT SYSTEM

We begin by describing the location of the **Intercity Transportation Terminals.** These are the stations that you will arrive at if you are not already in Boston, and they are also the terminals from which we shall start on some of the day trips to be described in this book. Then we shall describe the **MBTA (Massachusetts Bay Transportation Authority** or briefly, **the T**) system of trolleys, subway and commuter trains, and buses, which we'll use for trips in Boston, Cambridge, and Brookline, and in Greater Boston, including ones to the North Shore.

Intercity Transportation Terminals

Logan International Airport. Logan Airport, call **(800) 23-LOGAN**, located in East Boston, is connected to all points of the globe, and is served by all the major airlines, and some minor ones, too. There are fleets of taxis and limousines, and a water shuttle, to get you to the City Center, and there are also **free MBTA airport shuttle buses**, which, **at frequent intervals**, circle the airport stopping at various terminals and take passengers to the **Airport T Station on the Blue Line,** where you can take an inbound train directly to Boston's Center or make changes for Cambridge or Brookline.

Reflections in a Trolley

Train Stations. Boston has three train stations. The largest is South Station at the corner of Atlantic Ave and Summer St., amid the highrises of the financial district, on the **South Station T stop on the Red Line.** It is the terminal for the Boston to Washington, D.C. **AMTRAK trains (call (800) USA-RAIL or (617) 482-3660 for AMTRAK information)** and is also the terminal for several **T commuter trains (call (617) 722-3200 for T information). Near the train station is the handsome new South Station Bus Terminal used by several intercity bus lines (see below).** The **Back Bay** train station, which is a stop on the T's Orange Line, **is an AMTRAK train stop as well as a stop for some T commuter trains.** It is located on **Dartmouth Street just a few blocks from Copley Square** and the Copley Green Line T stop. So if you are in an area served by a Green Line, it is probably most convenient to get off at Copley and walk. **The third train station is North Station** which is across Causeway Street from the **North Station T stop on the Green and Orange Lines**. It is the terminal for several T commuter trains. Both South Station and Back Bay Station have recently undergone extensive refurbishing. **South Station offers an extensive food court**, news stands, book shops, and other services, even free entertainment programs. The other stations have more modest services. All three stations have rest rooms. Although not all cars on a commuter train have restrooms, each train that I have been on seems to have had at least one car with a rest room.

Intercity Bus Stations. Several intercity bus lines operate from **the beautiful new South Station Bus Terminal** at the South Station Red Line T stop. They are: **Greyhound Bus Lines, call (800) 231-2222 or (617) 526-1810; Vermont Transit, (800) 552-8737; Concord Trailways, (617) 426-8080 or (800) 639-3317; Plymouth and Brockton St. Railway, (617) 773-9401 or (508) 746-0378; Peter Pan Bus Lines, (800) 343-9999 or (617) 426-7838; Bonanza Bus Lines (617) 720-4110 or (800) 556-3815; C and J Trailways, (800) 258-7111; American Eagle (800) 453-5040; Bloom Bus Lines, (800) 323-3009.**

South Station

Boarding a Green Line Trolley

at Park St. T stop

NANCY

Getting About in Greater Boston; A Brief Description of the MBTA
   A combination of walking and using the MBTA (the T, for short), is the best way of getting about in Greater Boston. The official name of the T is: MASSACHUSETTS BAY TRANSPORTATION AUTHORITY. **For information call (617) 722-3200 or (800) 392-6100, or, if you are hearing impaired TDD 722-5146.**

   The T consists of three main components: (1) **a rapid transit system of light rail vehicles** (street cars or trolleys) **and trains** serving Downtown Boston and the inner suburbs; (2) **commuter trains originating at South Station or North Station** (see page 6), serving the outer suburbs; (3) **a supplementary system of buses and trackless trolleys.** Schematic maps of the rapid transit and commuter rail systems are given on pages 8 and 9. The most heavily used component of the T is the rapid transit system, **whose four lines are color coded Red, Green, Blue, and Orange.** Our maps are not in color but for easy identification the lines are labeled by strings of letters -- GG.. for Green, RR.. for Red, OO.. for Orange, BB.. for Blue, CC.. for Commuter Rail.

   The Downtown section of the T, which is underground, was built in 1897 and is **the Nation's oldest subway. The four lines intersect in pairs Downtown**, so you can transfer from one to the other. The intersections are at: **Park St. (Red, Green)**; **Government Center (Green, Blue)**; **Downtown Crossing (Red, Orange)**; **State St. (Orange, Blue)**. In listing attractions, we shall give the nearby T stops. In the Downtown area, the T stops are quite close to each other, and sometimes if you are

(continued on page 12)

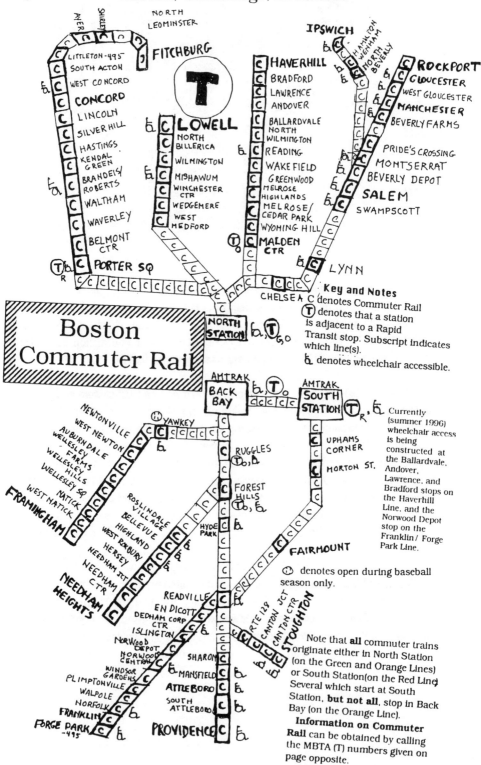

NORTH LEOMINSTER

FITCHBURG

T

IPSWICH

ROCKPORT
GLOUCESTER
WEST GLOUCESTER
MANCHESTER
BEVERLY FARMS

LITTLETON-495
SOUTH ACTON
WEST CONCORD
CONCORD
LINCOLN
SILVER HILL
HASTINGS
KENDAL GREEN
BRANDEIS/ ROBERTS
WALTHAM
WAVERLEY
BELMONT CTR
PORTER SQ

LOWELL
NORTH BILLERICA
WILMINGTON
MISHAWUM
WINCHESTER CTR
WEDGEMERE
WEST MEDFORD

HAVERHILL
BRADFORD
LAWRENCE
ANDOVER
BALLARDVALE
NORTH WILMINGTON
READING
WAKEFIELD
GREENWOOD
MELROSE HIGHLANDS
MELROSE/ CEDAR PARK
WYOMING HILL
MALDEN CTR

HAMILTON WENHAM
NORTH BEVERLY

PRIDE'S CROSSING
MONTSERRAT
BEVERLY DEPOT
SALEM
SWAMPSCOTT

LYNN

CHELSEA

Boston Commuter Rail

NORTH STATION

Key and Notes

C denotes Commuter Rail

(T) denotes that a station is adjacent to a Rapid Transit stop. Subscript indicates which line(s).

denotes wheelchair accessible.

AMTRAK
BACK BAY

AMTRAK
SOUTH STATION

NEWTONVILLE
WEST NEWTON
AUBURNDALE
WELLESLEY FARMS
WELLESLEY HILLS
WELLESLEY SQ
NATICK
WEST NATICK
FRAMINGHAM

YAWKEY

RUGGLES

FOREST HILLS

UPHAMS CORNER
MORTON ST.

Currently (summer 1996) wheelchair access is being constructed at the Ballardvale, Andover, Lawrence, and Bradford stops on the Haverhill Line, and the Norwood Depot stop on the Franklin/ Forge Park Line.

ROSLINDALE VILLAGE
BELLEVUE
HIGHLAND
WEST ROXBURY
HERSEY
NEEDHAM JCT
NEEDHAM CTR
NEEDHAM HEIGHTS

HYDE PARK

FAIRMOUNT

⊙ denotes open during baseball season only.

READVILLE
ENDICOTT
DEDHAM CORP CTR
ISLINGTON
NORWOOD DEPOT
NORWOOD CENTRAL
WINDSOR GARDENS
PLIMPTONVILLE
WALPOLE
NORFOLK
FRANKLIN
FORGE PARK -495

SHARON
MANSFIELD
ATTLEBORO
SOUTH ATTLEBORO
PROVIDENCE

RTE 128
CANTON JCT
CANTON CTR
STOUGHTON

Note that **all** commuter trains originate either in North Station (on the Green and Orange Lines) or South Station(on the Red Line). Several which start at South Station, **but not all**, stop in Back Bay (on the Orange Line).

Information on Commuter Rail can be obtained by calling the MBTA (T) numbers given on page opposite.

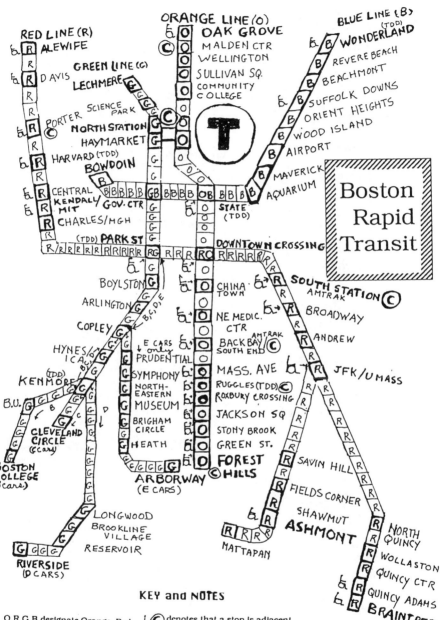

RED LINE (R)
ALEWIFE
DAVIS
PORTER
Science Park
NORTH STATION
HAYMARKET
HARVARD (TDD)
BOWDOIN
CENTRAL
KENDALL/MIT
CHARLES/MGH
(TDD) PARK ST
BOYLSTON
ARLINGTON
COPLEY
HYNES/ICA
KENMORE (TDD)
B.U.
CLEVELAND CIRCLE (C cars)
BOSTON COLLEGE (B cars)
LONGWOOD
BROOKLINE VILLAGE
RESERVOIR
RIVERSIDE (D CARS)

GREEN LINE (G)
LECHMERE

ORANGE LINE (O)
OAK GROVE
MALDEN CTR
WELLINGTON
SULLIVAN SQ.
COMMUNITY COLLEGE
GOV. CTR
STATE (TDD)
DOWNTOWN CROSSING
CHINA TOWN
NE MEDIC. CTR
BACK BAY SOUTH END AMTRAK
E CARS only
PRUDENTIAL
SYMPHONY
NORTH-EASTERN
MUSEUM
BRIGHAM CIRCLE
HEATH
ARBORWAY (E CARS)
FOREST HILLS
MASS. AVE
RUGGLES (TDD)
ROXBURY CROSSING
JACKSON SQ
STONY BROOK
GREEN ST.

BLUE LINE (B)
WONDERLAND (TDD)
REVERE BEACH
BEACHMONT
SUFFOLK DOWNS
ORIENT HEIGHTS
WOOD ISLAND
AIRPORT
MAVERICK
AQUARIUM

Boston Rapid Transit

SOUTH STATION AMTRAK
BROADWAY
ANDREW
JFK/UMASS
SAVIN HILL
FIELDS CORNER
SHAWMUT
ASHMONT
MATTAPAN
NORTH QUINCY
WOLLASTON
QUINCY CTR
QUINCY ADAMS
BRAINTREE

KEY and NOTES

O,R,G,B designate Orange, Red, Green and Blue Lines respectively. ♿ indicates wheelchair accessibility. Currently (summer 1996) access for wheel chairs is being constructed at Andrew and Quincy Center stops on the Red Line, and Wellington and Sullivan Sq. on the Orange Line. *TDD* indicates TDD service is available for the hearing impaired.

© denotes that a stop is adjacent to a Commuter Rail station.
After Kenmore, the outbound B Green Line cars make several stops along Commonwealth Ave. The C cars make stops along Beacon St., and the D cars make several stops in Brookline and Newton (not listed in the above schematic map). After Symphony, the E cars stop along Huntington and Centre.

For **MBTA (T) Information** call: **(617) 722-3200** or toll free **(800) 392-6100** or if hearing impaired **TDD - 722-5146**

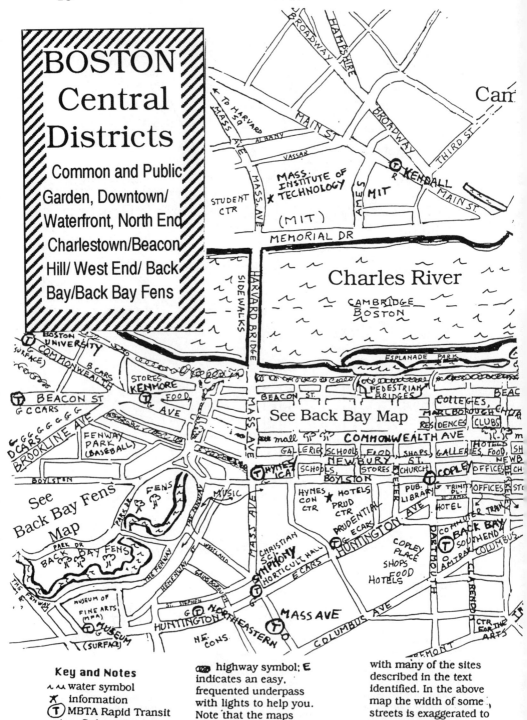

BOSTON Central Districts

Common and Public Garden, Downtown/ Waterfront, North End Charlestown/Beacon Hill/ West End/ Back Bay/Back Bay Fens

Key and Notes

∧ ∿ water symbol
✗ information
ⓉMBTA Rapid Transit stop. Subscripts G,R, O,B indicate which line.
🎋🎋 greenery symbol

🚗 highway symbol: **E** indicates an easy, frequented underpass with lights to help you. Note that the maps referred to are enlargements with more. streets indicated and

with many of the sites described in the text identified. In the above map the width of some streets is exaggerated to enhance legibility of street names.

Rooted arrows ⤝⤞ indicate type of district.

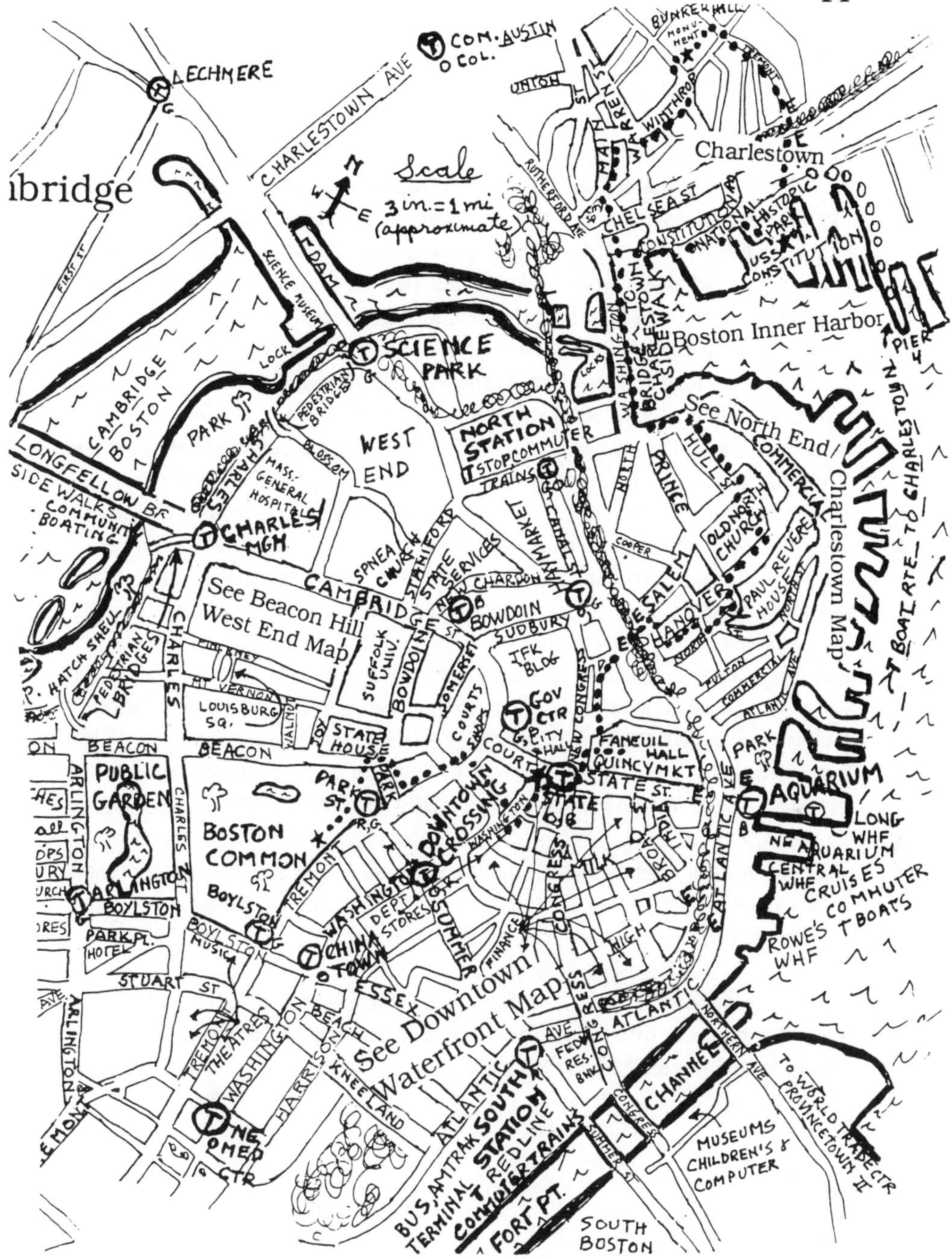

BUNKER HILL
MONU-MENT
COM. AUSTIN
COL.
LECHMERE
UNION
CHARLESTOWN AVE
Charlestown
bridge
Scale
3 in. = 1 mi (approximate)
RUTHERFORD AVE
CHELSEA ST
CONSTITUTION
NATIONAL HISTORIC PARK
USS CONSTITUTION
FIRST ST
SCIENCE MUSEUM
DAM
CHARLESTOWN BRIDGE
WASHINGTON
Boston Inner Harbor
PIER 4
LOCK
SCIENCE PARK
CAMBRIDGE BOSTON
PEDESTRIAN BRIDGE
PARK
CHARLES
See North End/ Charlestown Map
NORTH STATION
T STOP COMMUTER TRAINS
WEST END
MASS. GENERAL HOSPITAL
BLOSSOM
LONGFELLOW BR
SIDEWALKS
COMMUNITY BOATING
CHARLES MGH
NORTH
PRINCE
HULL
COMMERCIAL
OLD NORTH CHURCH
T BOAT RTE TO CHARLESTOWN
HAYMARKET
SPNEA CHURCH
STANIFORD
STATE SERVICES
CHARDON
CAMBRIDGE ST
See Beacon Hill West End Map
BOWDOIN
SUDBURY
JFK BLDG
SALEM
HANOVER
PAUL REVERE HOUSE
COOPER
FULTON
COMMERCIAL
ATLANTIC AVE
SUFFOLK UNIV.
SOMERSET
COURTS
GOV CTR
CITY HALL
NEW CONGRESS
FANEUIL HALL
QUINCY MKT
STATE ST.
HATCH SHELL
PEDESTRIAN BRIDGES
PINCKNEY
MT VERNON
LOUISBURG SQ.
WALNUT
STATE HOUSE
BEACON
COURT
STATE
PARK
AQUARIUM
LONG WHF
NE AQUARIUM
CENTRAL WHF
CRUISES
COMMUTER T BOATS
ROWE'S WHF
ARLINGTON
PUBLIC GARDEN
CHARLES ST
BOSTON COMMON
PARK ST.
DOWNTOWN CROSSING
WASHINGTON
MILK
BROAD
INDIA
CONGRESS
TREMONT
BOYLSTON
ARLINGTON
DEPT STORES
SUMMER
FINANCE
HIGH
PARK PL. HOTEL
MUSICAL
CHINA TOWN
ESSEX
STUART ST
See Downtown Waterfront Map
ATLANTIC
AVE
THEATRES
BEACH
HARRISON
KNEELAND
NE MED CTR
SOUTH STATION
RED LINE
COMMUTER TRAINS
BUS, AMTRAK TERMINAL
FED RES. BNK
CONGRESS
CHANNEL
NORTHERN AVE
TO WORLD TRADE CTR
PROVINCETOWN II
MUSEUMS CHILDREN'S & COMPUTER
SUMMER ST
FORT PT.
SOUTH BOSTON

Key and Notes (continued)

●●● Freedom Trail. ooo route from the T boat dock to the Constitution Park Visitors Center. **Complete identification of the sites of the Freedom Trail** is given on the Downtown/Waterfront and North End/Charlestown maps, pages15 and 26.

on one line, even though the T stop nearest an attraction is on another, it is best to walk rather than transfer.

The Park St. Station on the Red and Green Lines is probably the T's busiest. It is at the edge of **Boston Common**, on the **Freedom Trail**, and two short blocks away from the major department stores in one direction, and from Government Center in another. A five minute walk from Park St. takes you through an incredible variety of urban sights and sites. **From Park St., the Red Line provides an eight minute connection to Harvard Square in Cambridge**, one of Greater Boston's most popular meccas, and the **B, C, D Green Lines** provide transportation to Brighton, Brookline, and Newton, and the **E Green Line** takes you to the **Museum of Fine Art**s and other cultural attractions. The Green Line cars run as trains underground and as trolleys along the surface. They are delightful. **If you board surface outgoing cars your ride is usually free.** On the Common near the Park St T stop, is a **Visitors Bureau Information Center**, where you can get color maps of the T system as well as various types of passes and visitors "passports". You can also get these at the Harvard T Station, North, South and Back Bay Train Stations, and at many hotels. Senior citizens can obtain special passes by presenting proper identification at Downtown Crossing. The basic fare on the T is currently 85 cents. (But it may be higher by the time you read this.) Since service is curtailed at night, always call the T to be sure of the evening cut-off times. **A valuable guide to the T system with exhaustive lists of T destinations is** *CAR-FREE IN BOSTON*, **published by the Association for Public Transportation** (current price $6.95). **In writing this book, I referred often to the** *OFFICIAL T PUBLIC TRANSIT MAP, BUS, SUBWAY, COMMUTER RAIL,* **put out by the MBTA,** and sold at many news stands (current price $2.50). These references are especially valuable for bus routes. Current basic bus fare is 60 cents, exact change. For the longer trips to Greater Boston described in later chapters, the fares are higher. Pets are usually not allowed on the T except for the disabled.

In addition to the bus, subway, and commuter rail trains, the MBTA runs **commuter boats to Charlestown from Long Wharf and to Hingham and Logan Airport from Rowe's Wharf**. See maps on pp. 10, 11, and 15.

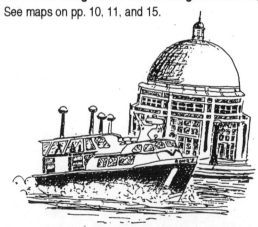

Airport Water
Shuttle Approaches
Rowe's Wharf

In the Public Garden

BOSTON'S CENTER, THE COMMON AND PUBLIC GARDEN

These two delightful historic parks are at the center of Boston. All around them is the bustle of the Downtown districts. **There are three T stations on their borders**; on the Tremont St. side of the **Common** are the **Park St. (Green and Red Lines) and Boylston (Green Line) T stops**, and on the Arlington St. side of the **Garden** is the **Arlington T stop (Green Line)**. See map on p. 11.

Boston Common, spreading over 40 acres, **is the Nation's oldest public park**. It was set aside for public use by the Puritans in 1634. Colonials socialized and pastured their cattle on its greens. During the pre-Revolutionary ferment, British soldiers sent to quell rebellious Boston, camped and drilled here. Today, under its pleasant trees, office workers, shoppers, and visitors relax and picnic. The corner of the Common near the Park St. T exit is the scene of a constant carnival -- vendors, political demonstrators, musicians, dance groups, school choirs. Everything happens. **At the Information Center on the Tremont St.** side (which has rest rooms), you can pick up an MBTA map as well as a guide to the **Freedom Trail**, the famous walk starting at the Common and stringing together several of Boston's most outstanding historical sites. (We describe it in the next section, pp. 16-30.) The graveyard on the Boylston St. side of the Common is the resting place of such notables as artist **Gilbert Stuart** and hymn composer **Reverend William Billings.**

PUBLIC GARDEN

In Colonial days, the waters of the Charles River came up to the Charles St. border of the Common. **Now across Charles St. is the Public Garden**, one of the country's first public botanical gardens, established in the mid-nineteenth century as part of the great Back Bay land fill-in project. **It is a lovely place of flowers, heroic and whimsical statuary, and labeled**

trees -- American Beech (fagus grandifolia), Kentucky Coffee Tree (gymnocladus dioicus), and so on. You are gently educated as you savor their beauty and enjoy their shade. The Garden, loveliest in the springtime, is an elegant walking link between the **Back Bay** and **Beacon Hill** districts. But for the very young and their doting uncles and aunts, parents and grandparents, from May to October, by far **the most popular offerings of the Garden are rides on the Swan Boats**, dating back to 1877, gliding motor-free under foot power along the central lagoon, trailed by ducks and geese devouring the tidbits tossed by many small hands. The lagoon and its vicinity also form the setting for Robert McCloskey's book, *MAKE WAY FOR DUCKLINGS*, a children's favorite, now celebrated by a bronze sculpture. (See at right.)

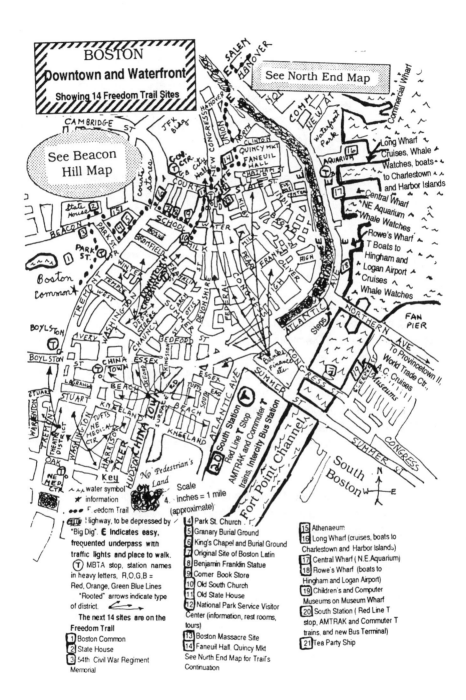

BOSTON
Downtown and Waterfront
Showing 14 Freedom Trail Sites

See North End Map

See Beacon
Hill Map

Boston
Common

Key
~~ water symbol
★ information
•••• Freedom Trail
⊞ highway, to be depressed by
"Big Dig". **E Indicates easy,**
frequented underpass with
traffic lights and place to walk.
Ⓣ MBTA stop, station names
in heavy letters, R,O,G,B =
Red, Orange, Green Blue Lines
"Rooted" arrows indicate type
of district.
The next 14 sites are on the
Freedom Trail
1 Boston Common
2 State House
3 54th Civil War Regiment
Memorial

Scale
4 inches = 1 mile
(approximate)

4 Park St. Church
5 Granary Burial Ground
6 King's Chapel and Burial Ground
7 Original Site of Boston Latin
8 Benjamin Franklin Statue
9 Corner Book Store
10 Old South Church
11 Old State House
12 National Park Service Visitor
Center (information, rest rooms,
tours)
13 Boston Massacre Site
14 Faneuil Hall, Quincy Mkt
See North End Map for Trail's
Continuation

15 Athenaeum
16 Long Wharf (cruises, boats to
Charlestown and Harbor Islands)
17 Central Wharf (N.E.Aquarium)
18 Rowe's Wharf (boats to
Hingham and Logan Airport)
19 Children's and Computer
Museums on Museum Wharf
20 South Station (Red Line T
stop, AMTRAK and Commuter T
trains, and new Bus Terminal)
21 Tea Party Ship

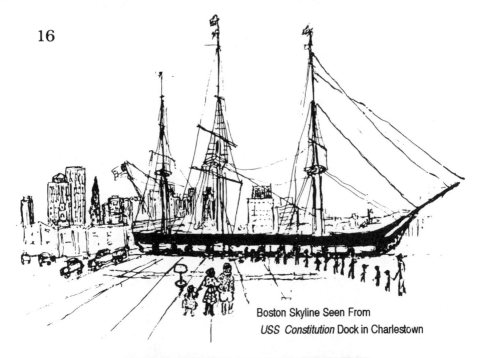

Boston Skyline Seen From
USS Constitution Dock in Charlestown

MEETING HISTORY ALONG THE FREEDOM TRAIL

Surrounding the Common, compact and beautifully walkable, is the amazing tight tangle of Boston's Downtown districts, the famous **Back Bay and Beacon Hill**, the shopping, financial, government, and theater districts, and beyond them the **waterfront** and **North End,** all crowded with sites of interest to the visitor. A fine way of getting your first introduction to several of these districts is by walking the **Freedom Trail**, a string of 16 historical sites, which takes you on a journey through the narrow cobbled streets of Puritan Boston into the Revolutionary conflict; but all the while you are in the midst of the crowds and high rises of Modern Boston, a truly remarkable experience.

The Trail is marked by a double line of bricks. You can start anywhere on it, take as long as you please, hours or days, and relax almost everywhere, on park benches or at nearby restaurants and sidewalk cafes. **Several T stops are close to Trail sites,** a number of which are run as museums, where you can linger and steep yourself in the Colonial past.

The **Boston Common** is, of course, one of the Trail's sites. Let's start there. At the **Information Center** near the Park St. T station (Green and Red Lines), you can pick up a map and brochure. (See maps on pp. 15 and 26.) The Trail leads from the information booth through the Common **to Beacon St. to the golden domed, Bulfinch designed "new" State House**, built in 1797 and currently the seat of the Massachusetts Legislature (called the General Court). The **State House** is on the border of the famed **Beacon Hill** district of which we write more later. The **Archive Library** on the third floor contains priceless original documents of the State's history,* including the *HISTORY OF THE PLIMOTH PLANTATION* written in Governor William

The State House

Bradford's hand and containing the **Mayflower Compact**, composed upon the Pilgrims' landing in Provincetown (see Volume 2), in which they covenanted themselves together in a "Civil Body Politick ... to enacte, constitute, and frame just and equall lawes." In this remarkable library is the first copy of the **Massachusetts Constitution**, written in 1780, still the basic law of the State, and a model for many features later adopted in the Nation's Constitution. **John Adams** was its chief author. Another Archive treasure is the **Royal Charter of the Massachusetts Bay Company** that the Puritans brought with them in 1630. For over 50 years, they enjoyed uninterrupted self-government under this Charter, electing their own Governors and making laws to form their ideal church-state. Those were years when the Mother Country was in the throes of political upheaval. When the tumult in Old

---

* Some of these Archive treasures traditionally kept at the State House may be moved to the new **Commonwealth Museum** (see Museums section).

England died down, attention was once more paid to the aggressive Bay Colony. Its Charter was revoked and replaced with a new one under which the Governor was to be appointed by the Crown. The General Court (Legislature) was still to be popularly elected, but its laws had to be approved by Parliament. It must be mentioned too that the new Charter widened the franchise, which the Puritans had restricted to Congregational Church members.

In the gardens, corridors, and chambers of this beautiful State House, many statues, paintings, and carvings tell the story of the Commonwealth. Early Puritan intolerance is represented by the statue of **Mary Dyer**, a Quaker, who was hanged for her religion in 1660 on Boston Common, and one of **Anne Hutchinson**, who was expelled from the Bay Colony in 1638 for daring to criticize the Puritan ministers. More about these two remarkable women on pages 185, 186. The gradual growth of religious freedom is symbolized by the painting showing **Samuel Sewall**, one of the judges in the Salem witch trials, publicly repenting his part in them.

Opposite the Speaker's chair in the House Chamber is the Sacred Codfish, carved out of wood, symbolizing the importance of fish as the foundation of the Commonwealth's early economy. In Colonial days, it was a chief food, and more; codfish was at the base of the sea trade. Prize fish were traded directly to Portugal and Spain. And less prized fish were traded to the West Indies for molasses, which in turn was used to manufacture rum, millions of gallons of it, the most important New England product, used as the chief medium of exchange with the Southern Colonies, with the Indians, and in the Newfoundland, European, and African trade. Rum was also the regional beverage of New England. Sailors, farmers, artisans felt that they couldn't get through the day without their drafts of rum. To restrict the troublesome New England sea trade, Old England in 1733 imposed a tax on molasses; but that was regularly eluded by wholesale smuggling. When in the 1760's the Mother Country started to crack down on smuggling by issuing Writs of Assistance giving customs officers the right to make searches where smuggling was suspected, bedlam broke loose on the streets of Boston. Years later, **John Adams declared that** it was no secret that **"rum was an essential ingredient of the Revolution."** And without the Sacred Cod there would have been no rum. The **Adams papers** are among the hundreds of thousands of precious documents in the State House Archives Library.

Free guided tours are conducted through the State House on Mon.-Fri., 10 to 4.

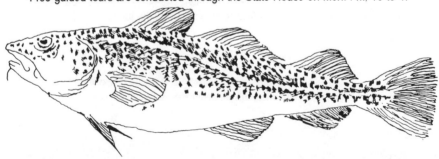

Across Beacon St. from the State House, on the Common, near the intersection of Beacon and Park Streets, a relief by St. Gaudens commemorates the heroism in the Civil War of **Colonel Robert Gould Shaw and the Massachusetts 54th Regiment of Black soldiers** under his command. The story of this regiment, **the first Black regiment organized in the North**, is celebrated in the film *GLORY.* (See also p. 36.)

A short detour to the north along Beacon St. brings you to the **Athenaeum Library** at no. 101/2, a repository of more precious documents and a treasury of art. The Athenaeum, founded in the nineteenth century by Boston intellectuals, was a forerunner of the Museum of Fine Arts, about which we write more on pp. 42, 43.

Park St. Church

From the State House the Trail goes along Park St. to its intersection with Tremont, the site of the handsome **Park St. Church**, with white steeple and telescoped towers in the Christopher Wren style, built in 1809 and known as the **Brimstone Church**, both because of the fiery preaching and because gun powder was stored in it during the War of 1812. **William Lloyd Garrison** gave his first anti-slavery speech here in 1829. Open in the summer. Free.

Following the Trail northward along Tremont, you come shortly to the **Granary Burying Ground**, next to the site of the town's first granary, the resting place of **Peter Faneuil, Paul Revere, Benjamin Franklin's parents, the victims of the Boston Massacre, and three signers of the Declaration of Independence: Robert Treat Paine, John Hancock, and Samuel Adams.** Samuel Adams' grave deserves a special pause, for **he was a prime mover in bringing the Colonies to the Revolution**. He was an organizer of the **Sons of Liberty**, a group which regularly planned rallies, riots, and boycotts to protest unpopular restrictions on Colonial trade and the various taxes that Britain imposed on the Colonies without their consent in the 1760's subsequent to the French and Indian War. He also organized the **Committees of Correspondence**, eventually formed throughout the Colonies, **first to record and communicate, and later the real executive branch of Colonial government**. A Harvard graduate, trained as a lawyer, he came from a merchant family and perceived the precariousness of fortunes based on commerce as long as the Mother Country could change the rules of the game at will. As a group New England merchants were early in thinking the unthinkable -- that resistance to Parliamentary law was justified if the welfare of the Commonwealth was at stake. **John Adams** later wrote to **Thomas Jefferson** in 1816 that the real Revolution had already taken place here "before a drop of blood was drawn at Lexington." **The real "Revolution was in the minds of the people, and this was effected from 1760 to 1775."** The shooting war itself was only an "effect and consequence." The **Burying Ground** is open from 8 to 4 every day. The stones are fascinating. Free.

Across the street, a little further along Tremont, you come to the handsome **King's Chapel**, built in 1754, designed by Peter Harrison. Before the Revolution, this church was Anglican and was attended by local Tories, including the Royal Governors. **In the ancient graveyard beside the church**, Boston's oldest burial ground, **lies Puritan John Winthrop, first Governor of the Bay Colony and leader of the Great Migration**. Beside him lie his son, John Winthrop, Jr., and his grandson, Fitzhugh Winthrop, both Governors of Puritan Connecticut. How does it happen that these arch-Puritans are buried beside the Anglican church? The tale is that no Puritan in good standing would sell the Royal Governor land for a church. So he simply allocated a portion of the ancient burial ground for the purpose. **After the Revolution, King's Chapel became the first Unitarian Church in America**. Religious tolerance had arrived in Massachusetts by then.

Another notable buried in King's Chapel graveyard is **William Dawes**. Dawes is not mentioned in Longfellow's famous poem on the *MIDNIGHT RIDE OF PAUL REVERE*, but he too rode out of Boston on the night of April 18th to warn "every Middlesex village and farm" of the impending march of the British to Concord. While Revere rode from the Charlestown shore after waiting for the famous lantern signals, Dawes rode out of Boston by an alternative route through Roxbury Neck. The two met in Lexington, whence they continued together. (More on the denouement of the

King's Chapel

Midnight Ride on page 89.) The church and graveyard are open from 10 to 4 except Mondays. Free. The interior of the church, with its rich paneling and separate pews, has been preserved in its original form.

Around the corner, on School St., on the sidewalk, a mosaic marks **the site of the country's first public schoolhouse,** built in 1635, later to become **Boston Latin** (now located on Ave. Louis Pasteur near the Back Bay Fens). This was the beginning of Boston's reputation for books and learning. The school, established so soon after their arrival in their "New Land in the Wildernesse," testifies to the Puritans' belief in the value of education for everyone. How else could you keep "Olde Satan" from deluding you but by knowing how to read Scriptures? They required every village of 50 families to build a schoolhouse as well as a church. In 1636, a year after Boston Latin, they founded **Harvard College** (see *Cambridge*, pp. 59-61).

Near the Latin School marker, in the yard of **Old City Hall,** now a restaurant, **is a statue of a former Boston Latin scholar, Benjamin Franklin.** Franklin left Boston at the age of 17 after a bitter quarrel with his brother James, a printer and publisher, to whom he was apprenticed. At the time, **in the early 1720's, the Boston marketplace was crowded with booksellers and printers,** New York had two booksellers and one printing house, and Philadelphia had no booksellers and two printing houses (both ill-equipped and unskilled in Franklin's opinion), and in all the Colonies to the south, there were neither booksellers nor printing houses. Franklin himself was to change the whole picture. The lack of printers south of Boston gave him a frontier into which he expanded and made his fortune. He established a printing and publishing house in Philadelphia and helped finance young printers that he had trained to go off to establish printing houses elsewhere. In Philadelphia, he started a subscription library, the country's first, a philosophical society, and many good public works in the Puritan mode, although he was far from being a Puritan in life style.

A little further along the Trail, at the corner of School and Washington, we come to the **Old Corner Bookstore,** built in 1713, but most famous for being in the nineteenth century the publishing house of **Ticknor and Fields** and a meeting place for such Boston literary lights as **Emerson, Longfellow, Hawthorne, Holmes, Whittier, and Howe,** another symbol of Boston's love affair with letters. In the late 1630's, on this site, stood **Anne Hutchinson's** house, where she held the meetings that so disturbed John Winthrop and the Puritan ministers. We continue her story on pages 185, 186. The Old Corner Bookstore is now owned by *BOSTON GLOBE* and specializes in New England travel books and maps.

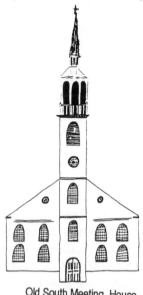

Old South Meeting House

If you look across the street and a bit south, you will see rising above the crowds of today's shopping district, the high-towered **Old South Meeting House**, built in 1729 on what had been the site of John Winthrop's house, **the true heart of Colonial Puritan Boston**. In the pre-Revolutionary ferment, this was a place of meetings too large for **Faneuil Hall,** the scene of fiery speeches on the hottest issues of the day, the taxes that the Mother Country was levying against the Colonies without their consent to finance the Empire, and the Writs of Assistance aimed at discouraging smuggling. From 1764, when the Stamp Act was passed, riots and demonstrations were born here.

From here was launched the single act of defiance which most outraged the British -- the **Boston Tea Party.** A marked side trail goes from the Meeting House along the route taken, on the night of December 16, 1773, by Bostonians dressed as Indians as they headed for Griffin's Wharf, where they boarded three tea ships -- the Beaver, the Dartmouth, and the Eleanor -- and dumped their cargo, 342 chests of tea, into the sea to prevent its landing and payment of the tea duties by the consignees. **The cruel over-reaction of the British to this action, more than any other single event, precipitated the Revolution.** They enacted what came to be known as the **"Intolerable Acts"**. They closed the port of Boston to trade, closed the Grand Banks fisheries to the fishermen, banned Town Meetings, moved the Colonial Government to Salem and Marblehead, increased their forces in the town, and demanded that the townspeople quarter their troops. The British thereby aroused intense sympathy for Boston's plight, and helped break the Great Barrier. For while New Englanders, partly due to their aggressive commercial competition with Old England, and partly due to their Puritan heritage as dissidents from the Anglican Church, were ready to challenge the supremacy of King and Parliament, other Colonies, although outraged by the new taxes, were far more royalist in their outlook and apt to regard the New Englanders as too radical. But the "Intolerable Acts" brought all to realize that more than taxation without representation was involved. Basic liberties, which as English subjects they took for granted, were threatened by the remote power across the sea. **The ball was set rolling**. Committees of Correspondence sprang once more into motion. Provincial Congresses met. Militia troops were formed and trained. Munitions were gathered and stored at various sites in the countryside. And the first Continental Congress with delegates from all Thirteen Colonies was planned to meet in Philadelphia in September, 1774.

The Old South Meeting House was saved from the wrecking ball in 1876 by a committee of 25 Boston women who raised the money to buy the building and restore it to its pre-Revolution form. The British had wrecked the interior by stabling their horses there in the year 1775-1776, when they occupied Boston, then under siege by the Continental Army (see the stories of **Bunker Hill** and **Concord**). Now the **Old South Meeting House** is run as a museum with exhibits on early Boston and various political movements that have shaped the City and Nation. Open 10-4 daily. Modest fee.

Following the Trail northward from the Old South Church, along Washington St., you find, near the intersection with Court and State Streets (called King and Queen Streets before the Revolution), the **Old State House**, built in 1712. Now restored are the Lion and Unicorn, emblems of the British Empire, which were removed after the Revolution. **This was the seat of the Colonial government. Here the popularly elected House of Representatives**, in defiance of the Royal Governor, **declared that the laws of Colonial Assemblies should be supreme**. In the Court of Justice in this building, **Colonial lawyer James Otis argued against the Writs of Assistance**, giving Customs Officers the right to make searches where smuggling was suspected. **John Adams later wrote "Independence was born that day."** From the

Old State House

balcony of this building, some of the hated Royal proclamations were read. But in July, 1776, after the British had been forced to evacuate Boston, **the Declaration of Independence was read here to cheering crowds**.

Today the building is maintained as The **Museum of Boston History** by the **Bostonian Society**. It houses an excellent collection of paintings, engravings, maps, manu-scripts, and memorabilia of Colonial days, like the blue ball that once advertised the candle factory run by Ben Franklin's father. Open 10-4, modest fee.

Near the Old State House, at 15 State St., is the Boston National Park Visitor Center, offering literature, restrooms, and free tours. Call **(617) 242-5642**.

A circle of cobblestones facing the Old State House marks the site of the **Boston Massacre,** where on March 5, 1770, a British guard of nine soldiers fired upon an unruly mob, killing five people, including Crispus Attucks, a Black Patriot. British troops had been stationed in Boston since 1768 in response to the violence and riots following enactment of the Stamp and Townshend Acts. To placate popular outrage at the Massacre, the soldiers were removed from the town and stationed in Castle William, a fortress guarding the entrance to the Harbor, and the officers involved were placed on trial. Had the British continued to act with the restraint that they showed on this occasion, we might still be part of the British Commonwealth!

Continuing along the Trail along New Congress St., to your left you will see steps leading **to the great open plaza of City Hall** (where there are rest rooms and tourist information folders) and to the **Government Center T station** (Green and Blue Lines), and to the right, you will see an important landmark of Colonial and Modern Boston, **Faneuil Hall**, built in 1742 by merchant **Peter Faneuil**, who presented it as a gift to the Town. The ground floor was used as a market place, and the second for Town Meetings, where citizens could voice and vote on their concerns. Because of the crucial Town Meetings held here, **John Adams called it the "Cradle of Liberty."** On November 22, 1772, the Town Meeting here elected a Committee of Correspondence consisting of **Samuel Adams, James Otis, Joseph Warren, Josiah Quincy**, and other popular leaders that was to become the effective government of Boston during the

Faneuil

Hall

Samuel Adams
1722-1803
Organized the
Revolution

Revolutionary period and a model for the Committees of Correspondence established throughout the Colonies.

Today there is a museum run by the Park Service on the second floor of **Faneuil Hall**. On its first floor, and in the granite **Quincy Market** behind it, **are hosts of shops and food stalls** (also restrooms). And what food!! You may not be able to move any further along the Trail. Counter after counter is piled high with delicacies of every ethnic origin. The Market is always thronged. People select delectables and eat indoors if the weather is inclement but vie for benches outside if it is benign. In addition to take-out counters, the Market has several restaurants, boutiques, and galleries. And in the **North and South Market** buildings flanking it is more of the same.

The **Quincy Market** was built in 1828 and is named after **Josiah Quincy**, a mayor of Boston and grandson of the Revolutionary War Patriot. One of the treasures of the **Museum of Fine Arts** is a **Gilbert Stuart** painting of Mayor Quincy with the Market designs under his arm. Near the market rises the pyramidal tower of the handsome granite **Custom House**, the highest building in Boston when its tower was added in 1913, but now exceeded by several skyscrapers. What, you may wonder, is a Custom House doing so far from the water? The answer is that the water was once here. **In the 19th century, Faneuil Hall and Quincy Market were adjacent to the waterfront.** In 1750, when Boston was America's foremost seaport, **Long Wharf** extended from here for a thousand feet into the deep water. The Harbor was then a forest of sails, and the Waterfront was a centipede of piers on which stood 160 warehouses crowded with cargoes being assembled for export and with the voluminous imports that brought to the Bay Colony the high standard of living that visitors marveled at. Today Atlantic Ave. cuts these buildings off from the waterfront that they were once a part of. However, **traffic lights facilitate the crossing from the**

Quincy Market, under the elevated highway (to be depressed), to the Waterfront Park and to the wharves, now devoted largely to recreational uses, and to hotels and condos. **From Long Wharf you can depart on cruises about the Harbor and to the Charlestown portion of the Freedom Trail**, to the **Boston Harbor Islands** and to **Provincetown** (see Volume 2). More about the offerings of Long Wharf on pages 40, 41. Near Long Wharf is the **New England Aquarium** (see pages 40, 41).

Custom House

BOSTON
North End and Charlestown
(Freedom Trail Continued from
Downtown / Waterfront Map)

KEY

⌃⌃⌃ water symbol
★ information
Ⓣ MBTA Stop
In the North End
1 Paul Revere's House
2 Paul Revere Mall
3 Old North Church
4 Copp's Hill Burying Ground
5 St. Stephens Church

●●● Freedom Trail, ₀₀₀ alternate
route
▨▨▨ highway, E easy underpass
with lights to help

Scale
4.5 inches = 1 mile
(approximate)

In Charlestown
6 Constitution National Historic
Park and Museum, with several
sites including the U.S.S.
Constitution, a Visitor Center with
information folders and rest
rooms, and a gift shop. Free
shuttle bus to take you around.
7 Bunker Hill Pavilion,
multimedia show on Battle of
Bunker Hill
8 Bunker Hill Monument, exhibits,
information, rest rooms, and 294
steps to a great view

Boston
Inner Harbor

See Downtown/Waterfront Map

As you can see from the map on page 15, several T stops are near Quincy Market and Long Wharf. The Government Center (Green, Blue), Aquarium (Blue), and State St. (Orange, Blue) T stops are closest. More about the many attractions of the Waterfront in our Waterfront section (see pages 40-42).

Although the temptations of Quincy Market are great, I recommend that you drag yourself away before you are completely surfeited and continue along the Trail. Go along Union St., itself a delightful chunk of Old Boston, miraculously saved from urban "renewal," go past the Oyster House, and the pushcarts of the Haymarket, and through the pedestrian underpass to the **North End, Boston's Little Italy.** You will want to experience the culinary delights of its ristorantes and panificios.

The North End has been the first American home of successive waves of immigrants. Before the Italians came the Jews. The store signs were then in Hebrew script. And before the Jews came the Irish. The North End was the birthplace of **Rose Fitzgerald Kennedy,** mother of **John F. Kennedy**. And here too was one of the villages of the Puritan town founded by John Winthrop. Here in Colonial days were several taverns, at one of which, the **Green Dragon, the small inner circle of the Sons of Liberty plotted the details of the Boston Tea Party** before it was taken up at the mass meeting of December 16, 1773 at the Old South Meeting House. Their headquarters was in Chase and Speakman's Distillery on Hanover St. These nests of intrigue are all gone. But remaining still in North Square, just off Hanover St., between Benet and Richmond, is the **Paul Revere House**, where the noted Son of Liberty raised his family, engaged in his engraving and silversmith trade, and **whence he set forth on his famous ride on April 18th, 1775**. Built in 1676, and almost 100 years old on that historic night, this house is one of the few Colonial residences made of wood spared by the many fires which swept early Boston. Open 10 to 4 daily. Fee.

On Salem St. rises the white steeple of the Old North Church, built in 1723, Boston's oldest standing church. In a predecessor on this site, Cotton Mather, the noted historian and witch hunter, preached. **But the Church is best known as the opening scene of Longfellow's all time hit poem, *THE MIDNIGHT RIDE OF PAUL REVERE,*** according to which, on the night of April 18, 1775, Paul Revere said to his

Paul Revere's House
in North Square off
Hanover St.

friend

> .... If the British march
> By land or sea from the town tonight
> Hang a lantern aloft in the belfry arch,
> Of the North Church tower as a signal light,
> One if by land and two if by sea;
> And I on the opposite shore will be
> Ready to ride and spread the alarm
> Through every Middlesex village and farm.

The Church has a serene courtyard adjoining the Paul Revere Mall, a favorite meeting and greeting place for the old timers of the present Italian neighborhood. The Church is open daily from 9 to 5. Visitors are welcome to attend services. Nearby rises the gold cupola and spire of **St. Stephen's Church,** designed by Bulfinch in 1803 as the "New" Old North Church, and now a Roman Catholic church.

Follow the Trail from the North Church along Hull St. to Copp's Burying Ground, where **Cotton Mather and his father Increase Mather**, both important Puritan preachers and leaders, are buried. From Copp's Hill, you see, across the water, **the Charlestown shore, to which Paul Revere rowed** with "muffled oar ... just as the moon rose over the bay" **to await the lantern signal**. On the night of Paul Revere's ride, near the Charlestown shore, "swinging wide at her moorings lay/ The Somerset British Man-of-War." Today the Somerset is, of course, no longer moored there, but you will see as you look toward the Charlestown shore a three masted Man-of-War!! A phantom ship? No, **the famous frigate** *CONSTITUTION* **(Old Ironsides)**, the next stop on the Freedom Trail. But before we head there, a few more notes on Copp's Hill Burial Ground. Here lies **Edmund Hartt, builder of the** *CONSTITUTION,* savoring his masterwork in perpetuity. Here also lies **Prince Hall, a leader of Boston's freed Black community**, who early in the nineteenth century petitioned the Massachusetts Legislature (in vain) to admit Black children to the public schools. And it was from this point that **British General John Burgoyne** trained his cannons on Charlestown during the **Battle of Bunker Hill** (see pp. 29, 30) and sent off the fireballs that engulfed the town in flames.

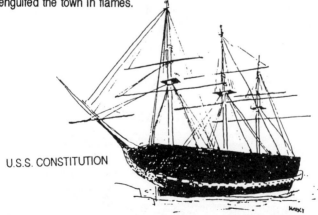

U.S.S. CONSTITUTION

The *U.S.S. Constitution*, the Trail's next stop, now forms the centerpiece of a **National Historic Park,** which spreads over several acres of the former Charlestown Navy Yard, a main builder of ships for the U.S. Navy from the 1790's until 1974 when it was closed. **To get to the *CONSTITUTION*, you can follow the Trail across the bridge from the North End to Charlestown** (there is a sidewalk for pedestrians). **Or you can take a commuter T boat to it from Long Wharf,** which is across Atlantic Ave from the Quincy Market and near the Government Center (Green and Blue Lines) and Aquarium (Blue Line) T stops. There are boats every half hour from about 7AM to 8PM, more frequently during rush hours. The boat docks on Pier 4 in Charlestown just a short walk from the Park entrance and **Visitor Center, where there are restrooms, and an information desk. Or you can take T bus 93 from Haymarket Square to Charlestown's City Square.** Haymarket Square is behind **Government Center Plaza** and is a stop on the Green and Orange Lines. From City Square it is a short walk to either the **Bunker Hill Monument** or to the **Constitution.**

The *CONSTITUTION*, **launched in 1797 from this Navy Yard, was never de-feated in battle**. It was Admiral Edward Preble's flagship during the wars against the Tripolitan pirates, and was named "Old Ironsides" in the War of 1812, when it sank the British *Guerriere* without sustaining much damage. After a long distinguished career, it was declared unseaworthy in 1830 and was condemned to be broken up; but it was saved by popular clamor sparked by Oliver Wendell Holmes' stirring poem *Old Ironsides*, which begins "Ay tear her tattered ensign down/ Long has it waved on high/ And many an eye has danced to see/ That banner in the sky."

You can board a fully restored *CONSTITUTION* and get an intimate glimpse of life aboard a U.S. warship in the early nineteenth century. One thing is immediately clear. Folks were much shorter in those days. Nearly all adults must stoop while moving through the living quarters of this fascinating ship. Nearby is the **Constitution Museum,** fee, with more exhibits and memorabilia about the career of this remarkable vessel, the oldest battleship of the U.S. Navy still afloat. **Call (617) 426-1812.** Several other sites in the Park can be visited on ranger-guided tours (free), which you can learn about at the Visitor Center.

Two hundred yards from the *CONSTITUTION*, in the Bunker Hill Pavilion, *THE WHITES OF THEIR EYES*, an excellent multimedia presentation of the **Battle of Bunker Hill,** is shown continuously. Fee. After the British were chased all the way from

Concord to Boston on April 19, 1775 (this story is told in our Concord section in Chapter 2), they were besieged by Colonial militia, who camped in a great circle about the City. For two months, Colonial militia kept arriving, first from nearby and then from afar, to join in the siege. Then on the night of June 16, the Colonials made their move. A contingent under General William Prescott tried to seize and fortify Breeds and Bunker Hills in Charlestown Heights, which were key positions overlooking

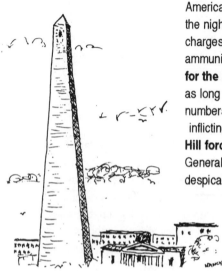

Boston. The next day, the British attacked to dislodge the Americans from the redoubts that they had dug during the night. The Americans repelled their successive charges, but were forced to retreat when their ammunition ran out. **Although the Battle was a defeat for the Americans, they considered it a moral victory**; as long as their powder lasted, they had faced superior numbers of British "regulars", and had driven them back, inflicting heavy casualties. **On the British side, Bunker Hill forced painful reassessment.** In his report home, General Gage warned that the rebels were "not the despicable Rabble too many have supposed them to be. They are now spirited by a Rage and Enthousiasm, as great as ever People were possessed of." **Three weeks later Washington rode into Cambridge to take command of the Continental Army,** of which the militia camped about Boston formed the basic core. (See our *Cambridge* and *Quincy* sections.)

Bunker Hill Monument

To get to the battleground, follow the Trail up to the Bunker Hill Monument. As you climb uphill you come to a charming district of handsome 19th century houses about **Monument Square**. The **Monument** is a great obelisk of Quincy granite. Its cornerstone was laid on June 17, 1825, the fiftieth anniversary of the Battle, amidst grand celebrations, and an oration by Daniel Webster. Inside the low building attached to the monument are exhibits showing the dispositions of the opposing forces during the course of the struggle, an information table, and **restrooms. You can climb the 294 steps to the top to savor a marvelous view of Boston from the Charlestown perspective.** Free. To return to Downtown Boston, you can retrace your steps, loop back to the boat dock, or you can walk to the Community College T stop on the Orange Line (see map) and take a train to Downtown Crossing, in the Heart of Everything.

Charles Street
Meeting House
(See pages 35,36.)

BEACON HILL

We've already met several of Boston's Downtown districts when walking along the Freedom Trail. The most famous is **Beacon Hill**, which rises across Beacon St. on the North Side of the Common, **and is dominated by the gold-domed "new" State House, built in 1795, designed by Charles Bulfinch**, who was later the architect of the Nation's Capitol and other major public buildings of his day. While on the Freedom Trail we paused to describe some of the treasures of the State House. (See pages 17 and 18.) The T stops nearest Beacon Hill are: Park St. on the Red and Green Lines; Charles/MGH on the Red Line; Arlington on the Green Line.

The elegant brick and stone buildings climbing the Hill were built after the Revolution, in the Federal Period from 1795 to 1848, for Boston merchants who had prospered in the sea trade. Puritans all, they nevertheless wanted their houses to reflect their worldly success. To design them they chose **Bulfinch**, who had returned to his hometown from his studies abroad, eager to transfer to Boston some of the architectural gloss of England and France. Originally, Beacon Hill was not one but three hills (Trimountain, after which Tremont St. is named), which were smoothed out to make the slopes more suitable for building. Later in the nineteenth century, when **Back Bay** was laid out, many of the Hill's original residents moved there, and their places were taken by some of Boston's most famous intellectuals and reformers.

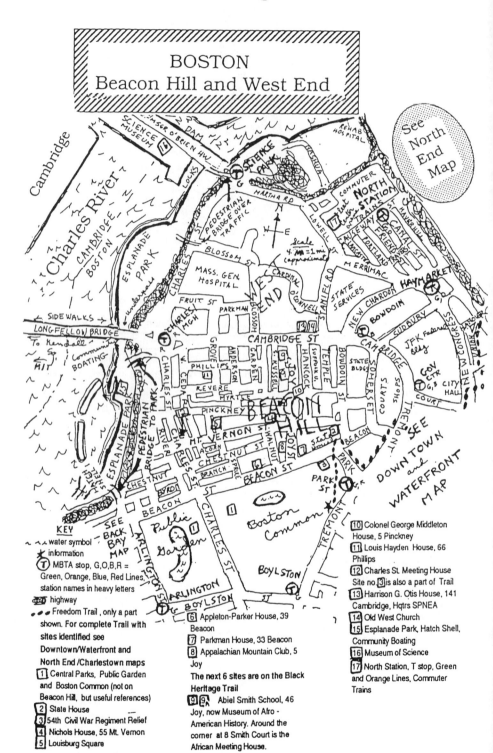

BOSTON
Beacon Hill and West End

KEY

~ ~ water symbol
★ information
Ⓣ MBTA stop, G,O,B,R =
Green, Orange, Blue, Red Lines,
station names in heavy letters
▱▱ highway
• • • Freedom Trail , only a part
shown. For complete Trail with
sites identified see
Downtown/Waterfront and
North End /Charlestown maps
1️⃣ Central Parks, Public Garden
and Boston Common (not on
Beacon Hill, but useful references)
2️⃣ State House
3️⃣ 54th Civil War Regiment Relief
4️⃣ Nichols House, 55 Mt. Vernon
5️⃣ Louisburg Square

6️⃣ Appleton-Parker House, 39
Beacon
7️⃣ Parkman House, 33 Beacon
8️⃣ Appalachian Mountain Club, 5
Joy

The next 6 sites are on the Black
Heritage Trail
9️⃣ 9️⃣a Abiel Smith School, 46
Joy, now Museum of Afro -
American History. Around the
corner at 8 Smith Court is the
African Meeting House.

🔟 Colonel George Middleton
House, 5 Pinckney
1️⃣1️⃣ Louis Hayden House, 66
Phillips
1️⃣2️⃣ Charles St. Meeting House
Site no.3️⃣is also a part of Trail
1️⃣3️⃣ Harrison G. Otis House, 141
Cambridge, Hqtrs SPNEA
1️⃣4️⃣ Old West Church
1️⃣5️⃣ Esplanade Park, Hatch Shell,
Community Boating
1️⃣6️⃣ Museum of Science
1️⃣7️⃣ North Station, T stop, Green
and Orange Lines, Commuter
Trains

To modern eyes, Beacon Hill is a special treat, with harmonious, beautiful buildings from another era on tree shaded cobbled streets, dense with the delights of half-hidden lanes and gardens. Although some of the houses are still single family residences, others have been recycled to apartments, and still others are now the homes of various institutions, in some cases the state headquarters of organizations who want to be close to the State House to monitor the activities of the Legislature. But although the uses are new, the beauty of the Hill is fortunately protected for future generations. It has been designated as a National Historic District so that purchasers of a property may not raze the buildings on it.

At the western edge of Beacon Hill is Charles St., a bustling street of coffee houses, food and bookstores, galleries and numerous antique shops. It leads to one of the few pedestrian bridges over the gaseous Storrow Drive to the popular **Esplanade Park**, which we describe in our *Emerald Necklace* section. A visit to **Beacon Hill** can be pleasantly combined with a stroll through the **Park.**

Virtually every place on the Hill has an interesting list of past tenants. Here are a few highlights. At 55 Mt. Vernon, the **Nichols House designed by Bulfinch** is one of the few houses on the Hill open to the public. Wed-Sat from 1 to 5. Fee. Its last occupant, writer and architect Rose Nichols, bequeathed it to the public as a museum when she died in 1960 at age 88. Next door to it, but not open to the public, 57 Mt. Vernon was the home of **Charles Francis Adams, son of John Quincy Adams**, and himself minister to England during the Civil War. His son **Henry Adams,** the historian, was born in this house. No. 59 was the home of **Thomas Bailey Aldrich, author and editor of *THE ATLANTIC MONTHLY***, and is still owned by his family. No. 83 was the home of **William Ellery Channing,** the famed apostle of Unitarianism. (See pages 39 and 183.) No. 85 was one of three houses built on the Hill for **Harrison Gray Otis,** a Boston mayor and U.S. Senator, and a speculator in Hill real estate.

Louisburg Square, named after the battle of 1745, of which we write more on pages 221 and 222, is a charming, well-shaded enclave of bow-front residences surrounding a central garden with statuary. It is just off Mount Vernon St, to your left as you climb along Mount Vernon from Charles St. **Louisa May Alcott** of *LITTLE WOMEN* fame lived at No. 10. **William Dean Howells,** editor of *THE ATLANTIC MONTHLY* and author of *THE RISE OF SILAS LAPHAM,* lived at No.'s 4 and 16. **Jennie Lind,** the opera star, was married in No. 20.

While exploring, don't miss Chestnut St., considered by many to be the Beacon Hill's loveliest. **Julia Ward Howe,** feminist, peace and anti-slavery activist, and author of *THE BATTLE HYMN OF THE REPUBLIC,* lived at No. 17. At No. 29a lived **Edwin Booth,** a noted actor and brother of Lincoln's assassin. No. 43 was the home of **Richard Henry Dana,** author of *TWO YEARS BEFORE THE MAST.* At No. 50 lived **Francis Parkman,** a noted historian, author of *THE OREGON TRAIL.*

Beacon St. has many of the Hill's most resplendent residences, now mostly the headquarters of various organizations. Another of the few Hill houses open to the public is No. 39-40, formerly the **Appleton-Parker House,** now the **Women's City Club.** Open Mon., Wed., Fri. in summer and Wednesday only in winter, fee. Here **Henry Longfellow,** the poet, married **Fanny Appleton,** whose family had made its fortune in textile manufacture. This is a chance to see an elegant interior of handsome fireplaces, fine wood paneling and furniture, cut glass chandeliers, and **windows overlooking the Common.** No. 33 Beacon, the **Parkman House,** was bequeathed to the City by the Parkman family, and is used to receive distinguished visitors. The Parkmans moved here from 9 Walnut St. after the murder of the head of the family, Dr. George Parkman, by Professor John Webster of Harvard Medical School, an event that shocked proper Boston. The family has also contributed generously toward maintenance of the Common.

In a brownstone at 5 Joy St. (see map on p. 32), open to the public are the offices of the **Appalachian Mountain Club,** with a pleasant library, peaceful courtyard, literature tables, and bulletin boards of the activities of various outdoor organizations and information about New England trails. In adjacent brownstones are the offices of other environmental groups including the **Sierra Club.**

The south slope of Beacon Hill, that we have been exploring, is famous for its mansions, **but the north slope, where workmen, artisans, and servants of the rich lived in modest houses, has fascinating sites, too.** Here are several sites of the **Black Heritage Trail.** Although slavery was declared unconstitutional by the Massachusetts Supreme Court in 1783, extreme discrimination against Blacks still existed. They were excluded from attending churches and schools with whites. Boston's Black families, many of whom lived on the north slope of the Hill, established their own **Meeting House** in 1806 at 8 Smith Court, off Joy St. It was in this church that

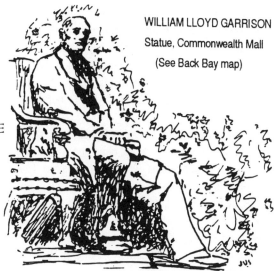

WILLIAM LLOYD GARRISON
Statue, Commonwealth Mall
(See Back Bay map)

I AM IN EARNEST
I WILL NOT EQUIVOCATE
I WILL NOT RETREAT...
AND I SHALL BE HEARD

abolitionist **William Lloyd Garrison** founded the New England Anti-Slavery Society in 1832. **The African Meeting House** has been restored and is open to the public. It is the first stop on the **Black Heritage Trail.** Nearby, at 46 Joy St., is the **Museum of Afro-American History**, housed in what was once the **Abiel Smith School**. The School was founded in 1834, by a gift of Abiel Smith, to educate Black children. Earlier Prince Hall, a Black leader, had petitioned the Massachusetts Legislature in vain to admit Black children to the public schools. Later, in the fight for integrating Boston schools, Garrison led a boycott to close the Smith School. **In 1854, at long last, the Massachusetts Legislature opened the public schools to Blacks.** The Museum has many exhibits on the history and contributions of Blacks in Massachusetts, and also conducts tours. **Call (617) 742-1854.** Near the Museum and Meeting House, on Smith Court, No.'s 7, 71/2, and 10 are early 19th century wooden structures, typical of those that Black families lived in then.

At **No. 5 Pinckney is one of the oldest buildings on the Hill**, built in the late 18th century. It was the home of **Colonel George Middleton**, a horse trainer, who led an all-Black company in the Revolution. During the era of the Fugitive Slave Law, **Louis Hayden and his wife** used their home at 66 Phillips as a station in the **Underground Railroad.** The house was also a meeting place for local Abolitionists. At 108 Charles St., lived **Dr. George Grant, the first Black instructor at Harvard Dental School.** He typifies the many Black professionals who lived in Boston after the Civil War. The **Charles Street Meeting House** at the intersection of Charles and Mt. Vernon was built in 1807 as the Third Baptist Church. Its original parishioners were south slope aristocrats, who excluded blacks from the services. However, later the Church was a platform for **Abolitionists Garrison, Harriet Tubman, Sojourner Truth,**

and Wendell Phillips. In 1876, the Meeting House was purchased by the **African Methodist Episcopal Church** and was a religious center for Blacks until 1939 when it changed owners again. Facing the **State House**, on the Beacon St. side of the **Common,** is a site of the Black Heritage Trail that we encountered while on the Freedom Trail, namely the monument to the **all-Black Massachusetts 54th Civil War Regiment,** organized and led by Robert Gould Shaw.

At the northern border of Beacon Hill, at 141 Cambridge, in a neighborhood of modern government buildings, is another of the **Harrison Gray Otis** houses. This one, built in 1793, was actually the first of the three designed by Bulfinch for his friends the Otises. It is now the headquarters of the **Society for the Preservation of New England Antiquities (SPNEA),** and houses its Library and Archives. After meticulous research, the SPNEA has restored the interior decoration and furnishings. Open to the public. Fee. **Call (617) 227-3956** for schedule. Next door to the Otis house rises another survivor from the 19th century, the **Old West Church**, whose congregation was gathered before the Revolution.

On Charles St., near the Charles River, lived real-life authors **Annie Fields and Sarah Orne Jewett,** and also **Olive Chancellor**, ardent fighter for women's rights in Henry James' *THE BOSTONIANS*, who typified the Boston woman of wealth concerned with social reform. Alas, the lovely water view which they all treasured has been marred by the gaseous Storrow Drive.

The Massachusetts 54th Civil War Regiment. Picture inspired by the St. Gaudens relief in Boston Common.

Trinity Church in Copley Square reflected in the Hancock Tower. The park in the foreground is a popular setting for concerts and dance festivals or just relaxing.

BACK BAY

Most of Downtown Boston consists of higgledy-piggeldy narrow streets, colliding at every angle. The single exception is **Back Bay**, the district west of the Arlington St. side of the Public Garden. Back Bay's neat grid with alphabetically ordered cross streets, Arlington, Berkeley, Clarendon, Dartmouth, Exeter, etc., resulted from a mid-nineteenth century project in which earth from the outer suburbs was used to fill-in about 430 acres of tidal flats of the Charles River. With no more space on Beacon Hill, wealthy Bostonians started to build their homes, churches, and cultural institutions here. Much of Back Bay is now protected as a National Historic District. It contains some of the country's most beautiful blocks of mid-to-late nineteenth century residential and church architecture. It is a pleasure to wander along the streets savoring the rows of elegant brick, granite, and brownstone buildings. **In the spring, in magnolia blossom time, the walk along Commonwealth Ave. under arching greenery toward the Public Garden is exquisite.** The Back Bay T stops are: Arlington, Copley, Hynes/ICA, and Kenmore of the Green Line.

Today, most Back Bay buildings have been recycled to new uses, stores galleries, restaurants, hotels, educational and cultural institutions, corporation head-quarters. Several of Boston's smaller arts groups are based here. Commonwealth Ave., Beacon, and Marlborough Streets are the homes of students and organizations, while Boylston and Newbury are primarily commercial. Boylston has large stores and office buildings for banks and insurance companies, while Newbury St. is noted for its

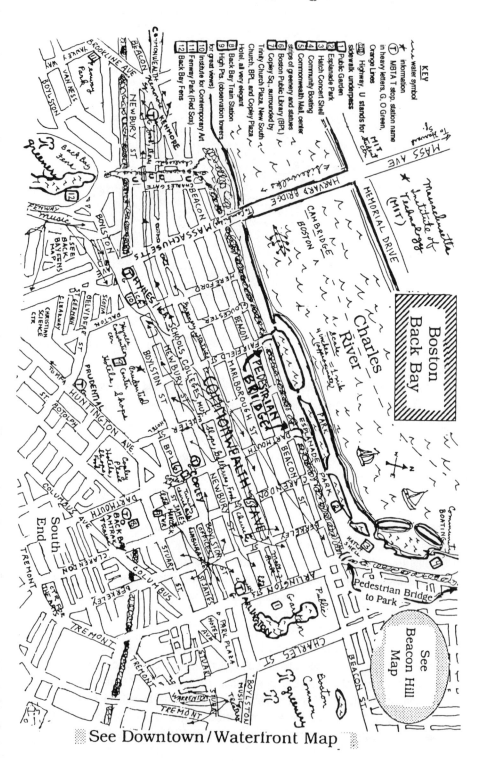

See Downtown/Waterfront Map

many elegant restaurants, galleries, and shops.

Sprinkled about the area are several strikingly handsome stone churches, some now serving as theatres, galleries, and residences. The architectural gem of the churches is **Trinity Episcopal Church**, on Boylston in Copley Square, overlooking a popular park, **which in summer vibrates with free concerts and open air dance festivals.** The Copley T stop on the Green Line is closest. Opposite Trinity, on Dartmouth St., is **Back Bay's crown jewel, the Boston Public Library,** a beautiful Renaissance palace, designed by McKim, Mead, and White. Halls with murals by **Sargent** and **Abbey,** carvings by **St. Gaudens**, and columns, floors, and stairways in marble of many colors welcome you graciously to the Realm of Knowledge. Fortunately, the courtyard of the "Old Building" was retained when the Annex was constructed in the late 1970's. It is an oasis of peace and quiet where a scholar can munch on lunch while surveying the day's finds, and weary shoppers can relax while enjoying the delicacies of the many nearby foodstores. The Library's collection is one of the world's finest, including rare documents and periodicals from around the globe, maps, tapes, records, and microprints. The Annex has an auditorium featuring films, concerts, and lectures, all free. **Call (617) 536-5400.** Adding to the elegance of Copley Square are the **New Old South Church**, to which the Old South's congregation moved in 1876, and the **Copley Plaza Hotel**. On Arlington St., opposite the Public Garden, near the Arlington stop on the T's Green Line, is the handsome brownstone **Arlington St. Church** (Unitarian), built by the congregation to which **William Ellery Channing**, the Apostle of Unitarianism, preached. He is honored by a monument across the street in the Public Garden, inscribed with "He breathed into theology a humane spirit and proclaimed a new divinity of man." His Unitarian preaching marked the transformation of Puritanism into tolerance and humanism. More about Channing on page 183.

In Back Bay, two high rise buildings offer the public, for a fee, spectacular views of the City: the glass sheathed, I. M. Pei-designed, 60 story **John Hancock Building** on St. James St. behind Trinity Church, and the 50 story **Prudential Tower** in the **Prudential Shopping Mall** on Boylston St., two blocks west of the Public Library. The Copley T stop on the Green Line is a short walk from both. The **Hynes**

The Muses Welcome Visitors at the Copley Square Entrance of the Boston Public Library

Convention Center, hosting shows, conventions, and sports, is also part of the Prudential Complex on Boylston St. The Hynes CC/ICA T stop on the Green Line is closest to it, and the Copley stop is about two blocks away.

Rowe's Wharf. In the foreground, T boat terminal, Boston Harbor Hotel, and Great Arch. In the background, financial towers across Atlantic Ave.

THE WATERFRONT

A marvelous way of experiencing Boston is from seaside. The many piered waterfront of this former maritime prodigy extends from Dorchester Bay, around the central peninsula to the heavy-duty container docks in Charlestown on the Mystic River. But we shall focus on the part bordering Atlantic Ave. and its feeder streets **between Long Wharf and South Station** (T Red Line), a distance of about 3/4 mile, a leisurely walk of 15 minutes even with the "Big Dig" in progress. See map on page 15. This section offers choice recreation -- cruises, Aquarium, museums, galleries, parks, restaurants -- amid hotels and condos and high rise office buildings of government and finance. The elevated highway, to be depressed by year 2004 by the Big Dig (hooray!), still casts a daunting gloom over Atlantic Ave. **But there are easy underpasses**, with traffic lights, and safety isles for pedestrians (marked with **E** on the map) **at** : (a) **State Street**, allowing you to go from the Quincy Market to the Long Wharf cruise docks; (b) **Broad St.**, where crowds of office workers cross over from the Financial District and pour through the **giant arch** to **Rowe's Wharf** to the docks for the **MBTA boats for Hingham** and the airport.

On Long Wharf, **Boston Harbor Cruises, call (617) 227-4321**, offers harbor tours, whale watches, trips to the John F. Kennedy Library on Columbia Point (see p. 46), and operates the **frequent T boat service to the Constitution Park** in Charlestown. (See Freedom Trail section.) Also on Long Wharf, **Bay State Cruises**, call **(617) 723-7800**, offers narrated harbor cruises, whale watches, trips to the **Boston Harbor Islands State Park** (see Emerald Necklace), and also provides a shuttle boat to **Commonwealth Pier on Northern Ave.** to its cruise ship, the **Provincetown II,** which makes daily trips to Provincetown in the summer. Next to the Commonwealth Pier, which is about 1/4 mile from Atlantic Ave., is the **World Trade Center**, host to a variety of trade shows. The MBTA is currently planning rapid transit from South Station to the Trade Center. On Northern Ave. near Atlantic is another passenger entrance to Rowe's Wharf. Beyond the Trade Center, at 290 Northern Ave., is the berth of the **Virginia C**, operated by the **A.C. Cruise Lines,** call **(617) 261-6633**, offering whale watches and daily trips to Gloucester's Rocky Neck during the warm season. See Chapter 3. About two blocks from South Station, just beyond the Congress St. Bridge (see map on page 15), are the **Computer and Children's Museums** (see p.45). Along Atlantic Ave. and Fort Point Channel, artists have converted many old warehouses to galleries, studios, and living spaces. **Mobius** at 354 Congress is an artist-run center for experimental work in all media, call **(617) 542-7416** or consult Web site **http://www.artswire.org/Artswire/www/mobius.html.**

The jewel of the Waterfront is the New England Aquarium, call **(617) 742-8870**, on Central Wharf, next to Long Wharf. The nearest T stop is the Aquarium stop (Blue Line), but Government Center (Green and Blue Lines) is only a five minute walk away via the Quincy Market. See map. Its 200,000 gallon see-through ocean tank -- one of the world's largest -- harbors huge sharks, giant turtles, and hundreds of smaller species. Clearly-written captions explain the details of habitat and life cycle of thousands of species in smaller tanks. Exhibits exploring marine ecology,

performances of sea lions and dolphins in the Discovery Barge, multimedia shows. **This is a great aquarium. Call (617) 742-8870** for schedule and fee information.

MUSEUMS

Greater Boston has a vast number of fine museums. Below is just a sampling of museum highlights on the Boston side of the Charles River. The excellent Harvard museums will be described in the next section when we cross the River to Cambridge.

Museum of Fine Arts (MFA), 465 Huntington Ave., near the Fenway and Olmsted's **Emerald Necklace. This is Boston's greatest.** Take the Arborway Green Line (the E Green Line) and get off at the Museum stop, or you can take the Green Line streetcars labeled Northeastern since Northeastern University is located only three blocks from the Museum, or you can walk to it from the Longwood stop on the Riverside Green Line (the Green Line streetcars marked D).

This is one of the world's great assemblies of art from antiquity to the present housed in a beautiful Greek Temple, designed by **Guy Lowell**, and a new West Wing Annex, designed by **I. M. Pei**. Many of the Museum's treasures were contributed by 19th century Brahmins. Their cost today would be unimaginable.

The Museum has superb collections of paintings ranging from the 11th to the 20th century, and is especially noted for its paintings by 19th century French Impressionists. But for visitors who have arrived after steeping themselves in history on the Freedom Trail, of special interest will be the collection of paintings by early American artists, including more than 60 by **John Singleton Copley** and 50 by **Gilbert Stuart.** The heroic statues of the actors in the Revolutionary drama that you saw on the Freedom Trail were produced several decades afterwards. But here you find life-

size portraits, by these celebrated artists, of their *contemporaries*, **Samuel Adams, John Hancock, Paul Revere, Joseph Warren, James Otis, Mercy Otis Warren, Josiah Quincy**, and many others, and the effect is stunning.

Another favorite of visitors fresh from the Freedom Trail is the collection of **American Decorative Arts and Sculpture from the Colonial Period to the Present,** especially period rooms of 18th century furniture and the superb collection of Paul Revere silver. **Occupying a place of honor in the Revere Silver Room is the great punch bowl dedicated to the *Glorious Ninety-Two.*** Who were they? They were the 92 members of the Massachusetts Legislature, who in 1767 **voted for a resolution calling for a Union of all 13 Colonies** to fight the British Tax Acts and Writs of Assistance. Only 17 members of the Legislature voted against the resolution, and those "wretches" were consigned to H--l in engravings and broadsides of the time. A sample from a broadside of 1767: May Heav'n its blessings shower/ On the Glorious Ninety-two/ But Seventeen devour/ Mean abject wretches ...

The Museum's collection of Asiatic Art, including scrolls, paintings, prints, sculpture, and ceramics of all periods from India, Japan, China, and Islamic countries, **is recognized as the world's most extensive assembled under one roof.** Undoubtedly Boston's headstart in collecting Far Eastern Art began early in the 19th century with the China Trade and was continued by Boston Brahmins with a zeal for travel and collecting. The collections of Ancient Egyptian and Near Eastern Art, of Classic Greek, Roman, and Etruscan Art, and of Roman Imperial Art are outstanding. The Textiles and Costumes Collection of weaving, embroidery, laces, printed fabric, and costumes of Eastern and Western cultures is ranked as the world's greatest. I could go on and on. **But I hope that I've conveyed to you the main idea, that this Museum is one of the Wonders of the Western World.**

The Museum also hosts rotating exhibits. In the new Annex are an excellent gift shop, an outstanding restaurant, a sidewalk cafe, a cafeteria leading out to a sculpture garden, and an auditorium for films and lectures. It also has an extensive library. **Call (617) ANSWERS or (617) 267-9300** for information about fees and schedules of special events and also *free days*. Current rates are: $8; elders and students, $ 6; ages 6-17, $3; under six, free. Currently, Wed. 4-9, free.

Isabella Stewart Gardner Museum, 280 The Fenway, near the Museum of Fine Arts. See above map. Directions for getting there by T are the same as for the MFA. Paintings of European masters, sculpture, and furniture collected by Mrs. Gardner with the advice ot art critic **Bernard Berenson**, and displayed in a lovely Renaissance Venetian palazzo. The center courtyard with its fountains and cascades of greenhouse flowers is delightful. The upstairs galleries are the setting for concerts of classical music, which regularly get rave reviews from an adoring public. Open Tuesday through Sunday from 11 to 5. **Call (617) 566-1401 for information.** Current rates are: $7; elders and college students, $5; ages 12-17, $3; under 12, free.

Institute of Contemporary Art, **(ICA)**, 955 Boylston St., in a recycled police station opposite the Prudential Center. The Hynes CC/ICA and Copley T stops on the Green Line are closest. **Call (617) 266-5152.** The Institute is "dedicated to presenting the most significant and exciting developments in present day art." The exhibits and modes of presentation *are* often exciting, and always intriguing. Movies and lectures, too. A visit here to see some of what artists strive for today is a fine supplement to the MFA and Gardner experience of the past. Current fees are: $5.25; students with ID, $3.25; children and elders, $2.25; Thurs. 5-9 p.m., free.

Museum of Science and Hayden Planetarium, Science Park, located near the Charles River Locks straddling the River. Take Lechmere Green Line and get off at Science Park stop, or walk there from the Charles/MGH stop on the Red Line along the Esplanade Park (see map on p.32). **Call (617) 723-2500. This museum has a host of educational, action-packed exhibits that focus attention on the wonders of the natural world**, and a rich array of things of science to play with. Youngsters love it and so do their parents, and everyone learns a lot. The range covered is vast -- mathematics, physics, astronomy, chemistry, biology, meteorology, geology, ecology, and archaeology. See ice crystals form, play with computers, learn how birds fly,

Isabella Stewart Gardner Museum

how the human body works, journey into the center of storms, etc., etc., etc. Films in Mugar Omni Theatre dazzle. Excellent gift shop. The 6th floor cafeteria offers good, moderately priced food and superb views. In the warm months, boat trips are offered from the Museum along the Charles River to the **Hatch Shell** in the **Esplanade Park**. Current fees are: $8; seniors and ages 3-14, $6; 2 and under, free. Additional fees for the Planetarium and Mugar Omni Theatre.

Children's Museum, located in a recycled Warehouse on **Museum Wharf**, 300 Congress St., call **(617) 426-8855. It is near South Station on the T Red Line.** Just walk north along Atlantic Ave., past the Federal Reserve bank, and turn right onto Congress St. **A giant milk bottle marks the wharf.** The Museum features a smorgasbord of hands-on activities for children. Fascinating permanent exhibits and some special ones, as well as shows featuring puppets, mime, magic, songs and stories. Kids walk on a giant's table, learn about construction, experience a Spanish neighborhood market, dress up in grandmother's attic, produce TV shows, work in a factory, learn how movies move, fly kites, enter calligraphy contests, make origami, blow bubbles, learn about creatures and plants living under the nearby docks, etc., etc. Current fees are: $7; ages 2-15 and seniors, $6; 1 year olds, $2. Fri. 5-9, $1 for everyone. In summer, sight-seeing boat tours leave from the nearby wharves.

On the same wharf as the **Children's Museum** is the new **Computer Museum**. Call **(617) 423-6758.** A spectacular array of computer games and robot demonstrations, a walk-through model of a personal computer the size of a two story house, exhibits and classes on accessing and traveling the information highway, guided tours, a helpful staff, all make this museum educational and entertaining for everyone. Current fees are $7; seniors, students, ages 5 and up, $5; 4 and under, free.

As you walk along Congress St. to Museum Wharf, you pass the **Beaver II**, a replica of the **Beaver, one of the three "Tea Party" ships** from which Bostonians dumped tea on the night of December 16, 1773. It was built in Denmark and sailed to Boston on the occasion of the Bicentennial celebration in 1973. It is run as a museum, with exhibits on the history of the events leading to the Party. Fee.

John F. Kennedy Library and Museum, at Columbia Point in Dorchester, next to UMass, Boston. **Call (617) 929-4574.** By T, take a Red Line train to the JFK/UMass stop, and then take a bus to the Library. Since the Library is near the UMass campus, you can also take a bus to UMass and walk to the Library from the campus. As you exit the UMass station, you will see a beautiful white gem-like building overlooking Boston Harbor. That's it, the JFK Library. It is unfortunately isolated from the rest of the City by the Southeast Expressway. It will be a cosmic improvement if someday there is a greenbelt to it with walking and bicycle paths. This should be one of the jewels of the **Emerald Necklace. In summer, a delightful way of getting to the JFK Library is by the Boston Harbor Cruises boat from Long Wharf.** (See Waterfront section, pp. 40, 41.) The Library is the repository of the papers of President Kennedy's administration. There are also films and video displays of the highlights of his presidency and political campaigns. You can relive his confrontation with George Wallace in support of the integration of the University of Alabama, and his speech proposing a ban on atmospheric testing of nuclear weapons, two of the Nation's finest moments. Current fees are: $6; seniors and students, $4; ages 6 to 15, $2; under 6, free.

Across the parking lot from the JFK Library and Museum is the new **Commonwealth Museum, call (617) 727-9268.** Free. This contains a variety of exhibits on Massachusetts history. The building also houses **an extension of the State House Archives Library.** In fact, some of the archives treasures described previously when we were at the State House while on the Freedom Trail may at some point be moved here. (See pages 17, 18.)

There are many excellent museums in the Greater Boston area to which you can daytrip by public transportation. Some of these will be described in later chapters. **Of these my favorites are the ones in Salem** (see Chapter 3, pp. 117-128), **only a half hour's train ride from North Station.** Recall also that we passed several museums while on the Freedom Trail and that we encountered the **Museum of Afro-American History** while exploring Beacon Hill (see pages 35, 36).

GALLERIES AND SHOPS
Of course, one of the treats of a large city is the splendor and variety of its stores and galleries. Here are just a few of Boston's shopping districts. We have already mentioned that Boston's major department stores, **Filene's and Jordan Marsh's (now Macy's),** are located at Downtown Crossing, the intersection of

Washington and Winter Streets, near the Old South Church on the Freedom Trail, and several T stops (see Downtown/Waterfront map on p. 15): the Park St. stop on the Green and Red Lines is one block away, and the Downtown Crossing T stop on the Orange and Red Lines opens right into Filene's famous automatic mark-down bargain basement. **Art galleries abound in Boston**, but the ones on **Newbury Street in Back Bay** are most famous. Try for starters the block between Exeter and Dartmouth (Copley T stop on the Green Line is nearest), which is dense with elegant galleries, boutiques, and pleasant restaurants and cafes. The displays of sculpture, paintings, and crafts are often breath-taking. **Also in Back Bay are two large shopping complexes,** both near the Public Library: the **Prudential Center,** on Boylston St., between the Copley and Hynes/ICA stops on the Green Line; and **Copley Place**, on Dartmouth St., near the Copley Stop on the Green Line and opposite the Back Bay train station on the Orange Line. The **Faneuil Hall and Quincy Market** area (see pages 24-27) teems with shops, galleries, and restaurants. The Government Center stop on the Green and Blue Lines is nearest. **Harvard Square** in Cambridge (only 10 minutes from Park St. on the Red Line) has a variety of shops, **but is most noted for its extraordinary array of bookstores.** The **Harvard Cooperative Society (The Coop)** in the Square is most famous. The exit of the Kendall/MIT (recently renamed Cambridge Center/MIT) stop on the Red Line is at the door of the **Tech Coop, the MIT branch of the Harvard Coop.** Next to it is a food court and shops. On the Main St. side of the Tech Coop you can board a free shuttle bus to the **CambridgeSide Galleria,** an extensive shopping mall. The chief shopping district of Brookline is near **Coolidge Corner,** the intersection of Beacon and Harvard Streets. Take the Cleveland Circle Green Line streetcar (labeled C) to it. See map on p.70.

MUSIC

Because of its Puritan Heritage, Boston got started late on theatre and music. It wasn't until after the Revolution, in the 1790's, that the first Boston theatre was built. But it has made up for lost time. Today Boston is bursting with music energy and talent. Music happens everywhere - in halls and auditoria, college campuses, theatres, museums, libraries, churches, synagogues, parks, streets, coffee houses, restaurants, nightclubs, and subways. Even venerable Faneuil Hall and King's Chapel regularly breathe out soprano cantatas, oboe solos, and violin concertos. The following is a small sampling. **The Boston Symphony Orchestra**, organized over one hundred years ago and one of the Country's finest, with Seiji Ozawa as its conductor, performs at **Symphony Hall**, designed with special concern for acoustics by McKim.

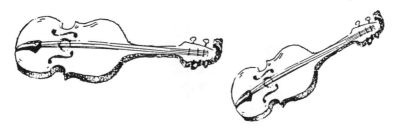

Meade, and White in 1900. It is located at the intersection of Massachusetts and Huntington Avenues. Take the Arborway Green Line streetcar (labeled E) and get off at Symphony. Since Northeastern University is a few blocks beyond it, you can also take a streetcar labeled Northeastern. Call **(617) 266-1492** for ticket information or **(617) CONCERT** for program information. The Symphony's regular season is from September to April. In the summer months, its home is in **Tanglewood**, in the Berkshires (see Volume 3). Low priced tickets are sometimes available for Wednesday night rehearsals. Friday matinees are a long tradition.

In May and June, when the Symphony vacates the premises, the **Boston Pops Orchestra,** with many of the same musicians, but Keith Lockhart conducting, takes over Symphony Hall, giving concerts of lighter classics, often with steamed-up arrangements, amid the popping of champagne corks for audiences sipping and supping while seated about tables. Pops Concerts are favorite fund raisers. Huge blocks of tickets are regularly bought up by organizations. In summer, the Pops also gives a very popular series of free concerts from the **Hatch Shell of the Esplanade Park** (see Parks and Emerald Necklace section, p. 53), the most acclaimed of all being the July 4th concert, attended by tens of thousands, which ends with Tchaikovsky's *WAR of 1812 OVERTURE,* climaxing in the shooting of cannons and a grand show of fireworks, a tradition initiated by the late maestro Arthur Fiedler, who invented the Pops. The **Handel and Haydn Society Choir**, organized in 1818, is Boston's oldest music group. It has a regular season at Symphony Hall, and traditionally sings Handel's Messiah at Christmas. **Call (617) 266-1492 or (617) 266-3605.**

For years Boston enjoyed the superb, innovative productions of the **Opera Company of Boston** directed by the incomparable **Sarah Caldwell**. But alas due to financial difficulties related to needed repairs of the Opera House at 539 Washington in Downtown Crossing, the Opera Company folded. But opera lovers devoutly hope that the building will be restored as part of the new Downtown revival plans, and the maestra will return.

The **Boston Light Opera**, **(617) 261-8866**, the **Lyric Opera**, **(617) 426-5000**, and the **Chorus Pro Musica**, **(617) 267-7442**, are outstanding among the area's smaller voice groups. Fine concerts, often at low ticket prices or free, are given at the recital

halls and auditoria of the area's music schools. Call **(617) 536-2412** to get the concert schedule at the **New England Conservatory of Music** at 290 Huntington Ave. See Back Bay Fens map, p. 54. Take the Arborway Green Line streetcar (labeled E) to the Northeastern stop. The New England Conservatory's **Jordan Hall has been praised as an acoustically perfect space** by many celebrated performers, some of whom were students there. Often the concerts are free. The Conservatory also provides performance space to several of Boston's smaller music groups, including the **Boston Philharmonic,** the **Cantata Singers**, and the **Gay Men's Chorus.** At 8 the Fenway, near the New England Conservatory but not to be confused with it, is the **Boston Conservatory**, which also offers the public a great range of concerts. Its specialties are opera, choral music, and dance. **Call (617) 536-6340.** The **Berklee School of Music** stages concerts at the **Berklee Performance Center**, 136 Massachusetts Ave., and the **Berklee Recital Hall,** 1140 Boylston St. **Call (617) 266-7455.** Both of these are near the Hynes/ICA stop on the Green Line. In Cambridge, the **Longy School of Music**, one Follen St., call **(617) 876-0956**, and **Harvard's Sanders Theatre** (in Memorial Hall at Quincy and Cambridge Streets), and local churches, provide performing space for several music groups including **Boston Musica Viva**, **Masterworks Chorale, Cecelia Society, Cantata Singers, Banchetto Musicale, Boston Camerata, Cambridge Concert Series,** and **Harvard-Radcliffe Collegium Musicum.** The **Harvard-Radcliffe Gilbert and Sullivan Society** performs in the **Agassiz Theatre** at Radcliffe. All these places are within walking distance from the Harvard stop on the Red Line. Watch the *HARVARD GAZETTE* for announcements.

    Beloved Boston Garden Arena, now closed and soon to be "redeveloped," used to host visiting spectaculars -- circuses and ice shows, big name bands, etc. Perhaps the **FleetCenter**, the new sports arena built near the old Garden site, will take up these roles. Like the Garden, the **FleetCenter adjoins the North Station commuter train station,** which is across the street from the North Station stop on the Green and Orange Lines. Visiting opera troupes generally perform at the **Wang Center**, 268 Tremont, in the **Theatre District** (see below). The Boylston stop on the Green Line is closest. Excellent jazz, dance and folk music can be heard in the area's nightclubs, coffee houses, and taverns. For information on who is performing where consult the *CALENDAR* in the Thursday *BOSTON GLOBE*. The subway and parks are the scene of much impromptu music, some of it very good. Of the many new groups rising to fame, my favorite is the **New England Klezmer Conservatory Orchestra**, which is reviving the almost-lost Yiddish music of the Eastern European shtetl.

THEATRE

Like music, good theatre happens in many places in Boston. The more lavish productions are apt to take place in the **Theatre District**, bordered by Tremont St. and the part of Boylston which is south of the Common. The Boylston T stop on the Green Line is closest. A walk along the edge of the Common from the Park St. stop on the Green and Red Lines also brings you to the District. **The Boylston St. T exit, at the corner of Tremont and Boylston, is opposite the grand matriarch of Boston's theatres,** the 1600-seat **Colonial**, at 106 Boylston, call **(617) 931-2787**, which recently has undergone a restoration refurbishing its magnificent prism chandeliers, gilded columns and friezes, and the classical, romantic wall and ceiling murals abounding in cherubs, muses, nymphs, and gargoyles. Another theatre-palace, with glorious marble floors and columns, sweeping staircases, and classical statuary, is the 3700-seat **Wang Center for the Performing Arts**, at 268 Tremont, two blocks away from the Colonial, call **(617) 931-2787**. The Wang hosts the performances of the **Boston Ballet** and visiting opera and dance troupes. The Boston Ballet's home season is from December to May. Opposite the Wang, at 265 Tremont, is the **Shubert, (617) 425-4520**, featuring blockbuster musicals and drama. Next door to the Wang, at 246 Tremont, the Wilbur Theatre, **(617) 423-7440**, offers dinner theatre -- currently comedy weddings cum receptions. At 219 Tremont, the **Emerson Majestic Theatre**, belonging to Emerson College, hosts dance and drama, often with student performers assisted by acclaimed professionals. **Call (617) 824-8000.** And two blocks west of Tremont, at 74 Warrentown, is the **Charles Playhouse and Cabaret**, call **(617) 426-5225** for Cabaret and **(617) 931-2787** for the Playhouse. The Cabaret has been home for 17 years to the mystery comedy *Shear Madness*. On the day of a performance you can sometimes get tickets at mark-down prices at the **BosTix Kiosks at Faneuil Hall** (Government Center T stop on the Green and Blue Lines) **and Copley Square Park** (Copley stop on the Green Line).

Several of the area's colleges are hosts to excellent repertory groups. Boston University's **Huntington Theatre Company** is based at 264 Huntington Ave., **(617) 266-0800**. Take the Arborway Green Line to it. The **American Repertory Theatre** performs at the **Loeb Drama Center**, 64 Brattle St., near Harvard Square in Cambridge, **(617) 864-2630**. Take the T Red Line to it. Also near Harvard Square, at 12 Holyoke St., **Hasty Pudding Theatre** hosts a variety of performing groups.

The above is a small part of Boston theatre. There are many small groups struggling for survival in the area, performing in improvised theatres, in churches or converted stores or warehouses or schools. They are often the nurseries of new talents and ideas, and form the living, leading edge of the theatre, which is greatly enlivened by the infusion of their energy and creativity. The **Boston Center for the Arts** at 539 Tremont, between Clarendon and Berkeley (see map on p.38), **call (617) 734-3988 or 643-9993 or 557-1255**, provides three stages in the old Cyclorama building for the productions of some of these groups. Two notable groups with their own home bases are: **Lyric Stage Theatre,** 140 Clarendon, **(617) 437-7172; Triangle Theatre,** 58 Berkeley, **(617) 426-3550**, which produces shows on gay and lesbian concerns. The closest T stops to these are Back Bay/South End on the Orange Line and Copley and Arlington on the Green Line. Another troupe in the Back Bay area is the **Children's Theatre**, performing at the New England Hall at the corner of Clarendon and Boylston, a short walk from either the Copley or Arlington stops on the Green Line. In Cambridge's Inman Square, **ImprovBoston** specializes in improvisational theatre stimulated by audience interaction. You can walk along Cambridge St. to it from Harvard Yard (about 1 mile). And many small groups visit Boston. This summer (1996), the acclaimed Bread and Puppets Theatre, based in Glover Vermont, performed at Mass. College of the Arts (near the MFA, take Arborway Green Line to it) and in Cambridge Common (near Harvard Sq., take Red Line). I remember fondly **the Nucleo Eccletico,** which gave magical performances in tiny theatres in the North End.

BEACHES

There are many good beaches in Greater Boston, accessible by public transportation. **Revere Beach** on the Blue Line is closest. **Marblehead, Manchester, Gloucester, and Rockport on the North Shore** all have beautiful beaches near public transportation, which make terrific daytrips from Boston. (See Chapter 3, *A NORTH SHORE SAMPLER,* for information on how to get to them.)

SPORTS

The Boston Red Sox play at Fenway Park. Take a Green Line streetcar to Kenmore Square and follow the crowd down Brookline Ave. to this beautiful baseball park. (See Back Bay map on p. 38.) The **Celtic**s play basketball and the **Bruins** play hockey in the new **FleetCenter** arena which adjoins the North Station commuter rail terminal and is across the street from the North Station stop on the Green and Orange Lines.

Note that in Back Bay and Beacon Hill there are pedestrian bridges to the Esplanade Park at Fairfield, Dartmouth, Arlington, and Charles Streets.

For Boston
Park Rangers
seasonal schedule
call or write
Boston Park
Rangers
(617) 635-7383
Boston Parks and
Recreation,
1010 Mass. Ave.
Boston, MA 02118

Emerald
Necklace
Schematically

Key
ᴧᴧᴧ water symbol
Ⓣ MBTA stop. GGG Green Line.
RRR Red Line. OOO Orange Line
outline of Necklace Gems,
not to be confused with ▬▬, the
symbol for a superhighway.
greenery symbol
⑯ number of Ⓣ bus route

BOSTON PARKS. OLMSTED'S EMERALD NECKLACE

**Boston has a beautiful park system, whose centerpiece is the Emerald
Necklace**, designed by **Frederick Law Olmsted**, author of New York's Central Park
and other great parks around the country. Although the Necklace is seriously marred
in places where traffic has been encouraged to pour through, nevertheless, what
remains intact still conveys Olmsted's vision and allows you to catch a glimpse of what
yet may be when we recover from our auto-mania. The **Metropolitan District Commission** (MDC), **call (617) 727-5250, and Boston Parks and Recreation, call (617)
635-7383,** jointly maintain the parks listed below. The **Boston Park Rangers** patrol
the parks and conduct educational programs. More about the Rangers on p. 57.

    **The Emerald Necklace consists of a series of the City's major parks, the
"emeralds" of the necklace**, linked by strips of greenery. Located near or on the
Necklace are some of the City's chief cultural institutions. The main connective tissues
of the necklace are the wetlands, or fens, as they are usually called, which start in
Jamaica Plain and drain through a sequence of ponds, marshes, and the
meandering brackish Muddy River (in Brookline) into the Charles River. It was

Olmsted's genius to view the fens, not as obstacles to be obliterated by fill-ins, but as natural areas whose beauty, once brought out by judicious draining and planting, would bring the refreshment of the countryside to urban dwellers. The landscaping appears minimal, just a path and benches in places, and here and there a lovely rustic bridge, and stairs leading down from a busy street to the quiet world of the fens, and plantings blending with the native shrubs and trees.

The jewels of the Necklace are described briefly below. They can all be reached separately by the T, and they are close enough together so you can walk from one to another nearby. The **Harbor Islands State Park** can be reached by boat from Long Wharf. (See Waterfront, pp. 40, 41.)

Boston Common and the **Public Garden**, which we have already described, are jewels of the Necklace. They were connected via the greenery of **Commonwealth Mall,** the walkway with trees, statues, and benches in the center of Commonwealth Ave, to the fens, which empty into the Charles River near Kenmore Square at Charlesgate St. Once the flow of the fens into the River was quite visible and lovely, but now it is hidden by pavement and rushing traffic.

Charles River Esplanade Park. This park consisting of a green strip and lagoons along the River is also a Necklace gem. In Olmsted's day, the streets of Back Bay led down to the Riverbank. Now, alas, six lanes of Storrow Drive separate Back Bay from what remains of the green strip, and you can get to it only where there are pedestrian bridges. **Nevertheless, what remains of the Park is heavily used,** the most popular section being between the pedestrian bridges at Charles St. (near the Red Line T stop) and Arlington St. (a few blocks from the Arlington stop on the Green

54

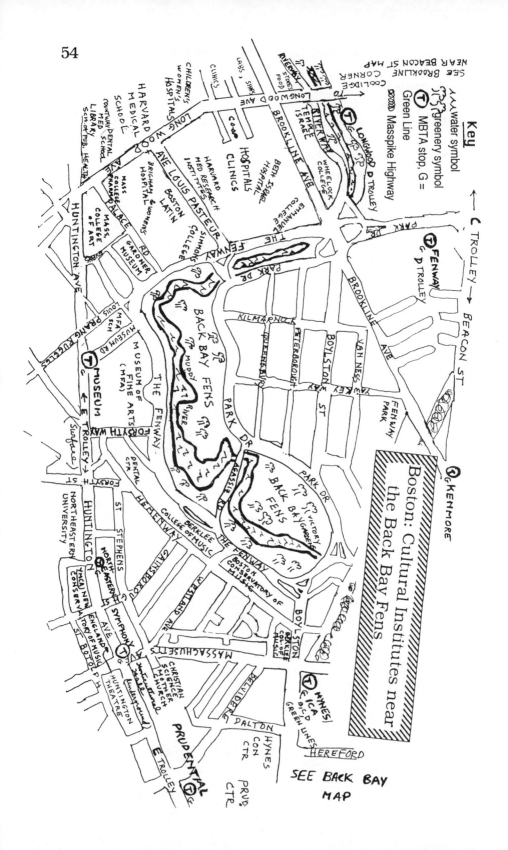

Boston: Cultural Institutes near the Back Bay Fens

SEE BACK BAY MAP

Key
~~~water symbol
~~greenery symbol
Ⓣ MBTA stop, G = Green Line
≋ Masspike Highway

Line). Two very popular features of the Park are the **Hatch Concert Shell** and the **Community Boat House.** In summer, the **Boston Pops Orchestra, the Boston Ballet, and other art groups give free performances from the Shell** to appreciative audiences reposing on the grass. (You'll see that many on the streetcar are carrying folding chairs, blankets, and picnic baskets.) The experience toward sunset, with sailboats gliding along side of you amidst waves of music, is enchanting, one of life's great treats. **At the Boat House, Community Boating, Inc. lets out boats** to resident members who demonstrate the required skills, and also sponsors sailing classes and social activities throughout the year. The membership rates are moderate. The goal is to make sailing a broadly based activity rather than one limited to a monied elite; and to judge from the legions of sails floating on the River on any fine day, the program is very successful. For more information **call (617) 533-1038.**

Along the River there is also a popular hiking-jogging-bicycling-roller blading paved strip, which gets very crowded. Six lanes of Storrow Drive for motorists and one, narrow, paved path for everyone else! **It's time to reassess!!** The bicycle path, named after **Paul Dudley White**, the heart specialist, who cycled daily until he was 86, extends along the River from Back Bay to Watertown. You can cross the River at Massachusetts Ave. on the Harvard Bridge (where MIT is) and then cycle along the north bank.

Cultural Institutions on the Back Bay Fens. In the vicinity of the fens west of Back Bay and south of Brookline (called the **Back Bay fens**) are a large number of cultural institutions. We list some of them. The **Museum of Fine Arts** (see p. 42), the **New England Conservatory of Music** (see p. 49), **Northeastern University, Symphony Hall, Horticultural Hall, Massachusetts College of Art, and Harvard Medical School** are all on Huntington Ave. near the fens, and the **Isabella Stewart Gardner Museum** (see p.44), **Simmons, Emanuel, and Wheelock Colleges, and the Boston Conservatory of Music** are all on the Fenway. All of these can be reached by the Arborway Green Line streetcar. One can also walk from the Hynes CC/ ICA stop on the Green Line or from the Longwood stop on the Riverside Green Line. Several noted hospitals are in the area including the **Children's, Brigham and Women's, and Beth Israel.** The present site of **Boston Latin High School,** the nation's first public school, founded in 1635, is nearby on Ave. Louis Pasteur.

COMMUNITY BOATING
Sailing For All

Back Bay Fens

Olmsted Park and Jamaica Pond. Further south and west along the fens, in the upper valley of Muddy River, is a small gem, **Olmsted Park**, featuring **Leverett Pond**, which, as Olmsted described it, is one of a "chain of picturesque, fresh water ponds, alternating with attractive natural groves, and meads ... the uppermost of these ponds being **Jamaica Pond**, a natural sheet of water, with quiet graceful shores, shaded by a fine natural forest..." (from *ARCHITECTURE BOSTON* by the Boston Society of Architects). Today there is a jogging trail around Jamaica Pond, and, on its Arborway border, an MDC boathouse renting rowboats and sailboats. Jamaica Pond can be reached by taking the Arborway Green Line E streetcar to Pond St.* and walking one block west. You can also walk there from the Longwood stop on the Green Line (D streetcars). At Longwood Ave., near the T stop, steps lead from the street into the Riverway section of the fens. One minute you are on a busy street, and the next in the midst of shrubs and trees beside a smooth slowly gliding river, with families of ducks quacking by.

Arnold Arboretum. About 1/2 mile from Jamaica Pond, along the Arborway, a street with much traffic, which, however, has pleasant, shaded sidewalks, **is the Arnold Arboretum, an exquisite jewel of the Necklace.** It can also be reached by taking the Arborway Green Line E streetcar,* or the Orange Line train, to the Forest Hills station, which is near one of the park gates. (See map on p. 52.) The Arboretum is maintained jointly by the **MDC, Boston Parks and Recreation, and Harvard University. Here are planted 6,000 varieties of ornamental shrubs and trees from around the globe on 265 wooded acres**, including (in Olmsted's words) "rocky

*With current (summer, 1996) construction on the E Green Line beyond Heath St., take bus no. 39 from Copley Square on the Boylston St. side of the Public Library. The bus goes along Huntington Ave., then Centre, and then South St. to the Forest Hills Station, the same route as the Arborway Green Line streetcar. Get off at: Pond St. for Jamaica Pond; at the intersection of South St. and the Arborway (also called Morton St. or Rte. 203) for the Arboretum. The bus driver will help you get off at the right stops.

hillsides, partly wooded with numerous great trees, and a hanging wood of hemlocks of great beauty" and "eminences commanding distant prospects..." Motor vehicles, except those for the aged and handicapped, are excluded. Near the main gate is an administration building (with rest rooms) where you can get a map of the grounds and schedules of events. Lilac and azalea time in the spring and foliage-fall time are especially glorious, but it is always a fascinating and exquisitely beautiful place to be, educational, too, since the shrubs and trees are labeled.

Franklin Park, 500 acres, with zoo, rose gardens, and golf course, call **(617) 442-2002**, is another great park, which, unfortunately, was in recent years the victim of neighborhood vandals. But it has been restored, and Boston Park Rangers patrol it in daylight hours. The **Bird's World**, including an outdoor aviary, and **The Range**, featuring camels, llamas, and zebras, are especially popular with children. Open 10-4 during the warm months. You can reach Franklin Park from the Arboretum by walking 1/2 mile along Morton St., which is an extension of the Arborway. Or you can take bus no. 16 from the Forest Hills station (Orange Line). Bus no. 16 goes from the Forest Hills station through Franklin Park and then to Andrew Station on the Red Line. Ask the driver where to get off for various attractions.

In addition to patrolling the Parks, **Boston Park Rangers conduct a number of excellent, educational programs** including hiking and bicycle trips through the Necklace. Although Boston is not a violent city, it's best to be cautious when visiting the parks, especially those away from the Central City. Go with companions, and during daytime hours. A good way to get your introduction to the Emerald Necklace is to join one of the hikes sponsored by the Park Rangers; call **(617) 635-7383** or write to Boston Parks and Recreation, 1010 Mass Ave., Boston, MA 02118 to obtain a schedule of Ranger programs.

The Boston Harbor Islands State Park. Olmsted visualised the park system as including the **Harbor Islands**, but it was not until 1970, when the Legislature created the **Boston Harbor Islands State Park**, that his grand scheme was realized, and the Necklace was completed. The Islands offer picturesque beaches and coves, and pleasant walks through a semi-wild, oceanside landscape, within sight of the Boston skyline, a unique experience. But that is not all. They abound in historical sites, old fortresses and lighthouses, and the remains of early Native American and European

settlements. **And they are easily accessible by public transportation. The Bay State Cruise Co., call (617) 723-7800,** runs several trips daily, from late spring until early fall, from Long Wharf to **Georges Island**, where the **Park Headquarters is located. From Georges, the Park Service runs a free water taxi service to Lovells, Gallop, Grape, and Bumpkin Islands**. As already mentioned in our Waterfront section, Long Wharf is: near the Aquarium stop on the Blue Line; a 5 minute walk from the Government Center stop on the Green Line; a 10 minute walk from South Station (Red Line). **Overnight camping, by special permit only, is allowed on Lovells Island. For information on how to get a camping permit call (617) 727-5250.** Brochures describing the Park are available at the **Bay State/Provincetown Cruises'** booth at Long Wharf, or by writing to the **Boston Harbor Islands State Park, Executive Office of Environmental Affairs, 100 Cambridge St., Boston 02203**. The boat trip to the Islands is a delight. As your boat wends its way out of the Harbor through the many islands, you'll begin to understand **John Smith's** wonder at the natural beauty of this place, which he called the **"paradise of all these parts"** in his exploration of the New England coast in the early 1600's. The Native Americans, whose gentle stewardship of the land had left the beauty of these islands intact, had been decimated by disease transmitted by Europeans by the time of the Puritans' arrival in the 1630's. The cultivated fields that Smith had seen on the islands then lay abandoned.

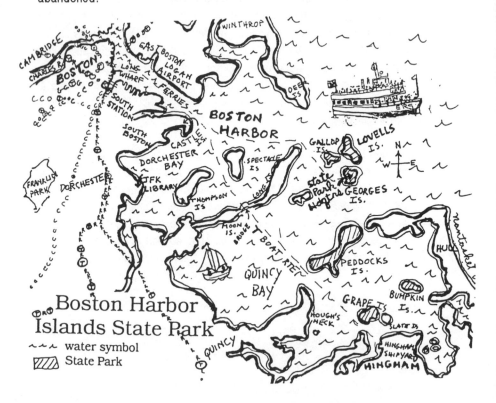

Boston across the Charles

CAMBRIDGE

After God had carried us safe to New England, and
wee had builded our houses, provided necessaries for
our livelihood, reard convenient places for God's
worship, and settled the Civill Government, one of
the next things that we longed for and looked after
was to advance learning and perpetuate it to posterity,
dreading to leave an illiterate ministry to the
churches, when our present ministers shall lie in the
dust.

From NEW ENGLAND FIRST FRUITS.
Inscribed on the Johnston Gate of Harvard Yard.

Cambridge, An Introduction

Cambridge, population 102,000, the seat of Middlesex County, across the
Charles River from Boston, is politically a separate city, and one with enough
fascination of its own to fill volumes. But, nevertheless, its life and history are so closely
intertwined with Boston's that it seems natural to write of both together. Cambridge's
chief claim to fame is that **it is the home of two of the world's leading universities,**
whose scholars have exerted an enormous influence on the intellectual and political

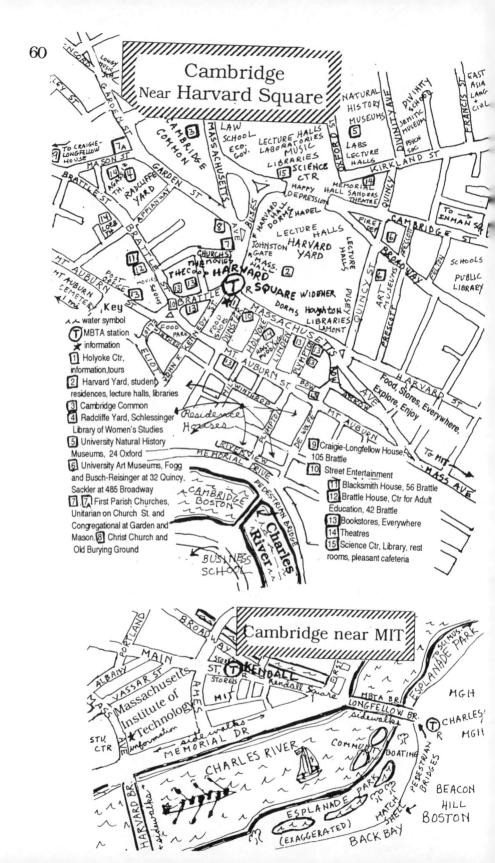

Cambridge Near Harvard Square

Key

∿∿ water symbol
Ⓣ MBTA station
★ information
[1] Holyoke Ctr, information, tours
[2] Harvard Yard, student residences, lecture halls, libraries
[3] Cambridge Common
[4] Radcliffe Yard, Schlessinger Library of Women's Studies
[5] University Natural History Museums, 24 Oxford
[6] University Art Museums, Fogg and Busch-Reisinger at 32 Quincy, Sackler at 485 Broadway
[7] [7] First Parish Churches, Unitarian on Church St. and Congregational at Garden and Mason. [8] Christ Church and Old Burying Ground
[9] Craigie-Longfellow House, 105 Brattle
[10] Street Entertainment
[11] Blacksmith House, 56 Brattle
[12] Brattle House, Ctr for Adult Education, 42 Brattle
[13] Bookstores, Everywhere
[14] Theatres
[15] Science Ctr, Library, rest rooms, pleasant cafeteria

Cambridge near MIT

life of our Nation, **Harvard**, the country's oldest, and the **Massachusetts Institute of Technology (MIT).**

Cambridge was settled in 1630 at the same time as Boston by several families of the **Great Puritan Migration**, led by **John Winthrop**, the first Governor of the Massachusetts Bay Colony, who founded Boston. It was first called **New Towne**, but in 1636, when **the College** was founded by act of the General Court (the Legislature) of the Massachusetts Bay Colony, the town's name **was changed to Cambridge, after the English university** which many of the Puritans had attended. In 1639 the College was named after **John Harvard**, a minister, who had settled in Charlestown, and who had died in 1637, at age 27, **bequeathing to it his 400 volume library and half of his residual estate, which amounted to 1500 pounds**. That the College was established so soon after their arrival in their new land attests to the importance that the Puritans attached to higher education for providing the moral leadership that they needed to survive in the "Wildernesse". One hundred years later, the College was providing leadership for another struggle. **In 1743, young Samuel Adams**, one of its graduates, wrote a master's thesis entitled **"Whether it be lawful to resist the Supreme Magistrate if the Commonwealth cannot otherwise be preserved."**

Getting There. Both Harvard University and MIT are near stops on the T's Red Line. The stop for MIT is **Kendall Square/MIT**, two stops away from Park St. which is in the heart of Boston and on the Red and Green Lines; the stop for Harvard is the **Harvard** stop, the fourth stop from Park St. The Red Line train from Park St. going to Cambridge will be labeled *Alewife.* Traveling by T, you feel the closeness of the two cities, a feeling which may elude car-drivers as they sit and fume in numerous traffic stalls and hunt for non-existent parking spaces. The T train crosses the Charles River on the Longfellow Bridge, near the **Community Boat House**. Looking out on a fine day, you catch an enchanting scene of sails and crewing shells on the River, with **Beacon Hill** and **Back Bay** rising in the background. At sunset, the view is magic.

Harvard University and Old Cambridge

Upon exiting the T, you are in Harvard Square, a bustling, bubbling commercial district of shops and eateries and wall to wall people afoot, whose sheer mass keeps the traffic at bay. Hooray!! Who are the people in the Square? Mostly young or youthful, they come from everywhere in the Boston area, and from the four corners of the earth, too, to judge from the accents you hear, to enjoy the ebullience of Harvard Square, its stores, restaurants, and multitudinous cultural offerings, and lively street scenes of musicians and peddlers, political demonstrators and petitioners. Among the variety of specialty shops here you can pursue any interest. **Most notable are the bookstores, the most fabulous collection in the whole country**. Bookworms can stop here and put the whole world behind them.

Close to the T exits is everything, the Harvard and Radcliffe Yards, the residence halls, libraries, theatres, a remarkable array of historical sites and museums, as well as the aforementioned numerous shops and eateries. To get your bearings, it is a good idea to make your first stop at the **Harvard Information Center, call (617) 495-1573**, on the ground floor of the **Holyoke Building**, the glass and concrete building near the main T exit, on Massachusetts Ave. near Kennedy St. (once called Boylston St.). Here you can get maps of the campus and walking tour guides of **Old Cambridge,** put out by the Cambridge Historical Commission. You can also pick up the *HARVARD GAZETTE* (free) listing the numerous events -- concerts, plays, lectures, political debates, films, exhibits, workshops, etc. -- which abound around the campus. For even more events, you can read the poster-laden bulletin boards about town. You may also inquire at the Information Center about the schedule and starting point of the **free, guided tours of the Harvard Campus.**

Harvard Yard's Johnston Gate, where the inscription at the head of this chapter appears, is just a stone's throw from the T exits. As you pass through it, you make a transition from the bustle of the Square to an attractive tree-shaded campus with a typical academic pastoral of students frisbeeing on greens surrounded by ivied buildings of various vintages. Most remarkable of all is the enclave of handsome 18th century red-brick buildings near the Johnston Gate, which are still used for residences classes and administration. Two of the oldest are **Massachusetts Hall**, to the right of

the Gate, built in 1718, and **Harvard Hall**, to the left, built in 1766 to replace an earlier structure. Although Harvard's first buildings of the 1630's have not survived, the Yard itself has been used continuously for residences and instruction for over 350 years, the oldest academic tradition of our young country, continuously, that is, except for a gap in the year 1775-1776, when **George Washington** ousted Harvard students from their dormitories and learning halls to quarter his soldiers.

Washington had ridden into Cambridge on July 2, 1775 to take command of the Continental Army, consisting then of bands of New England militia who were camped in a great semi-circle about Boston, laying siege to the City, which was then occupied by the British under General Howe. It was just two weeks after the **Battle of Bunker Hill** (see Freedom Trail, pp. 29, 30), and **a little over two months since some of these same men had chased the British all the way to Boston from Concord** (see Chapter 2, p.80). The formal ceremony initiating his command took place near the Yard on **Cambridge Common** (see map on p. 60), the focus for Old Cambridge's social life and pasture for its cattle. A plaque and three cannons captured from the British that year commemorate the event. With Cambridge as his base, Washington conducted the campaign **which culminated in the capture of Dorchester Heights and led to the British evacuation of Boston on March 17, 1776.** This date marking the first great victory of the Revolution, for the British prized Boston as the key city of the Colonies, is an official State holiday, called **Evacuation Day**. Since it coincides with **Saint Patrick's Day**, it is the occasion of a super gala celebration in the Irish Boston of today. Washington's campaign headquarters during his Cambridge stay was the **Wadsworth House,** a simple clapboard, built in 1726 as the residence of the College's president in the southwest corner of the Yard (and still standing).

Harvard Libraries. In the center quadrangle of the Yard is the opulently massive neoclassical **Widener Library,** built in 1913, **the central library of the University's system, containing the country's largest book collection, distributed about the campus in almost 100 separate libraries,** including several outstanding specialized collections. On the first floor of Widener are three splendid dioramas showing Cambridge as it was in the respective years 1667, 1776, and 1936. Behind Widener is the **Houghton Library** containing Harvard's rare document collection. The Keats room on the second floor, with a collection of the poet's manuscripts, is open to the public. Nearby is the **Pusey Library** with several floors built underground to avoid introducing high-rise into the Yard's skyline.

Entrance, Harvard Hall

Other Harvard Highlights Near the Yard. As you walk out the north gate of the Yard, to the left is the **Law School**, alma mater of many Supreme Court justices, and to the right is the somber Victorian Gothic, **Memorial Hall**, built to honor Harvard's Civil War dead, now housing lecture halls, a cafeteria, and **Sanders Theatre**. In front of you is the Sert-designed **Science Building**, a colossus, which, however, has a pleasant small cafeteria in a greenhouse, and rest rooms. Beneath you, out of sight and powerless to harm you, runs the traffic of Cambridge St., the happiest of all depressions, a definite improvement over the days when students had to battle with steel monsters to get to their classes.

The University Museums. Major attractions open to the public are the University's extraordinary museums. Outstanding of its kind is the cluster of natural science and anthropology museums at 24 Oxford called the **Harvard Museum of Cultural and Natural History, (617) 495-3045,** including the **Peabody Museum of Archaeology and Ethnology, the Museum of Comparative Zoology, the Botanical Museum, and the Mineralogical Museum.** Here are treasures that centuries of Harvard scholars have brought back from the four corners of the earth. Exhibits include pre-Columbian art and reconstructed dinosaurs, cases and cases of crystals and rare gems, acres of stuffed animals, and the renowned glass flower collection of the Blaschke brothers, painstakingly magnified reproductions in glass of the beauties and symmetries of the tiny world of flower parts. Modest fee. Currently open Mon.-Sat., 9 to 4.30.

　　The visual arts are well represented by a trio of museums, which have been combined to form the **Harvard Art Museum**. For information about all three call **(617) 495-7768 or (617) 495-9400.** The foremost of the trio is the **Fogg Art Museum**, 32 Quincy St., with a superb art collection displayed in galleries surrounding a 16th century Italian courtyard, including ancient Greek and Roman sculpture and pottery, Medieval Cathedral art, works of European masters, and modern art. The Fogg also has a 150,000 volume library and special exhibits oriented toward art education. **Along with genuine Rembrandts, Botticellis, Gainsboroughs, and Degas, are intriguing fakes and forgeries,** all part of the Museum's teaching function. There is also a laboratory, one of the world's oldest, for conserving paintings. With the growth of the Fogg's collection came the dilemma of how to house it. For a while paintings were hung three-high in the corridors outside the classrooms. But recently the problem was solved, at least for the present, by the opening of the **Sackler Museum**,

Dunster Hall - Harvard

nearby at 485 Broadway, where painting and sculpture are displayed in a delightful new building. The third museum of the trio is the **Busch-Reisinger**, now in the Werner Otto Hall at 32 Quincy, devoted to Northern European art from the Medieval period to the 20th century. Open hours are the same for all three museums, from 10 to 5 on Monday through Saturday, and on Sunday from 1-5. A combination ticket allows you to attend all three Call the above numbers for the current fees. Next to the Fogg Museum is the **Center for Visual Arts**, housing exhibits open to the public on its first floor. The building has the distinction of being the only one in North America designed by the renowned Swiss architect **Le Corbusier**.

Christ Church and
Old Burying Ground

First Parish Church
Unitarian

More Highlights Near Harvard Square. On Garden St., across from the southern tip of Cambridge Common, is Cambridge's oldest surviving church building, **Christ Church,** built in 1759, and designed by Peter Harrison, the architect of Boston's King's Chapel, and like the latter, an Anglican church. It was attended by the Tory elite before the Revolution, and by George and Martha Washington during their Cambridge stay. Next to the Church is the **Old Burying Ground**, where early settlers, including Harvard's first eight presidents, are buried. **None of Cambridge's early Puritan meeting houses remain**. However, the **First Parish Church, Unitarian**, built in 1833 on the site of the original meeting house of the 1630's (on the Church St. side of the

Burying Ground), and the **First Parish Church, Congregational,** at the corner of Garden and Mason, are both descendants of Cambridge's earliest Puritan congregation. The split occurred early in the 19th century, when Unitarianism won many converts from the "orthodox" Congregational churches, many of which underwent fission into Trinitarian and Unitarian components. The schism here in Cambridge shook the Congregational world, since Harvard, along with Yale, was a chief training ground for Congregational ministers. Old time religion would never be the same in New England, as the liberalizing influence of Unitarianism took hold.

On Garden St., just past Appian Way, is the entrance to **Radcliffe Yard**, which extends to Brattle St., an oasis of relative quiet, with ivied buildings about a green. **Radcliffe College** was founded by **Elizabeth Cary Agassiz, Alice Longfellow, and other Brahmin women,** as a means of obtaining the equivalent of a Harvard education for women. Harvard instructors came to Radcliffe to give the same lectures that they had just given on the other side of Cambridge Common. Today the merging of Harvard and Radcliffe is virtually complete, and the buildings here have been recycled to new uses of the joint coeducational university. Especially pleasant for quiet reveries is the little garden between Byerly and Longfellow Halls. On the Brattle street side of Radcliffe Yard is the **Bunting Institute,** a community of women scholars, whose goal is to help women, who have interrupted their academic careers, to reenter the academic world. The Institute's **Schlesinger Library** has an outstanding **Women's Studies collection**.

During the 1770's, Brattle Street was nicknamed **Tory Row** because of the loyalist sympathies of its residents. Along this street, in handsome mansions on spacious grounds stretching to the Charles River, lived a number of wealthy Tories, mostly officials of the Colonial administration. On the eve of Washington's arrival, they fled. **Miraculously, the mansions still stand, with modern Cambridge rising about them. Washington** used the mansions as living quarters for his officers, choosing for himself and Martha the most distinguished of them all, **the house at 105 Brattle**, a few blocks north of Radcliffe Yard. This house, built in 1759 by Tory John Vassal, and called the **Craigie-Longfellow House**, is today a National Historic Site administered by the Park

Service, and is open to the public from 9 to 4.30 every day. Modest fee. After the Revolution, it was bought by Dr. Andrew Craigie, who added to it substantially. His widow took in lodgers, one of whom was a newly appointed Harvard professor, **Henry Wadsworth Longfellow** (1807-1882). Upon Longfellow's marriage to **Fanny Appleton,** from one of Boston's wealthiest families, the young couple received the house as a wedding gift. It was here that Longfellow wrote his most famous poems. The furnishings are those left by the Longfellow family including a painting of the three heroines of the *CHILDREN'S HOUR*, "Grave Alice, laughing Allegra, and Edith with golden hair". Grave Alice was a founder of Radcliffe College. Longfellow Hall is named after her.

    Opposite Radcliffe Yard, at 54 Brattle, is the Loeb Theatre, now the home of the **American Repertory Theatre**. Just beyond it, at 56 Brattle, is the **Pratt House,** built in 1808, once the home of **Dexter Pratt, the village blacksmith of Longfellow's poem** that begins "Under the spreading chestnut tree, the village smithy stands..." A plaque marks the place where the tree once stood. The **Blacksmith House** itself is now a delightful coffee house, serving delicious pastries and hosting readings by local poets. At 42 Brattle, is another member of Tory Row, the **Brattle House,** now occupied by the **Cambridge Center for Adult Education**, whose courses range from how to write thrillers to how to do origami. In the 1840's, one of its occupants was the noted feminist, **Margaret Fuller**, editor of the influential Transcendentalist journal, *THE DIAL*. Among the visitors in this house were her friends **Emerson and Thoreau.**

    A pleasant place to walk near Harvard Square is along the riverbanks near the Residence Houses. To get to them, go down Dunster St. to the river. The white tower and blue cupola of Lowell House will guide you. The riverbanks are used for sunning, running, walking, bicycling, etc. A footbridge leads across the river to the **Business School** on the Boston side. The **Paul Dudley White Bicycle Path**, which begins near the Hatch Shell and crosses the river on the **Harvard Bridge** (which is at the Massachusetts Ave. end of MIT), passes by near here and continues all the way to Watertown. **The boat crews of four universities, Harvard, MIT, Boston, and Northeastern, practice on the rive**r, so in the warmer months there is always the spectacle of crew shells shooting up and down the stream. It is a three mile walk along the riverbank to MIT, but only 11/2 miles if you go to it along Massachusetts Ave. from Harvard Square (see pp. 68, 69).

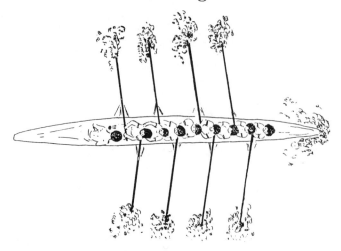

Another pleasant place to walk is **Mount Auburn Cemetery**, about a mile north of the Square on Mount Auburn St. **You can walk to it or take the Waverly or Watertown bus trolley from the Square.** The Cemetery was designed by the **Massachusetts Horticultural Society** in 1831. The Society regarded the project as a challenge to bring forth the best and most beautiful in landscaping while using the grounds to carry on horticultural research. It created what is generally considered a masterpiece, with a blend of formal gardens and memorial monuments, set amid ponds, shrubs, and magnificent trees, and paths winding through glens and glades up to a stone tower atop Mount Auburn, affording beautiful vistas of the city and countryside. **It is not at all spooky**, but a delightful place to walk with your friends; and **the spirits of the many notables buried here – including Longfellow, Winslow Homer, Charles Sumner, Mary Baker Eddy, Oliver Wendell Holmes, Julia Ward Howe, Henry Cabot Lodge – are guaranteed not to bother you**. The Cemetery is a favorite birding spot during the spring migration. In one tree, you may see as many as 15 species, a memorable experience, heightened by the trees in exquisite blossom all about you.

A Walk to MIT from Harvard Square

The Massachusetts Institute of Technology (MIT) is Cambridge's other great university, the country's first ranking engineering school, with outstanding departments in the natural sciences and mathematics, and numerous special institutes and research laboratories, and the country's oldest school of architecture. The MIT main campus is located in a series of connected granite buildings on Memorial Drive along the Charles River, between the **Harvard Bridge** (at Massachusetts Ave) and the **Longfellow Bridge** (near Community Boating), on which the

Red Line T train crosses the river. MIT is what you see when you look across the river from the Hatch Shell in the Esplanade Park. Harvard, also on the river, is hidden behind a bend. There are several ways of getting to MIT. You can take the Red Line T train and get off at the Kendall/MIT stop, which is at the eastern edge of the MIT campus and right at the door of the Tech Coop, the MIT branch of the great Harvard Cooperative Society store, based in Harvard Square. Adjacent to the Coop is a food court. To get to the Massachusetts Ave edge of the campus, you can take the Green Line to the Hynes/ICA stop and then walk along Massachusetts Ave. to the river and cross on the Harvard Bridge. Or you can take the Dudley bus from Harvard Square, which takes you along Mass. Ave. past MIT. **Or you can walk from Harvard Square**; MIT is only 1 1/2 miles eastward along Massachusetts Ave. **The walk gives you a glimpse of several different Cambridges.** On the first lap of the trip, you are in the midst of the multitude of activities near Harvard Square, the **Au Bon Pain plaza** with its chess players and entertainers, and further on, to the left, the **Baptist Church** with its bulletins boards plastered with ads of theatre, concerts, meetings, workshops, and rallies, and then more shops, and so on. Soon you pass on your left a beautiful brownstone castle, also known as **Cambridge City Hall** (restrooms). And onward past the crowds of **Central Square** (also a stop on the T Red Line), a commercial strip **with many far eastern and Indian restaurants** and used furniture stores resembling an oriental bazaar. And then the aroma of chocolate greets you as you pass the **Necco candy factory**, a reminder of old industrial Cambridge, which had numerous tiny factories making every species of whatnots -- furniture, cut glass, rain coats, stockings, novelties, toys. Successive waves of immigrants found work in these factories, Irish, Italians, Slavs, and most recently Portuguese and Spanish, accounting for the ethnically varied neighborhoods, with their churches and fraternal organizations, on either side of Mass. Ave. And then you are at MIT.

The **Information Center** is at 77 Massachusetts Ave. You can get maps of the campus, including an Arts Map guiding you to the many arts sites about campus, and you can pick up copies of *Tech Talk* and *The Tech*, which describe museum exhibits, arts events, and student activities. For MIT arts events information call **(617) 253-ARTS** or consult the *Boston Globe Calendar* or the Web address: **hhtp://web.mit.edu**. The **Student Center,** which is across Mass Ave. from the Information Center, houses: a smaller branch of the Tech Coop; a branch of Toscannini's Ice Cream, a local favorite; a student run information booth called *The Source*; a cafeteria serving good meals at reasonable prices. The **MIT Museum,** with galleries at 77 and 265 Mass Ave., has fascinating exhibits and a wonderful, science-oriented gift shop. At 20 Ames St. the **List Visual Arts Center** is a leading showcase of contemporary art, and mounts exhibitions which have earned world wide acclaim. The List Center oversees MIT's remarkable collection of outdoor sculpture, including works by Calder, Picasso, and Nevelson. Available at the List Center is a guide to the campus architecture, which includes several buildings by alumnus I. M. Pei and two by Saarinen.

The Excitement of Cambridge

I have concentrated mostly on Cambridge of the past and its present educational activities. But that is far from a complete picture. Cambridge today is an exciting place of advanced thinking and political movements, and much of what is significant is extra-curricular, although some distinguished academics are often involved. For example, some years ago, the Massachusetts State Civil Defense Authority had passed out their nuclear emergency plan, which boiled down to people taking their credit cards and bankbooks, and driving along Highway 2 with their windows rolled up to Western Massachusetts. Well, that impressed one Cambridge City Councilor as being like "a comic book, a cartoon, incredible." And so she organized the Cambridge response, which was to publish a booklet, advocating that the best defense against a nuclear attack was not to have one, and telling people how they could become active in sponsoring Nuclear Disarmament. The booklet became a bestseller of its kind as many other towns ordered thousands of copies.

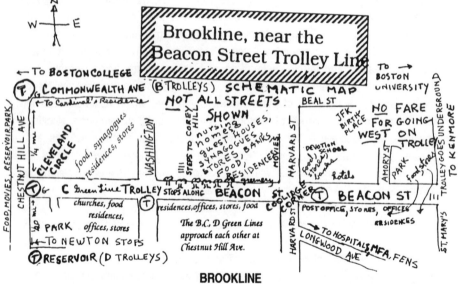

BROOKLINE

Brookline, population 50,000, a town of Norfolk County, politically separate from Boston, but almost surrounded by it, is not a tourist mecca, but I include it here because: it is a lovely place; it has a number of moderately priced accommodations, and good places to eat and shop; **located on the Green Line trolley routes,** it is a good base from which to explore Boston and outlying areas, and a fine base for walks into the fens and the Emerald Necklace. And last but not least, **it exemplifies an urban ideal**. It shows how the high population, necessary for the City's functioning and for the preservation of the countryside, can be achieved with grace and elegance and, at times, even splendor. As I write, I have in mind especially the region of Brookline about Beacon St., **near the Cleveland Circle Green Line trolley route (C car)**. On Beacon St., and on the hill slopes to either side of it, there is the greenery of arching trees, a plenitude of lovely parks and gardens, the charming architecture of castle-like apartment houses and Victorian homes, and there is the convenience of shops of great variety. People flow down the hills to the streetcars and the stores. **The streetcar strip itself,**

shaded by magnificent trees, exemplifies lovely landscape design. The side streets are leafy labyrinths, with turreted, bay-windowed houses, perched on terraces among cascades of stone and wooden steps, a pleasure to be lost in. Students and faculty from the many nearby colleges, descendants of Puritans, Orthodox Jews, Israelis, Chinese, Russian-speaking exiles from Eastern Europe, various professionals and retirees are some of the diverse groups sharing this attractive area. Once it was the site of summer estates of wealthy Back Bay residents.

A Brookline House

An Urban Walk Passing Near the John F. Kennedy Birthplace

One of my favorite urban walks is along the north side of Beacon St., starting near **Cleveland Circle**, and going eastward to St. Mary's, where the Green Line trolley goes underground, about 2 miles, but you can shorten as you please by taking the streetcar at any point. **A detour at Coolidge Corner takes you to the John F. Kennedy Birthplace.** The walk starts at **Cleveland Circle, which is the end of the line for the Green Line streetcars labeled C, and is near the Reservoir stop of the Riverside streetcars marked D**. Nearby on Beacon St., there is a commercial strip of stores and restaurants, and across Chestnut Hill Ave., there are parks and ball fields, an MDC ice skating rink, and the Chestnut Hill Reservoir, with a walking trail around it. You are near the **Boston College Campus** here. As you walk eastward along Beacon, you pass handsome brick castles, now next to not-as-lovely high rises. At Dean Road, behind the stone church, is a typical Brookline neighborhood park, with tall trees, tennis courts, and ball fields. The Riverside Green Line trolley passes on tracks on the south edge of the park. Continuing along Beacon, as you approach its intersection with Washington St., you see **Corey Hill** rising in front of you, a lovely urban scene, especially in fall when the trees are aflame, or in spring when they leaf out in shades of pale green. At Washington St., Beacon divides into two levels, and its north side passes under a canopy of tall oaks as it skirts the Hill. **This is the most pleasing part of the street.** The trolley track is below you to the right, with stone steps leading to it, on one of which is engraved **"In memory of Blakely Hoar, a lover of trees, this strip was planted in 1923."** To your left, at Summit Path, and other places too, are steps ascending through a series of terraces to the top of **Corey Hill**. A trip to the top rewards you with beautiful views of the City.

Coming back to Beacon St., you continue under the oaken archway past more apartments and a commercial strip of shops to **Coolidge Corner,** at the intersection of Harvard St. and Beacon. This is the major shopping center of the district with banks, shops, fruitstores, bookstores, bakeries, kosher delis, synagogues, restaurants, and an art deco movie house devoted to foreign and arts films and revivals. Also nearby is a special attraction, the **John F. Kennedy Birthplace,** now a National Historic Monument, run by the Park Service. To get to it, go north along Harvard St. to Beal St. and turn right. The modest house at 83 Beal is the Birthplace. It is furnished in the way it was at the time of John Kennedy's birth, and, in each room, by pushing a button, you can hear **Rose F. Kennedy**, the President's mother, reminisce about the house and family. At 351 Harvard St., which you pass on the way to Beal, is the **Edward Devotion School**, the public school that John Kennedy attended. In front of the school is a small one-story building, the **Edward Devotion House**, which, according to the plaque in front of it, was built in 1680 by Edward Devotion, who was a "perambulator, constable, fence viewer, and tithing man" for **Muddy River, which became the Town of Brookline in 1705.**

Near Coolidge Corner, just south of Beacon St., Longwood Ave. branches off Harvard St. It makes a pleasant route to the fens and to the cultural gems near them. (See pages 54, 55.) East of Coolidge Corner, Amory St. leads to **Amory Park** with tennis courts, ball fields, and **Hall Pond Sanctuary**, featuring a pond and ducks, an oasis of serenity.

FOOD, BRIEFLY

You will encounter delicious food in all price ranges everywhere in Boston, on main thoroughfares and off tiny alleys, at deli-cafeterias, cafe bakeries, food courts, and elegant restaurants. Below we list just a few eateries in districts we have visited in our text. *Moderate prices* means a good lunch can be had for less than $10, and a good dinner for less than $20, although quite often good lunches with elegant service and moderate prices can be had at restaurants rated expensive because of their dinner prices. Just look at the menus and decide. At the various gourmet take-outs, you can assemble a terrific meal at bargain prices. The following remarks are the opinions of my friends and myself.

On the Freedom Trail, as we have mentioned, **Quincy Market** is filled with delicacy laden take-out counters. Located in the Market are also a number of fine restaurants. **Durgin Park in the North Market building** is celebrated for its large portions of beef stew, steak, scrod, and a variety of old fashioned New England victuals served in an informal setting on long tables shared by several parties, a reminder of an earlier, rougher era when it was crowded with truckers who had just off-loaded huge slabs of beef for the many wholesale butcher stalls that then occupied the Market. Moderate prices. **Earlier on the Trail**, you pass, at the corner of School and Tremont, the **Parker House**, famous since the nineteenth century for providing food and good cheer to Boston's literary elite. Expensive for dinner but you can often get very good buys in lunch at its coffee shop. Nearby at 10 Bosworth (an alley off Tremont between Bromfield and School) is the **Marliave Cafe**, another venerable favorite, serving Italian food at moderate prices. The Park St. stop on the Green and Red Lines is close to these last two restaurants. Nearby on Winter Place, an alley off Winter St., is **Locke Ober's**, rated as one of Boston's best, expensive. On School St. near Ben Franklin's statue, in Old City Hall, is the **Maison Robert,** offering fine French cuisine, expensive. **In the North End** part of the Freedom Trail you pass within sight of many excellent Italian ristorantes and grocerias. The little bakery cafes with marvelous rum soaked layer cakes make wonderful trail stops. In summer evenings, the area is filled with strollers heading toward their choice of the many fine Italian restaurants.

In warm weather, umbrella-shaded tables blossom from the hotel restaurants on **Long and Rowe's Wharves. Along Atlantic Ave.** deli cafeterias specialize in lunch and breakfast for famished finance workers from the surrounding office towers. **On Northern Ave.**, a string of restaurants offer scrumptious sea food at moderate prices, from the **Barking Crab** on a barge near Atlantic Ave to **Anthony's** on Pier 4 near the World Trade Center. As you can see from the Downtown/Waterfront map, the closest T stops to these Waterfront eateries are South Station (Red Line), Aquarium (Blue Line), Government Center (Green and Blue Lines), and State (Orange and Blue Lines). If you walk along Beach St. (see map on page 15) from the Atlantic Ave. side of the South Station Bus Terminal, you encounter a **pagoda topped arch flanked by dragons** announcing the entrance to Boston's **China Town**, one of the country's largest, overflowing with exotic wares and wonderful, modestly priced restaurants, conveniently nestling among the buildings of the financial, theatre, shopping and clothing districts, and Tuft University's New England Medical Center. On a recent visit to Boston (summer, 1996), I walked from South Station along Beach to the **Dynasty Restaurant**, on Surface Rd. a few feet to the right of the arch, where I had an excellent lunch for $6.00 -- soup, appetizer, entree, rice, tea. This modern-looking yet traditional restaurant appeared to be very popular with financiers from the nearby towers as well as with local people. Many climbed to the second floor for dim sum. Around the corner, on Beach St. near the arch, **Imperial Seafood** also seemed very popular with local business people.

In the Beacon Hill area, Charles St. houses several restaurants of which my favorite is **Rebecca's** at no. 21. Good, hearty food, moderate prices, many vegetarian dishes. At 84 Beacon St., the **Hampshire House**, offers pleasant dining along with views of the Public Garden, expensive. In the basement of the same building is the **Bull and Finch Pub**, the inspiration for the TV show *Cheers*. Moderate prices, souvenirs.

Back Bay excels in food. On Newbury St. alone you'll find many delightful restaurants in various cuisine styles, French, Italian, Indian, Japanese, American. On a visit on Patriot's Day (April 1996), my companion and I had delicious lunches at **29**

On Beach St.
a pagoda
topped arch
welcomes
you to
China Town.

Newbury, near the Arlington St. stop on the Green Line, including salad, entree, crisp rolls, coffee, served elegantly in a pleasant atmosphere for less than $8 each. Near the Copley stop on the Green Line, at 159 Newbury, between Dartmouth and Exeter Streets (you can locate the building immediately by the marvelous, colorful mural), is **Du Barry's,** serving delicious French cuisine in a lovely flower bedecked courtyard. Moderate. Lunch recently (June 1996) with a friend cost less than $8 each. Across the street, at 190 Newbury, is the very popular **Stephanie's**, famous for its hearty breads, salads, and excellent desserts. Moderate. For Hungarian and Continental cuisine, the **Cafe Budapest** in the Copley Sq. Hotel at 90 Exeter, near the Copley Green Line stop, is rated frequently as Boston's best. Expensive. Back Bay has much more. Explore, explore.

Near the Theatre District, at 37 Stuart, a few blocks from the Boylston stop on the Green Line, **Jacob Wirth's** is another longtime favorite specializing in German style cuisine at moderate prices. Near the Arlington Green Line stop, the restaurant at **57 Park Plaza** is popular for its American food at moderate prices.

Harvard Square (Red Line) provides another cornucopia of good food. I mention only a few of the places I frequent between sessions at the bookstores, libraries, theatres, museums, and watching the chess players at the Au Bon Pain Plaza. For whole wheat pizza, I go to the food court at **33 Dunster**, near Mt Auburn. For a week day lunch with a delicious entree and a pass at an excellent salad bar, usually under $7, I go to **Grendel's,** located at 89 Winthrop, near JFK St., sharing a building with a Japanese restaurant at the edge of a small pleasant park. In the neighborhood are intriguing Middle Eastern restaurants, of which, except for an occasional lunch at the **Casa Blanca** at 42 Brattle (pleasant, moderate), I have little experience. My third most frequent lunch habitat is the **Yenching** at 1326 Massachusetts Ave just beyond Au Bon Pain Plaza. The luncheon special plate is usually well heaped, delicious, and always inexpensive, currently less than $5, with soup and tea included. The Square has a tremendous range of other restaurants in many ethnic varieties for you to explore. And then there are numerous coffee houses, where people get together for light fare -- soup, sandwiches, and pastry, coffee or tea -- and conversation, and, in some cases, entertainment-- poetry reading, music, games, etc. We have already mentioned the **Blacksmith House** on Brattle St. As you exit the subway, you can't miss the **Au Bon Pain Plaza** with its chess players. Another favorite is **Club Passim** at 47 Palmer St. (Palmer is the narrow lane running between

Church and Brattle, behind the front half of the Harvard Coop store.) It is one of the country's pre-eminent listening spots for folk music. The many successful recording artists who got their start in this intimate coffee house include Tom Rush, Joan Baez, Nanci Griffith, and Patty Larkin.

Now finally let's go to the area of Brookline bordering our urban walk. Along Beacon St. and near Coolidge Corner (the intersection of Harvard and Beacon) another plethora of food choices pleasantly confronts you. On the first part of the walk, my favorite is **Vinny Testa's** at 1700 Beacon, an Italian restaurant serving luscious giant-size dishes for modest prices, with emphasis on garlic. Before the main feast, crusty bread and garlic cloves sauteed in olive oil are brought to your table. Along and near the route of the walk you'll find kosher style delicatessens, Chinese, Japanese, Indian, and Mexican restaurants, and ones specializing in seafood. On Harvard St. are two of Boston's few kosher restaurants, **Rubins** at 500 Harvard, serving meat and vegetable dishes, and **Cafe Shalom** at 404A Harvard, offering meatless dishes, both modestly priced. The Coolidge Corner area has many food stores, coffee houses, and excellent gormet take-outs. Recently, I tried the lasagna at the Botecca Fiorentina at the corner of Babcock and Harvard (excellent). Further along on Beacon St., past Amory St., in the 900's and 1000's blocks, near the St. Mary's stop of the trolley, are several popular restaurants. On my last visit, my companion and I had dinner at the **Felucca at 1032b Beacon,** next to the trolley stop. Elegant service, lovely decor, delicious food in the North African and Greek style, featuring marvelous dishes of lamb, eggplant, sun-dried tomatoes with blends of garlic, olive oil, herbs, and excellent hard crusted fruited bread -- it was an outstanding experience. The entrees we chose were under $20.00. The next day we tried dinner at the **Elephant's Walk** at 900 Beacon, with French and Cambodian cuisine. Moderate prices, very pleasant. Both of these restaurants have moderately priced lunch menus.

LODGINGS, BRIEFLY

In this book, I assume that most of my readers are already in Boston. But in case you're not and are contemplating a trip and haven't yet received the excellent Visitors Guide (see page 4), below I list a sampling of possibilities taken from the (1995/1996) Guide. The prices quoted are either from the Guide (G) or resulted from my phone calls (C). Since prices vary with season, day of the week, location of room, furnishings, etc., the prices are to give you a rough idea.

Hotels

Boston Harbor Hotel, 70 Rowe's Wharf, Boston 02110, call (617) 439-7000, or (800) 752-7077. On dock of the water shuttle for the Airport and South Shore, near the Blue Line Aquarium stop and a 10 minute walk to South Station. A luxury hotel, the lowest double room rate is $250 on a summer weekend. (C) You are within an easy walk of Faneuil Hall, the Freedom Trail, the Aquarium, the financial district, and Everything.

Boston Mariott on Long Wharf, Boston 296 State St., Boston 02109. Call (617) 227-0800 or (800) 228-9290. Location almost the same as above. Weekday rates for a double are $189-249, and weekend rates are $139-199. (G) Again you are near Everything.

Boston Park Plaza, 64 Arlington, Boston 02116, call (617) 426-2000 or (800) 225-2000. Near Arlington St. Green Line stop in Back Bay. One block away from the Public Garden. Very popular. Doubles begin at $119. (C)

Omni Parker Hotel, 60 School St., Boston 02108, call (617) 227-8600. A historic hotel right on the Freedom Trail, across the street from the King's Chapel and Ben Franklin's statue. Near Park St. stop on the Red and Green lines. Rooms with a double bed begin at $169. (C)

The Copley Plaza, 138 St. James St., Boston, 02116, call (617) 267 5300 or (800) WYNDHAM. A beautiful grand old hotel in Back Bay overlooking Trinity Plaza, the Public Library, and the Hancock Tower. Near the Copley stop on the Green Line and Back Bay train station. Double, $210-265. (G)

Ritz-Carlton, 15 Arlington St., Boston 02117, call (617) 536-5700 or (800) 241-3333. Another grand hotel in Back Bay. Overlooks the Public Garden. Near the Arlington stop on the Green Line. Double $260-380. (G)

Midtown Motel, 220 Huntington Ave., Boston 02115, call (617) 262-1000 or (800) 543-4300. Near the Prudential Center, Symphony Hall,and Northeastern University. See Back Bay Fens map. On the E Green Line. Double, $139. (C)

Holiday Inn Boston-Brookline, 1200 Beacon St., Brookline 02146, call (617) 277-1200 or (800) HOLIDAY. On the Beacon St. Green Line trolley. Near Coolidge Corner (see Brookline section), a twelve minute trolley ride from Park St. and the Freedom Trail. Doubles begin at $129. (C)

The Harvard Square Hotel, 110 Mt. Auburn, Cambridge 02138, call (617) 864-5200 or (800) 458-5886, one block from the T. Doubles begin at $130. (C)

Marriott Hotel, Two Cambridge Center, Cambridge 02142, next to the MIT Coop and Kendall stop on the Red Line, call (617) 494-6600. Double $199. (C)

Economy Lodgings: Guest Houses and Hostels

Beacon Street Guest House, 1047 Beacon Street, Brookline 02146, call (617) 232- 0292, or (800) 872-7211. On Beacon St. Green Line trolley, about 10 minutes to Park St. and everything. In summer doubles range from $59 to $69, depending on whether you get a shared or private bath. In other seasons the prices may be somewhat lower, and singles at $45 may be available.(C)

Brookline Manor Guest House, 32 Centre St., Brookline 02146, call (617) 232-0003 or (800) 535-5325. Near Coolidge Corner shops and restaurants and near the Green Line trolley, about 12 minutes to Park St. Pleasant rooms, good location. The prices are the same as for the Beacon Street Guest House, above.

Newbury Guest House, 261 Newbury St., Boston 02116, call (617) 437-7666 or (800) 437-7668. Near Hynes Convention Center in Back Bay. Double $95-125. (C)

Berkeley Residence/ Boston YWCA, 40 Berkeley Street, Boston 02116, call (617) 482-8850. Near the Back Bay/South End Orange Line Station, the Hancock Tower and Copley Square. Private rooms, shared bath. $30 single; $44 double; $49 triple. Long term housing available -- $117 per week. For women only. (G)

YMCA, 316 Huntington, Boston 02115, call (617) 536-7800. On the E Green Line Trolley, near the New England Conservatory of Music and Northeastern and the MFA. See Back Bay Fens map p. 54. This is not listed in the Guide, but from everything I have heard it is a pleasant, convenient place to stay. Rates are $38 for a single, shared bath, and $56 for a double with twin beds , shared bath.

Boston International - AYH Hostel, 12 Hemenway Street, Boston 02115, call (617) 536-9455, dormitory style rooms near the Prudential Ctr. and the Hynes/ICA Green Line T station; 3 to 5 beds in a room; $15 a night for members and $18 for non-members. You must be a member June-September. See Back Bay Fens map page 54. (G)

A Bed and Breakfast in Cambridge, 1657 Cambridge Street, Cambridge 02138-4316, call (617) 868-7082 or (800) 795-7122. Near Harvard Yard. Double rooms, antique furniture, breakfast, shared bath $85. (C)

Chapter 2
MORE HISTORY IN GREATER BOSTON

CONCORD

LEXINGTON

PLYMOUTH

QUINCY

and

LOWELL

Transportation Summary

To Concord, take **Fitchburg/Acton Commuter T** train from **North Station** near **Green and Orange Line North Station T stop**. Trip takes about 50 minutes. **To Lexington,** take **T bus 62 or 76** from the **Alewife Station** on the **Redline**, and get offf at Lexington Center. **To Quincy,** take the **Braintree Redline T train**. Trip takes about 20 minutes from Park St. **For T information,** call **(617) 722 - 3200,** or **1 - 800 - 392 - 6100,** or if you are hearing impaired call **TDD 722 - 5146**. **For Plymouth,** take the 9 AM **Plymouth and Brockton** bus to Plymouth Center from the **South Station Transportation Center on the Red Line. Call (508) 746 - 0378.** **To Lowell,** take T commuter train from **North Station**, and then **LRTA bus to Lowell Center.**

MORE HISTORY IN GREATER BOSTON

Concord, Lexington, Plymouth, Quincy, and Lowell

INTRODUCTION

The Greater Boston area is crammed full of historic sites of great significance in our nation's beginnings to which you can daytrip by public transportation. In this chapter, we travel outward from Boston's center to Concord. Lexington, Plymouth, Quincy, and Lowell, using various components of the T system and intercity bus. The times of travel are about an hour or less in all cases.

CONCORD

By the rude bridge that arched the flood
Their flag to April's breeze unfurled
Here once the embattled farmers stood
And fired the shot heard round the world.
Ralph Waldo Emerson

A choice day trip, or several daytrips, from Boston is to Concord, Massachusetts, where the "shot heard round the world" was fired on April 19, 1775. On the night of April 18, eight hundred British infantrymen under Smith and Pitcairn rowed across the Charles River to Cambridge, and began their march toward Concord. Their object was to capture by surprise the munitions stored there. But thanks to **Paul Revere's famous ride**, and the less famous ones by **William Dawes** and **Sam Prescott**, the countryside was aroused, and four hundred armed militiamen from Concord and nearby towns were awaiting the British near the **North Bridge** on the morning of the 19th. The famous shot was fired when the Colonials refused to budge against the British advance. In fact, they charged the British column as it tried to cross the Bridge. The British, tired from their long night's march, and startled at the resistance, **retreated in disarray, chased by the Colonials all the way to Boston**, where they were held at bay. For days thereafter, Colonial militia kept arriving, first from nearby towns, and then from those further away. From Rhode Island, from Connecticut, from New Hampshire, and Maine, militia marched to join the Massachusettsmen as they camped in a great circle about Boston laying siege to the

city. **These New England troops would form the nucleus of the Continental Army** that Washington took command of when he arrived in Cambridge about 10 weeks later, on July 2, 1775. By that time the Colonials had shown their valor and determination in the **Battle of Bunker Hill,** which had taken place on June 17. (See Chapter 1, pages 29, 30.)

But that is not all. Even if Concord had not been the first battlefield of the Revolution, it would still have a great claim to fame because of the literary lights who lived there in the nineteenth century. **Thoreau, Emerson, Hawthorne, and the Alcott family were all Concord residents** for a significant period of their lives.

Today Concord is a lush, leafy suburb of Boston. Most of the farms of the "embattled farmers", who stood their ground against the British "regulars", have long been divided into residential estates. But the **townspeople have proudly preserved the beautiful traditional village center,** with meeting house, public buildings, and mansions about Monument Square, and also many major historic sites. In addition, because Concorders have a high degree of environmental consciousness and public spirit, **several lovely wild areas near the Concord River have been set aside as nature preserves.** So for the visitor, Concord offers a veritable smorgasbord of historic sites and natural recreationlands. There are even a few farms, with cultivated fields, orchards, and cows near the village. So Concord still manages the air of country. **It has much to offer for many visits.**

You can get to Concord by taking the Fitchburg/ S. Acton commuter T train from North Station which is adjacent to the **North Station T stop on the Green and Orange Lines.** The trip takes about 50 minutes. There are several trains a day. For schedule information, **call (617) 722-3200, or (800) 392-6100, or if you are hearing impaired (TDD) 722-5146.** The train stops in Porter Sq. in Cambridge, which is on the Red Line. So it is also possible to get on and off there.

The train trip to Concord is pleasant, through woods and by the backyards of country estates. You get a feel for the flow of life in Boston's affluent northwestern suburbs as troops of youngsters from the various academies along the way traipse on and off the train. **The Concord train station on Thoreau St.** is shared with a restaurant. Across the street is a small commercial strip with food stores, and a Friendly's Ice Cream, at the corner of Thoreau and Sudbury.

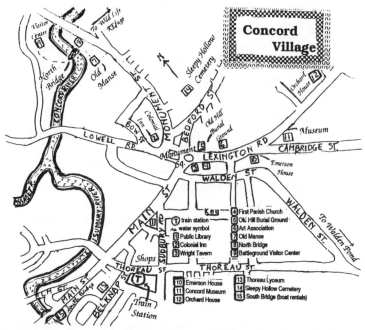

A pleasant walk from the train station on Thoreau St., along Sudbury Rd. (see map), brings you to the lovely **Concord Center**, with churches, public buildings, and shops about **Monument Sq.** On the way to it, at the intersection of Sudbury Rd. and Main St., you pass the **Public Library.** In the Center, are several interesting sites. Parts of the **Colonial Inn**, on Monument St. north of the **Square,** date back to 1716. Today it has a gift shop, restaurant, and rooms for guests, **(508) 369-9200.** Near it, the present day **Masonic Temple** was the **Schoolhouse** at the time of the Revolution. The **Old Hill Burial Ground** in the Center has the graves of many of the families whose sons stood at North Bridge.

The **First Parish Church,** near the **Square** on Lexington Rd., is built on the site of the **Meeting House** where the **First Provincial Congress** met in October, 1774, **John Hancock** presiding. In reprisal for the **Boston Tea Party**, the British forbad Town Meetings in Boston. So the Colonials moved their meetings to the countryside, to Concord, and continued their resistance to the British edicts, and, in addition, started to train militia and to gather military stores. **William Emerson**, grandfather of the Transcendentalist philosopher, **Ralph Waldo Emerson**, was the pastor here at the time. And like so many other Congregational ministers, he was glad to lend his church to the Patriot cause.

Next door to the Church is **Wright's Tavern**, built in 1747, and an important gathering place for the locals. The British command used the **Tavern** as their headquarters for the few hours of April 19th when they occupied the town. Earlier that morning, **after being aroused from bed by news of the British march, the Colonial militia had gathered at the Tavern**. But, upon arrival of the British, they moved on to take their stand at the **North Bridge**. Today **Wright's Tavern** houses a gift shop and the **Chamber of Commerce Information Office, (508) 369-3120**, where you can purchase the excellent *MAP AND TOURS OF THE TOWN OF CONCORD*, researched by the Junior League of Boston and the Concord Historical Commission. Other good information stops nearby are the **Concord Book Store and the Public Library**. The Tavern is open all year, Monday - Saturday, 9:30 - 5.

It is a pleasant walk of about 3/4 mile, along Monument St., from the Square to the **Battle Ground near North Bridge**, with a sidewalk all the way, shaded by tall trees. Before you get to the **Battle Ground,** you will see, on the left, a path leading to the **Old Manse,** built in 1770 by Reverend Emerson (see above), with grounds overlooking the Concord River. For awhile in the 19th century, **Nathaniel Hawthorne and his bride Sophia Peabody,** lived here. A path from the **Old Manse** leads to the **Battle Ground,** and the **North Bridge arching over the Concord River.** Here are plaques and monuments celebrating the momentous events of April 19, 1775, including the famous **Minuteman,** with gun in one hand and plow in the other, by sculptor **Daniel Chester French**, who also designed the statue of Lincoln in the Lincoln Memorial in Washington, D.C. You can cross the **Bridge** (not the original but a replica) and climb to the **North Bridge Visitor Center,** maintained by the **National Park Service**. At the **Visitor Center**, and, along the way, are exhibits and recordings explaining the sequence of events and the disposition of the forces. Most moving is the serene beauty of the scene, the river enclosed by great trees and brambles, wending its way through the rolling landscape, contrasted with the image of the farmers at the **Bridge**, anxiously watching the movements of the "regulars". The **Visitor Center has rest rooms** and is open year-round, but with hours depending on the season. You can always visit the **Bridge** and wander about the grounds.

Should you yearn for a longer walk, you can continue, from the **Battle Ground**, onward to the 3,000 acre **Great Meadows Wild Life Refuge**, a watery marshland rich in bird species, whose southeastern edge is nearby. In *COUNTRY WALKS NEAR BOSTON WITHIN REACH BY PUBLIC TRANSPORTATION,* **Alan Fisher strings together the sites that we have mentioned** -- the train station, Concord Center, the Old Manse, and Battle Ground - - **and a hike through the Wild Life Refuge**, into one grand walk. Some years ago, on a memorable cloudy-sunny October day, a companion and I took the train from Boston to Concord and followed the Fisher loop.

Of all the terrific trips enjoyed while researching for this book, that was one of the best. To get to the **Refuge** from the **Battle Ground**, go back across North Bridge (to get to the east bank of the river), and cross Monument St. to the parking lot (which has picnic tables and rest rooms). **There is a path from the parking lot, leading along the riverbank into the Refuge**. The trick is to find it. Here are Fisher's directions. "Follow a footpath to the left of some picnic tables at the back of the parking area, then pass through a gap in a fence, and turn left on an asphalt road. Follow a grassy path along the riverbank past a brown boathouse on the left. With a pond on your right, and swampy woods bordering the river on your left, head straight into the Great Meadow National Wild Life Refuge." We did, and it worked!! It was migrating season, and we made many sightings. A delightful way to cap our visit to the Battle Ground.

More pleasure was to come. Walking back to the train station, we were passed by troops of youngsters bicycling toward Friendly's Ice Cream, whose parking lot was filled with bicycles (hooray!). At the station were jostling youths from the Concord Academy. We felt like we were part of the community, a feeling that the car-encapsulated visitor does not get.

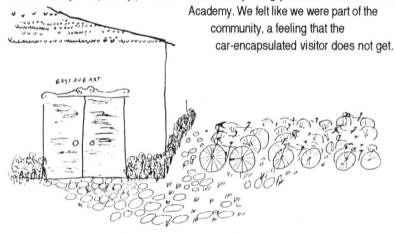

Concord has much more. About two miles south of the train station is **Walden Pond**, where **Thoreau** conducted his experiment in living the simple life and thereby coming to grips with life's essence. To get to it from the station, which is on Thoreau St., walk east along Thoreau, and then turn right onto Walden St., and keep walking

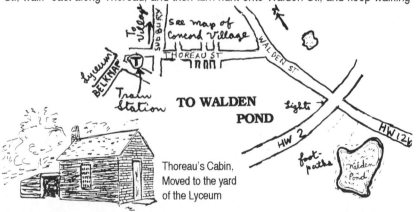

Thoreau's Cabin,
Moved to the yard
of the Lyceum

until you come to it. (See map.) The **Pond** is in a **State Park Reservation**, which borders on Walden St. There is a path around the **Pond,** a swimming beach, and a marker at the site of Thoreau's cabin. Fortunately, the parking lot has been kept relatively small. Arriving as you will afoot, you will be very much in the spirit of Thoreau, who was an inveterate walker, traveling in our mode -- by a combination of walking and public transportation. Thoreau fans may also be interested in the **Thoreau Lyceum**, located near the train station on Belknap St. (see map), a small museum abounding in Thoreau memorabilia, home of the Thoreau Society. Fee.

Going out from Concord Center along the Lexington Rd., you encounter a number of interesting sites. We have already mentioned the **First Parish Church** and **Wright's Tavern** in the Center. Across the street, near the **Burying Ground** is the **Art Association,** in a 1753 building. Fee. Further along, at 28 Cambridge St., near Lexington Rd., is the **Emerson House**, where Emerson lived from 1835 to 1882, and on Lexington just beyond Cambridge, is the **Concord Museum**, with rooms of period furniture, and many exhibits and memorabilia of Concord's history. Fee. About 1/2 mile further, on the opposite side of the road, is the **Orchard House,** where the Alcott family lived from 1857 to 1877, **the setting for Louisa May Alcott's** *LITTLE WOMEN.* Nearby is the **Wayside House**, another of the Hawthornes' Concord residences. **Going out from the Center, along Bedford St.**, in about 1/2 mile, you come to the **Sleepy Hollow Cemetery**, where Thoreau, the Alcotts, Emersons, and Hawthornes, all rest.

At the South Bridge, on Main St., a few blocks from the train station (see map of Concord Village), is the **South Bridge Boat House,** where you can rent a canoe to savor Concord from a riverside perspective. You can go past riverside mansions to the **North Bridge** (allow at least three hours to get there and back), or you can go southward along the **Sudbury and Assabet Rivers, where Thoreau and his brother loved to paddle** in the boat that they had built. **On the Assabet,** calm and peaceful in the summer, with an escort of domesticated geese, you pass by the backdoors of great estates and glide between flower bedecked banks, alongside turtles in the sun. **Along the Sudbury** are fewer houses. The banks are wilder, lusher with undergrowth, and shadowed by hemlocks and deciduous trees. Stopping places for picnics abound. The **Boat House** is open during the warm weather, daily from 10 to 8. On weekends, the rates are currently $8.25 per hour for one canoe, $38.00 per day. On weekdays, the rates are lower. A deposit of $20.00 and identification are required. **Call (508) 369-9438** for further information.

I have been thinking of Concord as a great daytrip from Boston. But there are accommodations for overnight stays, too. The **Colonial Inn, call (508) 369-9200,** has an ideal location in the Center. **The Hawthorne Inn,** 462 Lexington Rd., opposite the **Wayside,** is located about one mile from the center. **Call (508) 369-5610.** There are several food stores, take-outs, and restaurants in the Center and near the train station.

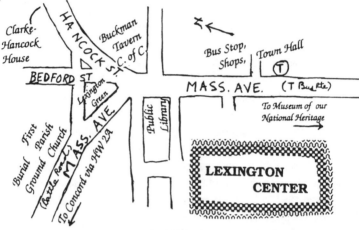

LEXINGTON

On their march to Concord on the fateful morning of April 19th, the British, 800 men strong, passed through Lexington. Aroused by the Village bell, sounded upon **Paul Revere's** arrival, seventy-seven Lexington militia, brave men all, whose names are recorded on the **Memorial** north of **Buckman's Tavern,** gathered on the **Green** to face the British as they advanced into the town, about 4 A.M. In the volley of shots of the next few minutes, eight Lexingtonians were killed and nine were wounded before the small band was dispersed. **These were the first casualties of the Revolution.** Today, Lexingtonians like to point out that the "shot heard round the world" was actually fired here, and not at the **North Bridge.** After the battle on **Lexington Green,** the British pushed onward and began the seven mile march to Concord. The fray at Lexington instilled them with a false sense of confidence. During their march between the two towns, the countryside was thoroughly aroused, for miles about, by the many horsemen who rode to spread the news of what had happened at Lexington. By the time the British arrived at Concord, four hundred Colonials had assembled there, and more kept coming. The cruel events at Lexington stiffened their determination to fight. (See Concord section.)

You can visit **Lexington Green** by taking **T bus 76 or 62 from the Alewife Station on the Red Line. These buses pass through Lexington Center** on their way to Hanscom Airforce Base and the Bedford V.A. Hospital respectively, and both have a frequency of about once an hour during the day. **No service on Sunday.** For more information, call **(617) 722-3200**, or **(800) 392-6100**, or, if you are hearing impaired, **TDD 722-5146.**

The **Green,** with the **Lexington Minuteman Statue, is on Massachusetts Ave.,** about two blocks away from **Lexington Center**, where there are shops, restaurants, the **Town Hall,** and, across the street, the **Public Library.** Lexington Center is a pleasant place, but there is none of the country village air that Concord has managed to retain. Massachusetts Ave., the main street, brims with traffic. There isn't a hint of cows in pasture nearby.

The **Chamber of Commerce** maintains an information desk in a pleasant colonial - style building in the park across from the Green. (It has restrooms.) Here are dioramas and exhibits describing the events of April 19th, and you can purchase a guide to Lexington's historic sites. Next to the Chamber of Commerce is **Buckman's Tavern,** built in the early 1700's, a social center for townspeople, and a refreshment stop for farmers bringing their produce to Boston. **On the morning of April 19th, the minutemen gathered here** before going out to take their stand on the **Green,** about 100 feet away. A guided tour through the **Tavern** gives you a glimpse into the life of Colonial Lexington. Donation requested.

Another fascinating site nearby is the **Clarke-Hancock House,** about 1/4 mile from the **Green,** along Hancock St. (see map). On the night of April 18th, **John Hancock and Samuel Adams,** who had been attending a Provincial Congress in Concord a few days earlier, lodged in this house, built in 1698 by John Hancock's grandfather, Reverend John Hancock, the second pastor of the local church. At the time of Adams' and Hancock's visit, the **House** was the home of Hancock's kinsman, Reverend Jonas Clarke. Not mentioned in Longfellow's poem, but **part of Paul Revere's mission on the night of April 18th was to warn these two arch-organizers**, at the top of the British "most obnoxious" list, of the impending arrival of the Redcoats. Warned, Adams and Hancock rode out of town before the British entered. Soon they would leave Massachusetts to participate in the **Second Continental Congress in Philadelphia**. (see Quincy section). Also a guest in the **House** on that night was Dorothy Quincy, Hancock's sweetheart, later his wife. The **House** is now run as a museum by the **Lexington Historical Society**. A visit here is a must, worth the modest admission fee. To prevent its destruction, at one time, it was moved across the street from its original site. But it was subsequently restored to its original location. However, the map that you get from the Chamber of Commerce may not show the correct position. As you walk from the **Green** along Hancock, it is currently on the left side of the street.

On the west side of the Green is the First Parish Church, whose congregation was gathered in 1692. Beside it is the **Burial Ground,** where many of the heroes of 1775 and their families are buried. A list of the church's ministers from 1692 to 1846 is inscribed on a stone beside the **Minuteman.** The stone also marks the site of the first three Meeting Houses

Massachusetts Ave. passing by the Church is the "Battle Road", along which the British marched toward Concord, and along which they were chased back to Boston.(See map.) As Longfellow describes the denouement of the events of the 19th,

> You know the rest,
> In books you have read
> How the Regulars fired and fled,
> How the farmers gave them ball for ball
> From behind each fence and farmyard wall,
> Chasing the Redcoats down the lane,
> Then crossing the fields to emerge again
> Under the trees at the turn of the road,
> And only pausing to fire and load.

If, like me, you become filled with the spirit of the occasion, you too can march the 7 miles along this road to Concord. **In hot weather, I advise you to provision yourself with much liquid in Lexington Center.** The first mile or so there is a sidewalk as you walk uphill out of Lexington. After you cross the bridge over Highway 128, there follows about a mile or so stretch of low traffic through a thin wooded strip. But then, as the road seems to end, you turn to right onto Highway 2 A. At the turn, you see the **Minuteman National Park** sign. Across the road at this point is a sign announcing the Minuteman Vocational School. Shortly after you turn to the right, you will see, on the right side of the road, a turnout with signs, a poster map, and legends announcing the Ebenezer Fiske Homesite. Continue along Highway 2A. This section of the road is laden with traffic although the surroundings are rural. Unfortunately, no provision has been made for walkers here, and it is best to walk beside the road

facing traffic. At about 31/2 miles out of Lexington, you encounter the **Battle Road Visitor Center** run by the National Park Service where you can stop to look at exhibits and collect literature describing the events at Concord and Lexington. There are restrooms, a water fountain, and benches on pleasant grounds. There is currently no pleasant car-free way for visitors to come here, no path for walkers through the fields that border the **Battle Road**. A car-free bicycle path between Concord and Lexington along the Battle Road is planned for completion in 1998. Add your voice to those requesting it so there will be no turning back.

About 3/4 mile further on, after you cross the boundary into the Town of Lincoln, a **plaque on the north side of the road marks an incident not mentioned in Longfellow's poem.** Here a British advance patrol surprised **Paul Revere** and his companions, **William Dawes**, the other night rider out of Boston, and **Dr. Sam Prescott of Lincoln,** whom Revere and Dawes met as he was returning from a late night courting session. Prescott managed to escape, and rode on toward Concord through the fields. But Revere and Dawes were captured. **So here, at about 2 A.M. of the morning of April 19th ended the famous "midnight ride."** Going onward, in about 1/2 mile, you enter the definitely rural outskirts of Concord. The smell of manure and the mooing of cows greet you. And if you are as lucky as I was, you will encounter a wonderful fruit stand at Merriam's Corner, with the sweetest peaches in the world. Soon the sidewalk begins. **You are entering Concord along the Lexington Rd., just as the Redcoats did on the morning of the 19th of April, 1775.** Never mind that you don't carry the 50 to 75 pounds of equipment that each "Regular" did. You have had to face rushing steel monsters all the way, and you can feel justly proud of your accomplishment. Rising above you to the right is the ridge from which the Colonials watched the advance of the British. It extends all the **way to the Old Hill Burying Ground in Concord Center. Soon you pass** the **Wayside**, the **Orchard House**, then **Emerson's House**, and before you know it, you are ` at **Wright's Tavern** in the Center of Concord. From Concord, you can return to Boston by the T commuter train, which takes you to **North Station** on the **Green and Orange Lines**. For schedule information, call **(617) 722-3200,** or **(800) 392-6100,** or, if you are hearing impaired, **(TDD) 722 - 5146.**

Another Lexington attraction is the **Museum of Our National Heritage,** 33 Marrett Rd., **call (617) 861-6559,** located just off Massachusetts Ave., about one mile east of Lexington Center, on the bus route. Ask the bus driver to let you off there. This

very attractive museum, on lovely grounds, run by the Society of Masons, has exhibits of early American history and other parts of the American experience, and hosts lectures, concerts, and many community activities.

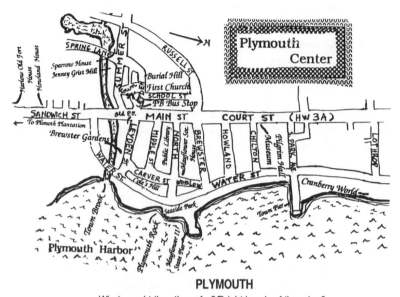

PLYMOUTH

What sought they thus afar?/Bright jewels of the mine?
The wealth of seas, the spoils of war?/They sought a faith's pure shrine!
Felicia Hemans

Plymouth, founded in 1620, the chosen home of the Pilgrims, and site of the first Thanksgiving, is another fine daytrip (or daytrips) from Boston. The Pilgrims were not the first English New World settlers. At the time of their voyage aboard the **Mayflower**, there were already along the North American coast several trading and fishing settlements established by London entrepreneurs. But the Pilgrims' story has captured the Nation's heart. Not adventurers seeking fortunes, but seeking to live according to their own religious lights, free of the dictates of church prelates or King, **they symbolize the hopes and strivings of millions who came afterwards,** driven to these shores by oppression and persecution.

The Mayflower II
gets under way.

Except that it has an unusually high density of historic shrines, Plymouth today, population 25,000, the shiretown of Plymouth County, is typical of Massachusetts' South Shore towns, with sandy beaches, and a harbor filled with fishing and pleasure boats. It is the commercial center for several smaller towns, and the home of the giant **Ocean Spray food processing cooperative**, organized by the cranberry growers of the South Shore and Cape Cod, where cranberries are the major crop. Retirees, commuters to Boston, and seaside summer villagers swell the population.

For an excellent booklet with maps, calendar of events, write to **Plymouth Area Chamber of Commerce, 225 Water St., Suite 202, Plymouth, Massachusetts, 02360 or call (508) 830-1620** or **(508) 747-7525**. A fine book on Pilgrim history is George Willison's *PILGRIM READER*, containing their own chronicles plus Willison's background notes.

The **Plymouth and Brockton Street Railway** (PB hereinafter) provides several buses daily from Boston to Plymouth Center. **However, the 9.00 A.M. is most suited for sightseers, because the last bus back to Boston from Plymouth Center is at 3.20 P.M.** There are later buses back to Boston from the PB terminal, in an industrial park on the highway, about 2 miles away. But there is no pleasant way to walk there, and there is no shuttle bus between the terminal and Center. The taxi fare is about $6.00. Call **(508) 746 - 0378**, for more information. In Boston, the bus leaves from the **South Station Bus Terminal near the T Red Line** South Station stop. The trip takes about 75 minutes. Going at 9 and coming back to Boston on the 3.20 gives you approximately a 5 hour visit in Plymouth.

As the bus nears Plymouth, going along Highway 3A, it makes several local stops. You can get off the bus at **Plymouth Center,** near the CVS store opposite the **Old Post Office,** at the corner of **Main and Leyden Streets**, in the midst of a pleasant business district with stores and eating places.

Leyden Street was named after the City of Leyden in Holland, where the Pilgrims took refuge for a number of years before venturing to the New World. Going downhill from the Old Post Office along Leyden St., itself a treasure trove of vintage houses, you will see **Plymouth Harbor** across the road, and a seaside park containing the portico-enshrined **Plymouth Rock**. Near the **Rock** is a statue of **William Bradford,** the second elected Governor of the Plymouth Colony and author of the chronicle, *THE HISTORY OF THE PLIMOTH PLANTATION*, the original of which is in the **State House Library** (see Chapter 1, page 17). According to Bradford's narrative, on

Portico-enshrined
Plymouth Rock

November 11, 1620, after a storm-tossed voyage, the Pilgrims first set foot on land, not here, but on Cape Cod, in what is now **Provincetown** (we shall tell the story in the Cape Cod section of Volume 2), whence a party under Miles Standish set forth to explore the nearby coast. **So the Rock symbolizes, not the first landing place, but that here the Pilgrims found their final home.**

Across the road from the Rock, atop Cole's Hill, stands Massasoit, Chief of the Wamponoags, without whose kindness the Pilgrims would not have survived their first year in the New World. As it was, **about half of them**, including John Carver, their first Governor, **perished in the first winter**, and are buried in **Cole's Hill**. Climb the steps to savor the view of the harbor sheltered by the long thin strand of **Plymouth Beach.**

Walking northward from the Rock through the seaside park, you come shortly to models of the first primitive, thatched roof huts that the Pilgrims built, and then further on, you come to the **State Dock,** and the **Mayflower II**, a full scale replica of the original Mayflower that carried 102 Pilgrims plus crew across the Atlantic. The ship is heartstirringly small. Aboard it demonstrations describe life at sea in the 17th century. Admission currently is $5.75.

Now let's go back to the foot of Leyden St.. On the land side, are the lovely **Brewster Gardens**, named after **Elder Brewster**, a pilgrim leader, **Bradford's foster father and chief mentor.** Announced by a large sign with a map of the grounds, so you cannot miss it, the **Park** is a belt of greenery alongside of the **Town Brook,** which gurgles happily on its way to the Harbor. A pleasant walk upstream takes you past several sites of interest: a spring that the Pilgrims drank from (and you can drink from it too); commemorative statues; the backyard of the **Sparrow House** (which fronts on Summer St.), built in 1640, **Plymouth's oldest surviving house;** the **Jenney Grist Mill,** water operated, a replica of the first one that the Pilgrims built; and finally you come to a pond, brimming with ducks and geese. **But the Brook itself is really the major exhibit.** One of the reasons that the Pilgrims abandoned Provincetown was that the fresh water supply there seemed uncertain. And here they found this bubbling brook promising everlasting refreshment. It was here, too, that kindly Indians taught them to catch herring (alewives) in the yearly run from the ocean to the spawning grounds upstream, and to use them for food and to fertilize their hills of corn.

A choice pastime when you are in Plymouth is to go uphill from the Old Post

Office along Leyden St. to the striking **First Church** in **Town Square**. It is the fourth
Meeting House on its site. The first Meeting House, the one that the Pilgrims
worshipped in, was not here, but in the fort that they built on top of **Burial Hill**, the
steep hill rising above the present church. **Climb the stairs behind the First Church
to the top of Burial Hill, the loveliest place in all Plymouth,** with superb views of the
town and harbor. Standing here savoring the views, you feel most strongly the
romance and mystery of the Pilgrim spirit, and can appreciate the poet's song,

> The Pilgrim Fathers where are they?
> The waves that brought them o'er
> Still roll in the bay, and throw their spray
> As they break along the shore.
> John Pierpont

**Many of the Pilgrim Fathers, and Mothers, too, are buried on the hill where you
stand**. There is a monument here for Governor Bradford and other Pilgrims buried in
unmarked graves. In marked graves, with headstones and monuments, lie many
prominent Colonials, active participants in the Revolutionary drama, including
members of the Otis and Warren families. Here rests **Mercy Otis Warren**, sister of
James Otis (see Chapter 1, page 23), **dear friend of Abigail and John Adams**, and
author of a three volume history of the Revolutionary period.

     You can also get to Burial Hill from the Jenney's Grist Mill (see above), by
crossing Summer St. to it. (See map.) A very pleasant walking loop is to start from the
bus stop at the Old Post Office, walk down Leyden St. to the sea side park and the
Rock, and then retrace your steps to the Brewster Gardens (see above) at the foot of
Leyden, and then walk upstream along the Town Brook to the Jenney Grist Mill, then
across Summer St. to Burial Hill, and then down the stairs to the First Church, and then
back to Plymouth Center along Leyden. **Off Town Square, in the area between the
Governor Carver Inn and the Church, are public restrooms.**

     Within a few blocks of the Old Post Office are several historic sites, all near
the main street, which is called Main St. in the vicinity of the Post Office, and then, to
the north, becomes Court St., and, to the south, becomes first Sandwich St. and then
Warren Ave. **About six blocks north of the Post Office, at 75 Court St., is the
Pilgrim Hall Museum, Plymouth's best,** with an outstanding collection of Pilgrim
possessions. An excellent slide show brings their real life drama home to you -- their
poverty, their life as toilers in Leyden, and their hopes and fears

and courage upon embarking for the New World. You will see pamphlets opposing the doctrines of the Anglican Church, which they printed on their underground press, and distributed despite the danger of being caught and imprisoned. Open daily from 9.30 to 4.30. The admission fee is currently $5.00 for an adult, $4.00 for seniors and students, and $12.00 for a family. **Call (508) 746 - 1620. If you have to choose just one Plymouth site with an admission fee, this should be it!**

On North St., two blocks north of the Post Office, are the **Public Library,** and the **Mayflower Society House**, built in 1754 by the descendants of **Edward Winslow**, the third Governor of the Plymouth Colony. About 3 blocks south of the Post Office is the **Howland House**, the only surviving house where Pilgrims are known to have lived. A block further south at 119 Sandwich is the **Harlow Old Fort House**, a working museum with demonstrations of 17th century crafts.

About two and one half miles south of the Post Office, off Warren Ave., is the **Plimoth Plantation**, **call (508) 746 - 1622**, open April through November from 9 to 5. During the Plantation's open season, **the 9 AM PB bus from Boston goes on from Plymouth Center to the Plantation,** so on one of your trips to Plymouth you can choose to get off there. The 35 acre Plantation contains a reconstruction of Plimoth Village as it was in 1627. The residents go about their daily tasks tending their kitchens, gardens, livestock, building houses, and crafting tools. You are invited to ask questions and join in their work and games. "Have the time of *their* life", the ad says. The Villagers are actors speaking with English accents, as the Pilgrims did, well trained so that they live their parts and try to get you to leave the 20th century and join them in the 17th. Within the Plantation grounds is a reconstruction of a **Wamponoag Village.** An admission fee of $15.00 entitles you to attend all activities for two days. There is also a combination ticket for $18.50 for admission to both the Mayflower II and the Plantation. There is a family rate of $60.00 good for 3 months participation.

Across from the Plantation begins the long strand of Plymouth Beach, so you can combine a trip   to the Plantation with a walk along the beach or a swim. Coming as you do car-free, you don't have to worry about the huge parking fee. The long beach strand channels the mouth of the Eel River, whose banks are protected as a wild life refuge. The area teems with shell fish and bird life. Eels, incidentally, behave reversely to herring. Herring live in the ocean and travel upstream to spawn, while eels live in fresh water and travel down to the salt water to spawn. All through the South Shore and Cape Cod, these two yearly migrations generate great excitement

among fisherpersons. You can return to the main road from the beach by crossing a footbridge over the river to a path leading via Manter's Point Road to Warren Ave., from which it is a two mile walk along a tree shaded sidewalk to Plymouth Center.

North of Plymouth, the PB bus from Boston passes by the edge of Duxbury and Kingston, two towns which were early spin-offs of the Plymouth Colony. The Pilgrims, as well as the Puritans, believed that everyone should be within walking distance of a Meeting House. So as the Colony grew, instead of letting the Plantation spread out from the center, groups of settlers went off to establish new centers, each with its own church. Kingston, the first spin-off from Plymouth, was founded in 1626. **And in 1632, three of the most famous Pilgrims, John and Priscilla Alden, and Captain Miles Standish,** the love triangle of Longfellow's *COURTSHIP OF MILES STANDISH*, **went off with Elder Brewster and others to found Duxbury.**

Not related to Pilgrim History, but a

hit with visitors, is Ocean Spray's Cranberry World, located on the Plymouth Waterfront, about 1/2 mile north of the Rock (a ten minute walk). Here are cranberry bogs, and exhibits on everything you might ever want to know about cranberries, including recipes and cooking demonstrations. Refreshments are served, too. **All free**. Open from mid spring to mid fall. **Call (508) 747 - 1000.**

Plymouth Harbor bustles with the usual activities of a New England coastal town. Offered from the docks are deep sea fishing trips, a variety of cruises, including one to **Provincetown,** and **whale watches**. Eating places abound in Plymouth, on the waterfront, and on Main St. The many lodgings within walking distance of Plymouth Center include the **General Carver Inn** in Town Square, call **(508) 746 - 7100**, and the **Governor Bradford Inn**, on the waterfront, call **(508) 746 - 6200**. Write to the Plymouth Area Chamber of Commerce, Plymouth Massachusetts 02360 or **call (508) 830-1620** for more information on accommodations.

QUINCY

I long to hear that you have declared an Independency and by the way, in the new code of Laws, which I suppose it will be necessary for you to make, I desire you would Remember the Ladies, and be more generous and favorable to them than your ancestors. Do not put such unlimited power into the hands of the Husbands. Remember all Men would be tyrants if they could. If particular care and attention is not paid to the Ladies, we are determined to foment a Rebellion, and will not hold ourselves bound to any Laws in which we have no say or Representation.

Abigail Adams to John Adams, March, 1776

Quincy was the birthplace of two American presidents, **John Adams and his son John Quincy Adams,** our second and sixth presidents, whose descendants include Charles Francis Adams, Lincoln's Secretary of State, and Brook and Henry Adams, noted historians. We know much about this remarkable family because of their profuse, articulate writings. Through John and Abigail's diaries and letters, we get a vivid picture of the drama of the birth of the new Republic and its first baby steps. An excellent book on the Adams family is Jack Shepherd's *THE ADAMS CHRONICLES*, upon which a popular Public Broadcasting series was based.

John Adams played a crucial role in pushing the Thirteen Colonies toward Independence. His career began as a typical Puritan success story. His father, a farmer and shoemaker, had managed to accumulate enough through thrift to send his son to Harvard. After Harvard, John Adams studied the Law. During the pre-Revolutionary ferment, he gained fame as a skilled apologist for New England's defiance of Old England, and was elected to be one of the Massachusetts delegates to the First Continental Congress, called to meet in September, 1774 in the aftermath of the British reprisals for the Boston Tea Party. The Congress was the first formal meeting of the leaders of the Patriot parties of the Thirteen Colonies, who until then had communicated mainly through messengers and circular letters of the Committees of Correspondence.

Although everyone disapproved of taxation without representation and other Parliamentary actions, the Congress was by no means in agreement about what to do. John Adams and other New Englanders earned the label "radical" because they advocated that the laws of popularly elected Colonial Assemblies should be supreme instead of those of Parliament. The allegiance to the Crown should be token and ritual, freely given as a result of their affection for the Mother Country, but not forced. Most delegates were more conservative, not ready to think in those terms. Even at the Second Continental Congress, which convened in Philadelphia on May 10, 1775, after the Battles of Concord and Lexington, and the "shot heard round the world" (see Concord section), even at that late date, many of the delegates were still advocating petitioning the King and Parliament to revoke the tax laws and the "Intolerable Acts," imposed as punishment for the Boston Tea Party. The New Englanders began to advocate Independence openly, and declared that it was time to fight: their land was already a bloody battlefield; it was time to form an Army, a Navy, to make a Constitution for a new Country, and to raise money for these goals. The words, "Army," "Navy," "Constitution," and above all "Independence," frightened many of the delegates.

Not being able to reach a consensus, the Congress remained split, but continued its work. One committee was formed to write a petition, and another to work out the details of raising money and waging a war!! On the War Committee, John Adams made two key motions. He proposed that George Washington, a delegate from Virginia, be named Commander in Chief of the Army to be formed, and that the various New England militia, then camped in a great circle about Boston laying siege to the British, be adopted as part of the official

"Continental Army." These were brilliant moves on Adams' part, which created an "instant" Army, and united immediately in the common cause New England and Virginia, the two power centers of the Thirteen Colonies. This coalition would eventually win the day for Independence. Also aiding the coalition was the Parliamentary edict closing the western frontier to settlement, which greatly upset the Southerners' ambitions to occupy new lands to replace their tobacco-worn soil. On June 15, 1775, **two days before the Battle of Bunker Hill** (see Chapter 1), the **Congress** as a whole adopted Adams' motions, and **named Washington, who "neither sought after, nor desired" the honor, Commander-in-Chief**. He soon set off for Cambridge to take command of his ready made army (see Chapter 1). During the August recess, many Congress delegates traveled north to Massachusetts to see first hand what they had wrought. **An Army, incredible!!**

But the impasse in Congress continued. A petition to the King was sent, and the forces of Independence received a very powerful boost when George III rejected it. Still many delegates shied away from explicitly opting for Independence. **Meanwhile the fighting continued in Boston,** and broke out in other places, too. **Washington and his troops captured Dorchester Heights, and forced the British to evacuate Boston on March 17, 1776.** The Continental Army had won its first really great victory, but the Congress was still debating the issue of Independence. On June 7, Richard Lee of Virginia proposed that the issue be brought to a vote, and specifically that Congress should consider the Resolution:

> Resolved: That these United States are, and of right ought to be, Free and Independent States; that they are absolved from allegiance to the British Crown, and that all political connection between them and the state of Great Britain is and ought to be totally dissolved.

Several of the delegates from New York and Pennsylvania argued against the Resolution, and Virginia, Georgia, and all of New England argued for it. It was decided to postpone the vote until July 1, so that delegates could go home to consult their respective Legislatures. In the meantime, the pro-Independence group decided to prepare a **Declaration of Independence** to be ready in case the Resolution passed. **Thomas Jefferson** was chosen to do the actual writing because his pen was deemed most elegant, **but the outline of the Declaration was laid out by a committee of five consisting of Jefferson, Adams, Franklin, Roger Sherman, and Robert Livingston.**

Jefferson   later wrote that his Declaration did not cover any new ground but summarized ideas discussed in the Congress during the previous two years.

On July 1, 1776, when the delegates returned from their home bases, the debate on Lee's Resolution was resumed. John Dickinson of Pennsylvania gave a long eloquent speech against, and then John Adams rose and delivered a long reply. He spoke extemporaneously and without written notes, and afterwards could not remember his words to record in his diary, so we don't know precisely what he said. When the vote was taken, it was 12 to 0 for Lee's Resolution with New York abstaining. Years afterwards in 1813, Jefferson commented on Adams' contribution. **"He was the pillar of its support on the floor of Congress,** its ablest advocate and defender against the multifarious attacks that it encountered." **On July 4**, after further debate, **the text of Jefferson's Declaration of Independence was approved. The Nation was born.**

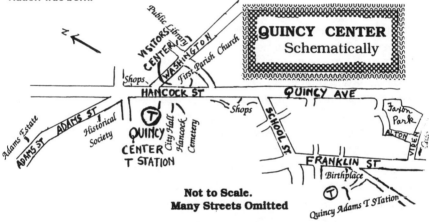

Quincy today, population 91,000, a commercial and manufacturing center, home of a U.S. Navy Yard, is nothing like the farming village where Abigail Adams raised her young family, while her husband John traveled in service of the embattled, embryo Republic. **But although the landscape is completely changed, several Adams shrines have been preserved.**

You can get to Quincy by taking the Braintree T Red Line train and getting off at Quincy Center (about a 20 minute ride from the **Park St. T station on the Green and Red Lines**). There are two Quincy T stops, Quincy Center and Quincy-Adams. **Our visit starts from the former. The Quincy Center T station** opens upon a pleasant plaza, with benches and statuary,

facing Hancock St., in the midst of the City's business
and government district. Just south of the T station is
City Hall, and beside it is the **Hancock Cemetery**
in which the area's early settlers lie, including
John Adams' and John Hancock's ancestors.
Across Hancock St. from the T station is the
impressive **First Parish Church,** built in 1828
of Quincy granite. **Here both presidents and
and their wives are buried.** The **Church's**
congregation traces back to the first settlers.
John Hancock's father was a pastor here.

First Parish Church

   The two major Adams sites, the
Adams Estate at 135 Adams St. and
the **Adams Birthplace** at 133 and 141
Franklin (see map), are located 3/4 of a
mile in opposite directions from the Quincy
Center T Station. **The National Park
Service will take you on trolley tours to both.** You can sign up for the tours at the
Adams National Historic Park Visitor Center at 1250 Hancock St., in the Presidents
Place Galleria next to the First Parish Church, **across the street from the T station**
(see map). **Call (617) 770-1175** for schedule information.   A fee of $2.00 includes
trolley transport and admission to the two sites, which are open from April to
November. The **Adams Estate**, a handsome mansion but not extraordinarily
luxurious, with lovely formal gardens, and a separate library building, became the
family home after John Adams had served his term as President. Four generations of
Adamses actually lived here. In this respect the house is unique among Presidential
homes. You get a warm intimate view of the family, upon seeing their portraits and
personal possessions, and the furnishings and decoration accumulated over the
years. The library contains the family's book collection, but not their own papers which
are stored in the **State House Archives** (see page 17). The **Adams Birthplace**

Adams Estate

consists of two simple clapboard houses, one was John Adams' birthplace, the home of his parents, and the other was John Quincy Adams' birthplace, the first home of John and Abigail after their marriage. John Adams inherited both houses and the farm on which they once stood from his father. Now they stand incongruously in the midst of a strip of residences converted to business offices. **These two humble dwellings dating from 1680 are the oldest surviving birthplaces of Presidents.**

A side trip from the Birthplace of about one half mile along Franklin to Viden Rd (see map) brings you to the cairn (now beside a green house retail store) from which, on June 17, 1775, Abigail and her 7 year old son, John Quincy, watched the flames and pillars of smoke rising from the **Battle of Bunker Hill** (see Chapter 1). The events of those fearful days are described vividly in her letters to John, who was then in Philadelphia at the second Continental Congress. **Abigail's most famous letter to John is the one quoted at the beginning of this section.** John's reply was not as memorable, so I shall not repeat it here. John was ahead of most of the Congress delegates on the matter of Independence for the Nation, but Abigail was ahead of John in wanting human rights for both halves of the race. **This remarkable woman was ahead of her time in wanting rights for all persons.** "I wish there were not a slave in the Province" was another of her impassioned pleas to John.

A good way to learn about other interesting Quincy historical sites is to get the Quincy Historical Trail brochure from the **Quincy Historical Society** located at 8 Adams St. (see map) in a Romanesque building built in 1792 as the **Adams Academy**, a boys school founded with John Adams' encouragement. At this site once stood the birthplace of **John Hancock**, the famous merchant prince, generous supporter of the Sons of Liberty, flamboyant signer of the Declaration of Independence, a presiding officer of the Continental Congress, and of numerous Provincial Congresses, Revolutionary War general, and Governor of the Commonwealth of Massachusetts. Hancock married Dorothy Quincy, a kinswoman of Abigail Adams, and daughter of the prominent family after whom the City and also Boston's **Quincy Market** are named.

Near the Quincy Center T station, on Washington St. (see map), is the handsome **Public Library**, designed by **H.H. Richardson**, the architect of Boston's **Trinity Church**. The Quincy Center T station is the terminus for several buses which fan out to various sections of Quincy and nearby South Shore towns. The Center abounds in good food at reasonable prices and interesting stores for bargain hunting.

Adams Birthplace, an early view

Lowell Cotton Mill
(c. 1915)

LOWELL

The New England that spearheaded the Revolution was almost completely rural and of English descent. But today's New England is a rich ethnic mosaic, residing mostly in cities or their suburbs. The great transformation, the American Industrial Revolution, started in the beginning of the nineteenth century, when, freed from the restrictions the former Mother Country had imposed, Americans reinvested fortunes made in the sea-trade in canals, railroads, textile mills, and large scale industrial enterprises of all kinds calling for much new labor. And the poor of Europe and Canada responded in legions bringing their strength and aspirations. At first it must have seemed that they had traded one kind of poverty for another. As they struggled to improve their working conditions, the American Labor Union Movement was born.

The saga of Lowell, site of a National Historic Park established in 1978, symbolizes these many new beginnings. The new revolution began with the attempt to produce textiles with water powered machines, the most jealously guarded, and profitable, of the Mother Country's industries. One of the Americans' first tries, a water run cloth factory, was built in 1814 in Waltham on the Charles River by a coalition of wealthy Bostonians and North Shorites led by **Francis Cabot Lowell**, who had surreptitiously studied English power looms while on vacation in 1810, ostensibly to regain his health. In 1821, after Lowell's death, the coalition, also known as the **Boston Associates**, launched a far more ambitious project -- **creation of a complete, new town**, later named in Lowell's honor, in farmland in East Chelmsford near the Pawtucket Falls on the Merrimack River, to be devoted totally to textile manufacture. Its initial design included not only water-run factories, but housing for the workers, and other institutions to supply their needs. **Lowell was a completely planned community**, with buildings and streets bordering an elaborate system of canals built to harness efficiently the power of the Merrimack, and to transport passengers and supplies. **The mills, the canals, and the gatehouses governing water levels were considered marvels of hydrotechnical engineering** for their day. A novel feature was that the new factories combined under one roof the complete manufacturing process from raw material to finished fabric. Even as the Boston Associates planned this extraordinary project, they fought (successfully, it turns out) for U. S. tariff protection of their infant industry.

      The first workers were mostly single women recruited from New England farms, yearning for opportunities to earn money and enlarge their lives. Lowell's founders tried initially to create a model community with decent living conditions and afterhour cultural stimulations to attract these women. Later, however, with increased competition, as textile mills sprang up on most of New England's many rivers, profit making won out over idealism. As early as the 1830's, these daughters of the Revolution showed their independence by protesting and "turning out" (we would say striking) against decreasing wages and worsening working conditions. Their places were taken by immigrants from many nations eager to improve their lot.

      Although large scale industry began in New England with intensive use of water power for textile manufacture, within a few decades, steam-run factories, large and small, were manufacturing consumer and industrial goods of every kind, seemingly everywhere. The skills and mechanical ingenuity developed in constructing and running textile machinery were soon being used to produce a variety of precision tools including tools that could make tools. And the industrial know-how acquired here was rapidly transferred to other sections of the growing Nation. And so **the whole country was launched into the Industrial Revolution.**

The Boston Associates'
first mill, in Waltham
on the Charles (1814)

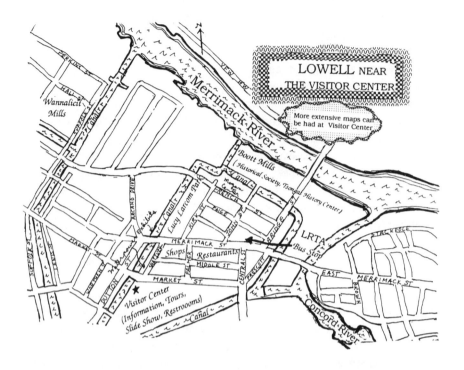

In appreciation of Lowell's unique role in this country's **beginnings as a leader in industrial technology,** and the **enrichment of the national heritage with the best of many cultures**, in 1978, under the leadership of then Congressman **Paul Tsongas**, a Lowell native and descendant of Greek immigrants, the U.S. Congress laid the foundation for establishment of a **National Historic Park** in the City. The intent was to preserve and restore existing sites and artifacts, including buildings, canals, and machinery, to research the lives of Lowell's workers and founders, and to prepare exhibits and sponsor tours to recapture this important chapter of our history and to make it accessible to all. The concept of an urban National Park celebrating the country's labor and industrial history was entirely new. **Today a visit to the Park makes a fascinating day trip.** But there are so many excellent exhibits and tours and special events arranged by the Park Service with the aid of local and state cultural and preservation organizations that you will probably want to come back again and again.

   To get to the Lowell National Historic Park Visitor Center take the T commuter train from North Station, which is across the street from the North Station stop on the T's Green and Orange Lines. When you get to the Lowell train station, which has rest rooms, I recommend taking an **LRTA (Lowell Region Transit Authority) bus** (they run every 15 minutes, and the fare is only 30 cents) downtown to Merrimack Street a few short blocks from the **National Park Visitor Center at 246 Market St**. (The driver will help you get off at the closest stop.) The Lowell train station, on Thorndike St. opposite the South Common Park, is only a mile away, but the walk along Thorndike is unpleasant and unsafe due to traffic and a disappearing sidewalk.

   At the Visitor Center, which is open daily except for holidays year round, you can sign up for any of the many tours that the Park Service conducts to the many exhibit spaces about town. Call **(508) 970-5000 for schedule information and to make advance reservations** (which are advisable during the busy season). **The town itself,** with its numerous ethnic enclaves, and restored and recycled 19th century buildings and its repaired canal and lock system, **is a major exhibit.** Knowledgeable and enthusiastic Park Service personnel will explore ethnic neighborhoods with you, take you to restored power run mills, to restored early boardinghouses, to exhibits on water power technology, on canal tours, and to exhibit halls and museums. Although most of the sites are within a mile of the Visitor Center, the Park Service uses a variety of conveyances, bus, open air trolley, and boat, to chauffeur visitors around. **They are great fun.** In the warm months visitors can take delightful guided cruises on the canals and the Merrimack, or enjoy miles of restored canal walkways.

   At the Visitor Center itself there are exhibits, free brochures, maps, restrooms, of course, and a bookstore where you can buy literature on Lowell's history including the fine Park Service publication, *LOWELL, An Industrial City,* by Thomas Dublin, a bargain at $4.95. **Be sure to see the outstanding wide screen slide show on Lowell history.**

   On my first visit some years ago, in the Park's early development stage, I went on a **totally delightful three hour ranger-guided tour.** I hasten to say that not all tours are this long. First we began with a brief tour of the Downtown District near the **Merrimack Gatehouse** on the Merrimack Canal. (See map.) We paused at **Lucy**

Larcom Park beside the Canal. It commemorates one of the most famous of the "mill girls", educator **Lucy Larcom** (1820 - 1893), who worked at the Lowell mills from age 11 to age 20 (age 11!) and wrote of the experience in her autobiographical *A NEW ENGLAND GIRLHOOD*. She was one of the contributors to the *LOWELL OFFERING*, a journal published by mill workers, whose literary quality astonished **Charles Dickens** on his 1843 visit to Lowell. Next to the park is Lowell's oldest church, St. Anne's.

Afterwards we were taken by bus to the **Wannalicit Mill and the Lowell Museum**, which had working power looms and exhibits of local history, such as portraits of the founders and the original plans for the city. But the best part of the museum visit was our guide's non-romanticized presentation of the workers' lives. When one of us sneezed, she spoke of the miseries of working in a lint-filled factory for 14 (14!) hours a day. When we had listened to one flying shuttle power loom in operation, she asked if we could imagine the noise of hundreds. Yes, she said, many of the "Lowell girls" suffered from partial loss of hearing. We were shown a bedroom with two beds. Ah, we thought, at least they had decent housing. But, we were told, not two but eight to ten women had occupied this room, sleeping crosswise on the two beds. And all their trunks and belongings had somehow to be fitted into it too. We were told how little remained of their pay after deductions for their room and board. And when we learned of their "turn outs" for better pay and working conditions, so transported were we that we were ready to join them on that earliest of picket lines.

Next we took a walk alongside the shrubbery and flowers on the **Northern Canal Walkway** overlooking the river rapids. The Lowell residents among us kept exclaiming on its beauty. They had never before experienced the river from this pleasant walkway, which had once been a promenade for mill workers on their day off. The Walkway is part of the **Great River Wall**, which extends for 1,000 feet, retaining the canal some thirty feet above the river bed. The wall and the canals were built by Irish immigrants. After a stop at the **Northern Gatehouse** where the mechanics buffs among us could admire what were described as the "finest examples of 19th and 20th century hydrotechnology," we boarded a boat which took us to the Pawtucket Canal.

On a recent (1995) visit, after seeing the slide show at the Visitor Center, which is itself in a restored mill building, we walked a few blocks to the **Boott Cotton Mills Museum**, in the restored Boott Mills buildings (see map), an exhibit space

Eliza Adams, an early labor organizer, one of many workers whose stories are told in the exhibits.

One of many art sites commemorating Lowell's workers.

developed since my earlier visit, with 100 working power looms (you get ear plugs to protect you from the din) and with terrific exhibits and slide shows tracing the country's early industrial history. On the way to the Boott Museum, you pass the **Mogan Cultural Center** occupying a restored boarding house, named after **Patrick J. Mogan**, an educator whose vision inspired the Park. The Boott Mills buildings also house offices of historical and educational organizations, including the **Tsongas Industrial History Center.** The exhibits are not static but a product of continuing work and study.

I hope that I have conveyed some of the excitement of this unique park, which encompasses the entire downtown of the city and has helped revive Lowell from the depression to which it descended after most of its mills closed. The exhibits I've mentioned are only part of the story. Everywhere you go you will see significant sites and commemorative statues. In addition there are a host of special events like the **Lowell Folk Festival** held in July celebrating Lowell's ethnic diversity.

Of course, you are going to be hungry at some point of your visit to Lowell. There is a cafeteria adjoining the Visitor's Center, but there are also many fine eateries nearby on Market, Palmer, and Merrimack Streets, and interesting stores too.

More on the Lowell Folk Festival

The Lowell Folk Festival, initiated ten years ago, has grown into the "premier traditional food and music festival in the Northeast .... a must visit for anyone seriously interested in folk music and culture." (Scott Alarik, *Boston Globe*) The success of the festival can be attributed to a happy collaboration of local civic organizations, national art groups, and the Park Service. The attendance over the years has averaged 200,000. Music and dance performances go on at stages all over town -- Boarding House Park, near the Mogan Cultural Center; in St. Anne's Churchyard; at the Park Service Visitor Center, etc. The ethnic range is vast: Native American; African Jazz; A Cappella Gospel; Polish; Greek; Armenian; Irish; Scots; Kentucky Blue Grass; Mexican; Inca; Brazilian; and more. A rollicking good time is had by all.

A T Update and More on Current PT Fares

An Update: On the latest T Commuter Rail schedules, a new information phone number appears **(617) 222-3200.** The number **(617) 722-3200,** given in the text on page 7, however, seems to be valid still. In addition, on the newest schedule is given T Web Site http://www.mbta.com and Smar Traveler 374-1234-8-*.

More About Fares. As mentioned, the basic T bus fare is 60 cents. (You must have exact change, but the driver will accept a train token, worth 85 cents.) But trips to the suburbs may cost more. The one-way fare to Marblehead (see pages 111-117) is currently $2.25. T Commuter Rail fares depend on the number of zones crossed. A one-way fare to **Salem**, which is 3 zones away from Boston's North Station, is currently $2.50, and the one way fare to **Rockport** (8 zones) is $4.00. The **RIPTA** basic fare is 85 cents, and increases according to zones crossed. The one way fare from **Providence to Newport** (4 zones) costs currently $2.50. There are bargains, however. When the B, C, D and E Green Line trolleys emerge from the subway going westward, you pay zero fare when you board, and zero fare when you leave. So, for example, you can jog or walk from Cleveland Circle to Coolidge Corner (see map on page 70), and go back **all free.** This happy state of affairs possibly results from the troubles attendant on the old system (when the MBTA was still called the MTA and Government Center was Scollay Square). You then had to pay a fare when you got off the surface Green Lines. This situation led to a hit song of the fifties by Jacqueline Steiner and Bess Hawes about the hapless Charlie who was stuck on the trolley because he didn't have a nickel to get off: (continued on page 241)

Chapter 3
A NORTH SHORE SAMPLER
MARBLEHEAD,
SALEM,
CAPE ANN,
and
MANCHESTER

TRANSPORTATION SUMMARY

To **Marblehead**, take **T bus 441 or 442 from Haymarket Sq. T stop on the Orange and Green Lines.** Trip takes about 1 hour.

To **Salem, Manchester, Gloucester, Rockport,** take **Ipswich/Rockport T commuter train from North Station adjacent to Orange and Green Line T stops.** Trip takes about 30 min. to Salem, 50 min. to Manchester, 65 min. to Gloucester, and 75 min. to Rockport.

For information call (617) 722-3200, or toll free 1 - 800 - 392-6100, or if you are hearing impaired TDD 722 - 5146.

A NORTH SHORE SAMPLER

Marblehead, Salem, Cape Ann, and Manchester

INTRODUCTION

Boston's North Shore offers visitors a variety of superb cultural and natural attractions -- outstanding museums, intriguing historic sites, art galleries, beautiful beaches, oceanside cliffs topped by woods and castles, and harbors brimming with sailing and fishing boats. Like Boston, the **North Shore** towns were founded in the 17th century by Puritans of the **Massachusetts Bay Company.** Closely allied by religion and politics, they also collaborated in the web of economic activities -- fishing, shipbuilding, and manufacturing -- supporting the extensive sea trade that brought so much wealth to Massachusetts in the 17th, 18th, and early 19th centuries. At the time of the **Revolution**, Massachusetts had several thriving ports. To the British, the Bay Colony was a many-headed hydra. As they tried to clamp down on Boston's freewheeling sea trade and smuggling, the **North Shore** ports carried the torch, trading, smuggling, and, after the start of the shooting war, privateering and providing ships for the fledgling **U.S. Navy**. After the war, Boston and the North Shore ports entered into a new golden era of round-the-globe trade, carrying them way beyond their former trading routes, to the **Far East**, the **South Pacific**, the **Baltic**, and the **Pacific Northwest**. An excellent book giving the total picture of early Massachusetts prowess on the seas is Samuel Eliot Morison's *MARITIME HISTORY OF MASSACHUSETTS.*

Several of Boston's most prominent families came originally from the **North Shore**, where they founded their fortunes on sea ventures. They settled in Boston after the Revolution. While Boston merchants had suffered as a result of the British occupation, these North Shore aristocrats had prospered from fabulously successful privateer operations attacking British shipping, and they continued to expand their fortunes in the **Golden Era** after the War. In politics, Federalists all, they were ardent supporters of a strong federal government that would protect and promote Massachusetts' maritime interests.

Today the **North Shore i**s a mixture of industrial cities and "gold coast" towns. Our sampling includes both types. What they all have in common are fascinating historical sites, wonderful views, and delicious seafood. And, of course, they all have given up attacking British shipping and smuggling molasses from the West Indies.

All of the **North Shore** places to be described can be easily reached by public transportation from Boston. The times of travel are short enough (about an hour or less) and the trips frequent enough so that you can conveniently explore the North Shore on day trips from Boston. However, there are also many pleasant accommodations so that you can choose a longer stay, as do hosts of summer colonists. Maps, brochures, lists of accommodations and events can be obtained in advance by writing to the various Chambers of Commerce at the addresses to be given in the text. When you write be sure to emphasize that you are traveling car-free, and ask for the schedules of the local transit system. The *CALENDAR* of the Thursday *BOSTON GLOBE* lists many **North Shore** events.

MARBLEHEAD

A wondrous place is Marblehead, to which you can go by taking the **T bus 441 or 442** from the **Haymarket Square T stop**, which is on the **Green and Orange Lines**. For schedule information, **call (617) 722-3200 or 1-800-392-6100, or,** if you are hearing impaired, **TDD 722-5146.** In the last lap of the trip, the bus takes you along Washington St., in Marblehead's **Old Town**, to Franklin St.. You will then be within a block or two of Front St.(see map), where you will find yourself looking down at a spectacularly picturesque harbor filled with sails and fishing boats.The rest of the world fades as you gaze at the marvelous scene before you.

Once a busy seaport, today this beautiful harbor, enclosed by rocky headlands, is bordered by yacht clubs from which, on a fine summer's day, as many as 2,000 sailboats issue forth. From May to October, sailing enthusiasts come from near and far for the **weekend races.** And **July's special racing week** draws even more. **Several parks set in the rock cliffs** above the harbor provide superb vantage points for scene savoring, picnics, or daydreaming.

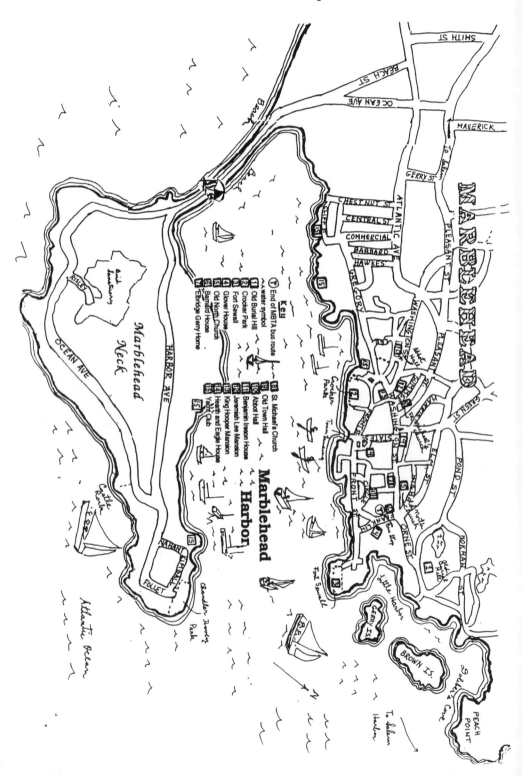

In the summer months, at the **Town Landing,** near the foot of State St., you can **board a sightseeing cruise or rent a boat** and row yourself about to explore. There are a number of sandy beaches too. The most popular, with lifeguards, spectator stands, rest rooms, and snack bar, is along the **Causeway to Marblehead Neck. At the Town Landing and the parks are restrooms, open during the summer months**. However, although some of the facilities are then closed, I recommend going to Marblehead in the late spring and early fall, when the crowds have thinned and the crisp air lends wings to your feet and sparks to your spirit as you spring along to explore this miracle of a town.

The exhilaration of the harbor is not Marblehead's only delight; **the Old Town itself is a major marvel.** In the narrow winding streets, crowded with wooden dwellings and the charms of hillside gardens, you encounter a complete town almost as it was laid out in the 18th century. As you wander about reading the signs on the houses, you discover that 18th and 17th century buildings are the rule rather than the exception. Even though these houses, formerly inhabited by shipowners, merchants, artisans, and fishermen, are now the homes of bankers, lawyers, and teachers, who commute to Boston during the day, or writers, artists, and shopkeepers, nevertheless the shape of the past is still here. Miraculously, the Colonial town has survived as townspeople have voted down streetwidenings, parking lots, and highrises. Even though some twentieth century houses have been added in the crevices, and the former rocky lanes have been paved, this is **IT, a real Colonial town, and not a reconstruction. Most of these buildings were here THEN!!**

As you might expect, amidst all this ancient treasure, there are many places that deserve pauses and pondering. **Of course, you should take your first walk along Front Street** to enjoy the doings at the **Town Landing** and the **magnificent views** from the two harborside parks, **Crocker Park** and **Fort Sewall,** the latter dating back to the French Indian Wars. What follows are just a few of the many special places of the **Old Town.**

Atop **Old Burial Hill** (see map) was the **first Puritan Meeting House.** Here are the graves of the earliest settlers, and also of 600 who served in the Continental Army. Six hundred!! A vast contribution for a Colonial town. But, relatively speaking, **Marblehead was not a small town at the time of the Revolution.** Its population of 6,000 was among the top ten in all thirteen Colonies, after Philadelphia population 34,000, New York and Boston, both 18,000, Newport 9,000, and Salem 8,000. After the **Battle of**

Concord (see page 80), Marblehead troops rushed to help in the siege of Boston and the **Battle of Bunker Hill** (see pages 29, 30), and following the evacuation of Boston by the British, a Marblehead regiment under **Colonel John Glover** accompanied Washington southward to New York and New Jersey. Skilled in seamanship, Glover's men rowed Washington's army across the Delaware, and were the advance contingent in the **Battle of Trenton**. Later, after the War, John Glover became the first general of the U. S. Marines. **Glover's home**, built in 1762, still stands at **11 Glover St.**

At **161 Washington St.**, the elegant, authentically furnished **Jeremiah Lee Mansion,** built in 1768, and now owned by the **Historical Society**, is a good example of the kind of house that could be built with fortunes made in the West Indies trade. Open daily except Sundays from mid-May to October, from 9.30 to 4. Fee. Diagonally opposite, on Hooper St., is the house of another merchant prince, the **"King" Hooper Mansion**, built between 1728 and 1745. Now owned by the **Art Association**, it makes a lovely setting for art exhibitions, and is open from 2 to 5 daily, except Mondays. Fee.

At **41 Washington St.** is the **Old North Church**, built in 1824 to replace the **Old Meeting House** on **Burial Hill**. Its congregation was organized in 1635, at the time of the first settlement. **John Barnard**, who was the parson of this congregation in the early 18th century, lived at **7 Franklin.** Across the street from the church, **44 Washington** was the home of **Elbridge Gerry**, a delegate to the **Continental Congress** and signer of the **Declaration of Independence**, later Governor of Massachusetts and Vice-President of the United States during Madison's administration. **"Gerrymander"** was a term coined by Gerry's opponents to describe the salamander-like voting districts formed during his term as Governor. Number **65 Washington** was the home of **Captain Trevett,** who led the Marblehead troops at Bunker Hill. **St. Michael's Church**, near the intersection of Washington and Summer, built in 1714, was the Anglican church attended by the local Tories. It is the oldest surviving Episcopal church in the country.

Old Town Hall, built in 1727, and still standing at the corner of Washington and State, is Marblehead's equivalent of Boston's **Faneuil Hall** (see pages 24, 25), the stage in Colonial days for Town Meetings protesting the Parliamentary edicts. Today's Town Meetings -- Marbleheaders are still resolutely devoted to them -- are

An Early Gerrymander

held in **Abbot Hall**, the imposing Victorian
brick building on Washington St. at the top
of the hill, whose tower dominates the skyline
as you look landward from **Crocker Park.**
On your visit there, be sure to drop in at
the **Selectman's Room**, where the original
of A. M. Willard's famous *"THE SPIRIT OF
76"* hangs. The painting was a gift to the
town from General John Devereaux whose
son posed for the drummer boy figure.
Many other interesting historic memorabilia
are to be found in **Abbot Hall,** which is
open year round, Monday through Friday,
and has rest rooms, which are especially
welcome in the off-season when park rest rooms are closed.

Abbot Hall

Those fond of **John Greenleaf Whittier's** poems will undoubtedly be intrigued by
the **Skipper Ireson House** on Circle St. Yes, this is the Skipper Ireson, celebrated in
the verse, Scores of women, old and young/ Strong of muscle and glib of tongue
Pushed and pulled up the rocky lane/ Shouting and singing the shrill refrain
Here's Flud Oirson fur his horr'd horrt/ Torr'd and furtherr'd and corr'd in a corrt
By the women of Morblehead.
Translation: Here's Floyd Ireson, for his hard heart, tarred and feathered and carried
in a cart by the women of Marblehead (presumably to the courts of justice in Salem).
What was Ireson's crime? He had "Sailed away from a sinking wreck/ With his
own town's people on her deck." On the sign announcing the **Ireson House** (now a
private residence), are two amendments to the Whittier poem: Ireson's first name was
Benjamin not Floyd; and there is a brief declaration that he was "An innocent man!!"
What do historians say? In his *MARITIME HISTORY*, Samuel Eliot Morison says that

SPIRIT of '76

Captain Benjamin Ireson was tarred and feathered and *rowed in a dory* to Salem by the *men* of Marblehead, and adds that Ireson *was* innocent.

What is not in dispute is that the women of Marblehead were much suffering. Many were left widows by the **Revolution**. The town was then impoverished, reverting from a flourishing trading port to a fishing village. In 1846, a storm on the Grand Banks of Newfoundland destroyed a large portion of its fishing fleet. The final stab of fate came in 1877, when a great fire demolished the shoe industry that had come to be Marblehead's mainstay. And so nothing was left for this poor town but to develop into the yachting capital and golden bedroom community of today. And thus did past adversity help bring about today's miracle. Anya Seton's novel *THE HEARTH AND THE EAGLE* is a pleasant way of learning about Marblehead's history from the 17th to the 20th century. The house at **30 Franklin** (a private residence) was a major setting for the book.

All the above sites are close together in the **Old Town** on the west side of the harbor. A walk of one or two miles, up and down and around, on the winding streets, passes them and many others, the modest houses of artisans and fishermen, dating to the 17th, 18th, and 19th centuries, marked with plaques indicating the occupations of the original occupants. But should you, on some occasion, want to go on a longer walk, I suggest crossing the causeway to **Marblehead Neck** (there is a sidewalk on the causeway, but when the tide is low, you may prefer to walk along the beach) and walking along the eastern edge of the harbor past the yacht-clubs there to the **Chandler-Hovey Park,** another fine vantage point for watching the sailing fleets. To complete your walk, you can circumambulate the **Neck** by returning via Ocean Ave, on which you pass great estates facing the Swampscott shore. Along the way, are some small parks for scene savoring. A turn-off from Ocean Ave. leads to an Audubon Sanctuary. The total walk to **Chandler-Hovey Park** and back to **Abbott Hall** is about 4 or 5 miles. You can shorten it somewhat by getting off the bus at Ocean Ave., which leads to the causeway. But, on a first visit to Marblehead, I recommend going to the end of the line, to Franklin St., which is lined with 18th century houses, and spending the day exploring the **Old Town.**

Along Washington and State Streets, housed in 18th century buildings, are enough shops with arts, crafts, books, maps, and everything nautical to make shopping and browsing in the **Old Town** an enjoyable experience. Don't miss the **Rusty Rudder** at 134 Washington, a cooperative selling the crafts of local artists. A fine children's attire shop is the **Bus Stop,** on Washington St. at the intersection with State, where the bus schedule is posted.

The **Old Town** has several good restaurants. Everyone likes **The Barnacle** on Front St. with waves lapping up on the rocks beneath it. The prices are reasonable, the chowders are delicious, and the views superb. **The Landing** on Front St. at the foot of State has a great location for harborwatching. **The King's Rook** on State St. is another popular place for sitting and sipping, playing games, and chatting. Open year-round. On Washington St. are several stores and cafes providing salads, sandwiches, and fresh juices.

There are several inns in, or within walking distance of, the **Old Town**. For more information, or help in making arrangements, call or write ahead to the **Marblehead Chamber of Commerce, 62 Pleasant St., P.O. Box 76, Marblehead, Mass. 01945. Call (617) 631-2868.**

Dining Seaside

SALEM

Also fascinating to visitors, but very different from neighboring Marblehead, is **Salem,** population 38,000, the seat of Essex County, **founded in 1626**, from which Marblehead was an early spin-off. Today, while Marblehead is a playground for sailing buffs, **Salem** is industrial with a long list of manufactures. Its most famous firm is **Parker Brothers Game Company**, producers of the best-selling **Monopoly.**

Founded before Boston, **Salem** was **an advance outpost** for the Puritans of John Winthrop's expedition. The Salemites who greeted Winthrop had already survived the hardships of several winters, started farms, and built a village. They had also

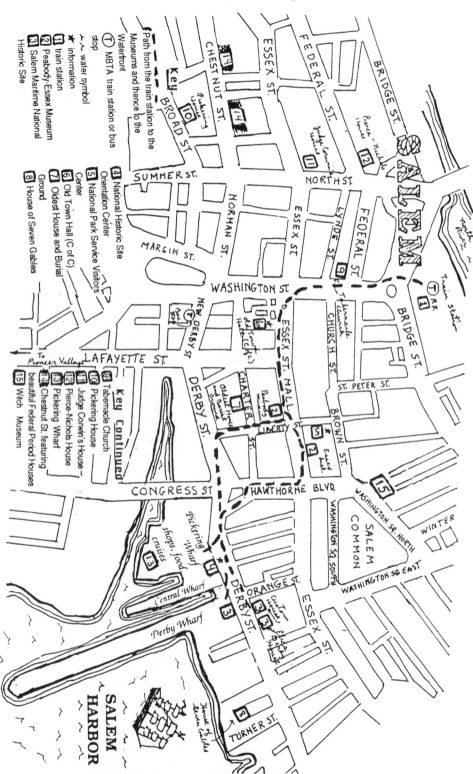

founded the first Puritan church in the New World, establishing a pattern of democratic decision making that was to be followed in Congregational Churches throughout New England. The Puritans had not originally intended to separate from the Anglican Church, but to "purify" it, and to separate themselves only from what they regarded as its corruption. But once in the New World, after consultation with the Pilgrim ministers from Plymouth, who were avowed Separatists, the Puritans adopted a church organization very similar to that of the Pilgrims, in which congregation members, and not a church hierarchy, made all the crucial decisions on church affairs, which, in the early days, embraced all communal affairs.

For visitors today, Salem's main attractions are its outstanding museums and historic sites recalling its past -- the early Puritan village, the witch persecutions of the 1690's, and the maritime glories of its West Indies and Far Eastern trade. Also standing among its old treasure are the settings for some of Nathaniel Hawthorne's works. Hawthorne, a Salem native, was a descendant of a witch court judge. **You will find in Salem much for many visits.**

GETTING   THERE. Salem is one of the early stops on the **Ipswich/Rockport commuter T train from Boston's North Station**, which is adjacent to the **North Station T stop on the Green and Orange Lines.** There are several trains during the day. The train trip to Salem takes **about 30 minutes**. For schedule information call **(617) 722-3200 or (800) 392-6100,** or if you are hearing impaired **TDD 722-5146**. T buses also connect Boston to Salem, but I recommend the train.

THE MUSEUMS. Two superb museums, now combined to form the **Peabody Essex Museum,** are located close together on **Essex St.**, a few short blocks from the railroad station **It is a pleasant walk to them from the station.** You cross Bridge St., whose intersection with Washington (see map) is adjacent to the station, and walk a few blocks along Washington to Essex St. and turn left. (**Daniel Low's** store marks prominently the intersection of Washington with Essex.) After turning left onto Essex from Washington. you will be on a car-free mall. You will pass shops and fountains, all quite pleasant, and then you will see on your right, at **161 Essex**, the **East India Marine Hall, the home of the Peabody Museum branch of the Peabody Essex.**

The collections of the **Peabody branch of the Peabody Essex** are described in its brochures under the headings of **Maritime History, Ethnology, and Natural History**. What those headings don't tell you is that the exhibits are **stunning in quality and in the manner of their display.** You ask yourself, how does it happen that a town of 38,000 has a museum like this? As explained in the exhibits themselves, the answer lies in Salem's extraordinary part in the Far Eastern trade that revived New England's economy after the Revolution, when Britain closed the ports of its empire to its former American colonies.

Trade of the newly founded American Republic with China was initiated in 1784, when the *EMPRESS OF CHINA* out of New York was permitted to join the line of foreign traders in Canton Harbor. The *EMPRESS* was soon followed by the *GRAND TURK* out of Salem. By 1787, of sixteen American ships trading in Canton Harbor, five were from Salem. So frequent were visits from Salem ships to Far Eastern ports that merchants in those countries thought that Salem must be a separate nation!! Perhaps the customs figures tell the story best. In the early days of the Republic, before income tax, customs duties comprised over 90% of the Federal budget. In 1805, the duties provided by the Salem Custom House totaled $1,019,706 or about 8% of the total for the whole nation. **Clearly, Salem was a giant in those days,** even though its population was less than 10,000.

The remarkable collections of the **Peabody Museum** originated from the "natural and artificial" curiosities gathered from the four corners of the earth by the **East India Society,** organized in 1799 by a group of captains and supercargoes. (In case you are wondering, the supercargo on a ship was the officer in charge of all the business transactions involved   in assembling and selling a cargo, and arranging for a return cargo. Astuteness was a prime prerequisite; many supercargoes were Harvard graduates.) In 1867, the **Museum** was officially founded with the generous endowment of philanthropist George Peabody, who also endowed the museums of archeology and ethnology of Yale and Harvard.

The Museum's rich collection of nautical objects includes paintings of Salem ships and shipmasters by the best artists of the day, marine prints, navigational instruments, wharf and shipyard dioramas, fully rigged and half-hulled boat models,

ship figureheads, whaling gear and scrimshaw. Among the Salemites to whom you are introduced are: **Captain Jonathan Harraden**, privateer extraordinary, **who captured 60 British vessels** during the Revolution; **members of the Derby and Crowninshield families,** Salem's wealthiest merchant-shipowners, leaders in the West Indies trade before the Revolution, and afterwards in the China, Far Eastern, and St. Petersburg trades, **whose ships captured 454 British "prizes" during the Revolution; Nathaniel Bowditch**, born in 1773, the son of a cooper, who went to school only to age ten, rose from clerk to supercargo to shipmaster, but is most famous for his after hours passion, the study of mathematics, which he applied to navigation, producing his *PRACTICAL NAVIGATOR,* long used as the standard authority by the U.S. Navy. Bowditch was one of the first American mathematicians to achieve international fame, a harbinger of the flourishing of mathematics and the natural sciences that was to come to this country.

Especially intriguing among the Museum's superb collection of art objects are the handsomely wrought games and puzzles from many lands. One wonders whether the status of Salem as today's board game capital is somehow related to this fine assemblage. Over the years several enlargements have been made to the original **East India Marine Hall** to accommodate new acquisitions and exhibits. But **the most extraordinary parts of the collection are still the exquisite China Trade artifacts**, the works of the best Cantonese artisans of the day, some made expressly for the American market. These beautiful works not only rejoice the eye but have provided scholars with invaluable knowledge of life in 19th century China.

The **Peabody Museum** also has a large book and manuscript collection, including original log books, ship accounts, plans, maps, etc., open to scholars, and a fine gift shop and a pleasant cafe, open to everyone. The current admission fee is $7 with discounts for seniors and students. Group and family rates are also available. **The admission fee entitles you to entrance to both branches of the Peabody Essex Museum,** the exhibits in the **East India Marine Hall,** which we have described above, as well as those in the **Essex Institute,** to be described next. And it entitles you to participate in many of the activities, tours to historic houses, lectures, slide shows, etc., sponsored by the **Museum.** Open hours are currently Monday - Saturday 10 - 5, Thursday until 8, Sunday noon - 5. **For information call (508) 745-9500.**

Now about the **Essex Institute,** the other half of the **Peabody Essex Museum.** Not far from the **East India Marine Hall**, on the opposite side of Essex, **at 132-134 Essex,** are two Victorian Italian Revival Buildings, **Daland House and Plummer Hall,** housing the **Essex Institute, its Museum and Library.** In **Daland House**, the **Library** contains one of the country's largest collections of early American manuscripts, broadsides, and printed literature -- about two million manuscripts and five hundred thousand printed items. It is a mecca for scholars of the period. **The Museum in Plummer Hall has** changing exhibits and rich permanent collections, including rooms of period furniture, clothing, paintings, toys, glassware, and decorative and utilitarian objects associated with the history of Essex County since the 17th century. In an enclosure behind **the Essex Institute** are several restored historic houses, dating from 1690 to 1819, several of which are open to the public.

As you might expect from the scope of the Essex, there are exhibits devoted to the witch "hysteria" of 1692, which started when two Salem children fell fainting in church, and later claimed that they had been bewitched by certain Salem residents. In the chain of events that followed, several Salemites were tried and executed for witchcraft. The nation has regarded the episode with fascinated horror ever since, and it has provided the theme of numerous novels and plays. On display at the **Essex** are early manuscripts written by and about the protagonists, and various treatises which attempt to put the Salem phenomenon in the wider context of 17th century beliefs in the supernatural. **Cotton Mathe**r, the minister of **Boston's North Church (**see pages 27, 28), had written an extensive treatise on *WITCHCRAFT AND POSSESSIONS* that greatly influenced the ministers and judges of Salem, as it had those of Boston (which also had its witch trials). Invited to investigate the Salem accusations, **Mather added fuel to the flames** with his ranting on the "invisible world". It was a time of terror in Salem, since any person could be accused by his/her neighbor of having occult powers that caused misfortunes to others. About 150 people were accused of witchcraft, including nine children. **The witch hysteria in Massachusetts did not die out until Lady Phips, wife of Governor William Phips, was herself threatened.** Then the Governor, who until then had been a pliant tool of Increase and Cotton Mather, decided that things had gone far enough. He pardoned all those being held for trial. Once the convictions stopped, the accusations also stopped.

In 1992, the **Peabody and the Essex,** both superb institutions of world wide renown, joined forces with the goal of helping to illuminate the present of our nation through an understanding of its past. Over the years they have sponsored many community outreach programs with special exhibits and lectures. Long may they thrive. For convenience, I repeat their telephone number: **(508) 745-9500.**

Near the **Essex Institute,** in the handsome former Unitarian Church at the northwest side of **Salem Common,** is the **Witch Museum,** where the "witch hysteria" is given a more sensational treatment than at the Essex. Here the latest in audiovisual and multimedia techniques are used to recreate the bizarre atmosphere of the episode -- the "possessed" children, accusations, trials, and executions. **Call (508) 744- 5217 for information.**

The ominous figure with tall, wide brimmed hat and great cloak, standing near the entrance to the Witch Museum **is not a witch.** It is **Roger Conant**, Salem's founder.

Salem Harbor and Derby Wharf about 1800 (Drawing inspired by a 19th century painting)

THE WATERFRONT. As you emerge from the **Peabody Essex Museum**, you are not immediately aware of the **Waterfront**. But, of course, this former maritime giant has one, and you are actually quite close to it. Paralleling Essex St., about two blocks away, is **Derby St**. (see map), bordering the piers, named after **Elias Derby**, the wealthiest of Salem's merchant princes. He was the owner of the GRAND TURK and other vessels of the China and Far Eastern and St. Petersburg trade. The Derby family seems to have had a stake in almost every grand sea adventure of those heady days. The family was part owner of the historic vessel *COLUMBIA* (Captain Robert Gray), after which the Columbia River is named. The Columbiamen "discovered" the river when exploring the Pacific Northwest to obtain furs as a medium of exchange for the China trade. (Of course, you and I know that the Columbia River was actually discovered by the Native Americans who sold furs to the Columbiamen.)

For visitors, the most interesting part of Derby St. is the 1/2 mile strip extending northeastward from Hawthorne Blvd. After your visit to the **Peabody Essex Museum**, a good place to begin your exploration of the **Waterfront** is the **Salem Maritime National Historic Site**, located on Derby St., near the corner of

Orange. To get to it, walk along Essex to Hawthorne Blvd., then turn right and walk down to Derby, and then turn left and walk along Derby to its intersection with Orange. Across the street you see a very long wharf, **Derby Wharf**, once the clamorous center of the bustling sea port. To the right of **Derby Wharf** as you gaze toward the sea, on **Central Wharf**, a sign announces the **Visitors Orientation Center** of the **Maritime National Historic Site,** where you can get literature and see slide shows bringing to life Salem's remarkable maritime history, including the early days of the Revolution, when privateers from this town of 8,000, sailing in ships especially designed and outfitted locally, captured over 500 British ships, and auctioned the cargoes of these "prizes" on the wharves. Part of the **Historic Site** is the handsome building on the land side of the street, formerly the **Custom House**, the very one whose outstanding role in providing revenues for the young Republic has already been mentioned (on page 120). **Nathaniel Hawthorne** spent several years as a customs official in this building. By pressing a button in the room that once was his office, you can hear it described in his own words. The **Maritime National Historic Site** includes, in addition to Derby and Central Wharves and the Custom House, a **Bonded Warehouse**, a **West India Goods Store**, and also the **Derby Mansion**, from which Elias Derby himself kept track of the doings on the wharves. **Entrance to all of these sites is free,** except the Derby Mansion, for which there is a modest fee. For more information **call (508) 740 - 1660.** At **2 Liberty St.**, around the corner from the **Essex Institute,** is the **National Park Service Visitor Center (call (508) 741-3648)**, which has additional exhibits, and literature on the early history of Salem and Essex County. **All free.**

If you walk eastward along Derby St. from Derby Wharf, and turn right on Turner, you come to the **House of Seven Gables**, built in 1688, the inspiration for Hawthorne's novel of the same name. Fee. For schedule information, **call (508) 744 0991**. This sea side compound also includes coffee and gift shops, and **Hawthorne's birthplace,** moved here from its original site on Union St.

At the foot of Hawthorne St., just to the right of Central Wharf, is Pickering Wharf, now crammed with specialty stores, food take-outs, and restaurants. **Also on Pickering Wharf, is the East India Cruise Company,** offering **whale watches** and **narrated cruises of Salem Harbor and the North Shore**, from May to October. Call **(508) 741-0434** for schedule information. **Benches on the wharf** provide ideal perches for **scene savoring and picnics**.

MORE HISTORY IN SALEM. Salem abounds with historic places. Here are just a few highlights. Much of the information in this section comes from *OLD NAUMKEAG* by Webber and Nevins, published in 1877. but still an excellent guide to Salem's old buildings. (Naumkeag was Salem's Indian name.) On the way from the train station to the Museums, you passed, at the corner of Essex and Washington, **Daniel Low's Department Store**, which stands on what was the **site of Salem's first Meeting House of 1629, the first Puritan New World Church**. The present structure was built in 1826 as the congregation's fourth Meeting House. It was designed to have commercial tenants on the first floor and a place of worship on the second. Daniel Low's has been a tenant here for over a century, but the building is no longer used for worship. The congregation tracing its descent to that of 1629 has broken into fragments, one of which worships at the Unitarian Church next to **Judge Corwin's House** (see page 126), and another at the **Tabernacle Church**, at the corner of Federal and Washington, which you pass on your way between the train station and the Museums. A pause there allows you to read a plaque which gives the covenant signed by the worshipers of 1629.

> We covenant with the Lord and with one another:
> and doe bynde ourselves in the presence of God,
> to walk together in all his wais, according as he is
> pleased to reveale himself unto us in his blessed
> word of Truth.

That is all. **No mention is made of King or Prelate**. The congregation proceeded to elect its own teacher and pastor, setting the pattern that has been followed in Congregational Churches until this day. The break with the King's Church that occurred here in 1629 facilitated the political break with the King himself in 1775.

The nineteenth century buildings near Daniel Low's also are crammed with interest. Near the Naumkeag Bank, an alley leads from Essex St. to the **Old Town Hall** in the ancient Market Square (**now called Derby Square**). The present building of 1817 was actually the **fifth of Salem's Town Houses,** which combined the functions of government center, court house, and market place. The second Town House was the one in which the iniquitous witchcraft trials took place. **But the most famous of Salem's Town Houses was the third one built in 1720.** It was in this House that Salemites denounced the Stamp and Townshend Acts and lent support to Boston's defiance of December, 1773. And when the Colonial Government was transferred to Salem in the aftermath of the **Boston Tea Party**, it was here that the General Court locked the doors to bar entry to the Royal Governor's secretary, and, under the adroit leadership of Samuel Adams, voted to participate in the Continental Congress and elected the Massachusetts delegation. It was in the third Town House also that the plans were laid for a Provincial Congress to meet in Concord. **So it was here in Salem, in the third Town House, that preparations were made for the momentous events of April, 1775, and July, 1776.**

The present **Old Town Hall** is no longer used as a seat of government (City Hall is on Washington between Essex and Federal Streets), and it can't boast of heroic events, but it is a fine example of Federal period architecture. On the ground floor is the **Chamber of Commerce**, which produces an excellent information folder containing a map and listing services and historic sites. **Call (508) 744 - 0004**, or write to **Chamber of Commerce, Old Town Hall, 32 Derby Sq., Salem, MA 01970**. The graceful upstairs hall often hosts concerts, dramas, and movies.

On Charter St., about 2 blocks from the Peabody Museum, is the Goult-Pickman House, built in 1638, Salem's oldest. Open in summer. Fee. **Call (508) 745 -1638.** Next to it is Salem's **oldest burial ground** with headstones dating back to 1637. Free. Buried here is John Hathorne, a witch trial judge and ancestor of Nathaniel Hawthorne.

Several magnificent mansions built by merchant shipowners from 1790 to 1820, when Salem was at the height of its prosperity, can be seen by **walking about the border of Salem Common and in the Chestnut St. Historic District,** a few blocks west of Washington (see map on page 118). **Samuel McIntire,** a native Salemite, designed Salem's grandest Federal houses. A block south of Chestnut, at **18 Broad St., is the Pickering House, built in 1651,** and continuously occupied since then by the Pickering family, whose most famous member was **Timothy Pickering,** who commanded the regiment of 700 Salem men, accompanying Washington to fight in New Jersey. After the War, he held several national offices including Congressman, Senator, Postmaster General, Secretary of War, and Secretary of State. The House is open to the public on Mondays. **Call (508) 744 - 1647**. Fee. A block up from Chestnut, at the corner of North and Essex, is the **"Witch House,"** the home of **Jonathan Corwin,** a chief justice of the "Witchcraft Court." Here he examined some of the accused before their trials. Open seasonally. Fee. Call **(508) 744 - 0180.**

Judge Corwin's House

A block north of the **Corwin House**, at **80 Federal St.**, just west of North St., is the handsome **Pierce-Nichols Mansion**, notable as **McIntire's** first important commission. McIntire's achievements as an architect are all the more remarkable because he was self-taught. However, growing up in Salem, he had the advantage of access to the collections of books, manuscripts, and periodicals that early Salem leaders loved to assemble, which eventually became the basis for the **Essex Institute. Nathaniel Bowditch** (see page 121), McIntire's contemporary, also self-taught, benefited greatly from the scientific library of a British scholar, seized by a Beverly privateer during the Revolution and sold at low cost to Salem collectors. Another notable poor boy who benefited from Salem's bookish atmosphere was **Benjamin Thompson,** who, in 1766 at age 13, came to Salem to serve as an apprentice to a storekeeper. In his later years **Thompson was responsible for formulating and demonstrating a fundamental law of physics, the equivalence of mechanical work and heat energy**. Yet most Americans hardly know anything about him. Why? Probably because he was a Tory!! He is best known among physicists as **Count Rumford**, a title that he acquired during an adventurous career in Europe.

The above highlights will get you started on exploring Salem's historical sites. Salemites have strung together most of them and others into a **Heritage Trail,** marked by red lines on the sidewalk, their answer to Boston's **Freedom Trail** (see pages 15-30). A walk of one or two miles up and down and around will reach them all. Should you on some visit yearn for a longer walk, go south along Lafayette St. (see map on page 118) and then to your left along Clifton (about 1 and 1/2 miles from Pickering Wharf); you will then come to the **Forest River Park,** a pleasant waterside park with fine views of Salem Harbor and the Marblehead Shore, featuring benches, picnic tables, beaches, rest rooms (open seasonally), duck pond, and ball fields, and, in summer, a special attraction, **Pioneer Village,** a re-creation of early Salem of the 1630's, with reproductions of the first buildings and exhibits on the lifestyle of the founders. **The Village** is open from June to mid-October. Fee. Call **(508) 744 - 0180.** The rest of the park is open year round. Should you not want to walk all the way, you can also take the Lynn T bus, from the T stop near the supermarket on New Derby St.; it goes along Lafayette past Clifton.

FOOD IN SALEM. At some point all that history is going to make you hungry. Like any place that attracts so many visitors, **Salem has many good restaurants and food take-outs.** Going to the Museums along Washington and then the Essex Mall, you will be tempted by the aromas issuing forth from several cafes. The **Peabody**

Museum itself has a pleasant restaurant. The **Hawthorne Hotel** on Salem Common provides elegant dining. Call **(508) 744-4080. Pickering Wharf** is crammed with restaurants and food take-outs, providing pizza, strudel, ice cream, cheese cake, juices, everything. And one block up from the Wharf, on Derby St., there are many cafes featuring fish and shell fish, with low prices posted. **Derby Fish and Lobster** at **215 Derby**, near Pickering Wharf, call **(508) 745 - 2064,** has high ratings and low prices. On my last visit to Salem, my companion and I chose to eat lunch at **Victoria Station**, because we wanted a close-up view of the Harbor doings, but we weren't disappointed in the food. It was tasty and moderately priced. Of course, you can get plenty of food in the supermarket on New Derby St., next to the T bus stop. At **43 Church St.**, one block north of Essex Mall (see map pn page 118), in the historic **Lyceum Building**, once an important culture center, is the   popular **Lyceum Restaurant, call (508) 745 -7665**, moderate prices. In 1876, **Alexander Graham Bell gave the first public demonstration of the telephone in the Lyceum Lecture Hall.** Bell's connection with Salem began when he tutored a deaf child, whose relatives in gratitude sponsored the difficult years of early experiments with his great invention. Oops, we're slipping back into history. That's what happens when you're in Salem.

LODGING IN SALEM. Salem has several lodgings in historic buildings, within easy walking distance of all that I've described, including the **Hawthorne Hotel,** in the center of everything, at the border of Salem Common, and several guesthouses on the neighboring streets. For more information on lodgings, write the **Chamber of Commerce, 32 Derby Sq., Old Town Hall, Salem, MA 01970, or call (508) 744-0004.** Ask for their excellent map, which shows the locations of services and attractions.

Pioneer Village

CAPE ANN: ROCKPORT AND GLOUCESTER

For sailors on the way to Maine, Cape Ann is the last rocky outcropping of the Massachusetts coast, cut through, since 1642, by the Annisquam Canal. But to land lovers, it is a bundle of endearing oceanside charms. An astonishing natural variety is concentrated in Cape Ann's twenty square miles. The peninsula is ringed by rocky cliffs interrupted by sandy beaches and the salt marshes of the Annisquam. The shore line forms many little harbors, formerly fishing villages and now vacation resorts, and one great harbor, **Gloucester.** The population is concentrated on the rim of the peninsula, while much of the interior, once covered by farms, has been allowed to revert to a wilderness of swamps and forest, growing in pockets of soil distributed among great granite cliffs. Ponds in abandoned quarries are seemingly everywhere. A profusion of great boulders and odd rock formations, part of a terminal moraine left by the ice age glacier, and numerous highland swamps in holes gouged by glacial action, all contribute to the wild beauty of the Cape and its great variety of habitats for birds, animals, and plants.

   Gloucester and **Rockport**, the two towns that share **Cape Ann**, can be reached by train or boat from Boston, and also have their own local bus system **CATA (Cape Ann Transportation Authority)**, circulating about the Cape. Their natural and cultural attractions have drawn a large and loyal summer colony and a celebrated art colony, whose tradition dates back to the nineteenth century when **Fitz Hugh Lane** and **Winslow Homer** painted Gloucester Harbor scenes. Cape Ann makes a delightful day trip from Boston, or, since it has many accommodations, a fine vacation spot.

   Gloucester (population 27,000) has been a fishing port since it was founded in the 1620's. In Colonial days, when fish was the basis of the Bay Colony's economy, no port was more successful in harvesting the "Sacred Cod." Its fishermen sailed to far seas in search of the richest fishing fields. The courage and endurance of its twentieth century fleet, largely of Portuguese and Italian ancestry, were celebrated in Kipling's *Captains Courageous.* The Town's many industries -- paints, varnishes, glues, heavy overclothing, nets, seines, boxes -- emerged from its fishing industry. Today the emphasis is on fish processing rather than fishing. Gloucester's plants process fish from many fleets, and have one of the world's largest outputs. Not coincidentally, **Clarence Birdseye,** of food freezing fame, was a Gloucester resident. Gloucester's large art colony is centered in the **Rocky Neck** section of East Gloucester, where fishermen's cottages overlooking the Harbor have been recycled to art galleries and artists' residences.

   Rockport (population 6,000) was once a granite port and fishing village. Now it is primarily a combination of vacation resort, bedroom community for professionals who work elsewhere, and the residence of many recognized artists who attract students from everywhere.

   Rockport has a clapboard-white, picture postcard prettiness, and is dense with fine guest house lodgings. **Gloucester** is mostly a rougher, workingperson's town.

Between the two, they offer the visitor the variegated charm of two contrasting worlds as well as historical sites, terrific sea food, and numerous natural splendors -- beaches, grand seaside parks, woodlands, and marshes.

INFORMATION. There are two Chambers of Commerce in the area: **Cape Ann Chamber of Commerce**, 33 Commercial St.., Gloucester 01930, **(508) 283-1601,** and the **Rockport Chamber of Commerce,** Board of Trade, Rockport 01966, **(508) 546-6575.** The first lists services and attractions in both Rockport and Gloucester, and also Manchester, at the gateway to Cape Ann. The other focuses on Rockport services and accommodations.. It publishes an excellent map of Rockport showing footpaths and secondary less-used roads, by the sea and into woodlands, and including a guide to the shops of **Bearskin Neck** and **Whistle Stop Mall.** When you write be sure to emphasize that you are going car-free and ask for the schedules of both the **T** train and the local **CATA** bus.

GETTING THERE. There are several commuter trains a day to Gloucester and Rockport from Boston's **North Station**, on the **Green** and **Orange Lines.** For commuter train schedule call **(617) 722-3200,** or the toll free number **(800) 392-6100,** or, if you are hearing impaired, **TDD 722 - 5146.** To get information about the local **CATA** bus call **(508) 283-7916.**

The train trip is very pleasant, still much as described by Lucy Larcom in the 19th century,

> You may ride in an hour or two if you will,
> From Halibut Point to Beacon Hill,
> With the sea beside you all the way,
> Through pleasant places that skirt the Bay.

Halibut Point, in case you are wondering, is the Cape's outermost point with splendid views to Maine and the Isles of Shoals.

You can also get to Cape Ann by boat. This way you encounter Gloucester at its prettiest as it rises out of the sea, its church spires gleaming and *Our Lady of Good Voyage* welcoming. During the summer months, the **A.C. Cruise Lines, (617) 261-6633,** offers trips to **Gloucester** at 10.00 A.M. daily from Boston's Northern Ave. Pier 7 (a twenty minute walk from **South Station** on the **T Red Line,** or take **T bus 7** from **South Station** or a taxi). The boat arrives in Gloucester's **Rocky Neck** about 12.30 P.M. and departs about 3 P.M., so those taking the round trip can enjoy the

galleries and eateries and harbor sights of **Rocky Neck** for about 2 hours. For a longer stay you can go back by train. During week days there are special rates for senior citizens.

GETTING ABOUT ON CAPE ANN

It should be a joy to bicycle in Cape Ann. The distances are ideal, only about 15 miles about the peninsula. But alas the traffic is too much and too fast for the narrow two lane roads. Until the speed limit is lowered to 15 miles per hour everywhere, I recommend getting about by **walking** and the local **CATA** bus. Many people do cycle about the Cape, and I admire them for their heroism. If their numbers increase sufficiently, perhaps they will succeed in changing the prevailing consciousness and obtaining the lower speed limits necessary to make car and bicycle traffic safely compatible.

Below I shall try to describe how Cape Ann unfolds as **you walk from each of the area's train stations** with a possible assist from **CATA** buses whose routes circumnavigate the peninsula and pass by all of the historical and natural attractions to be highlighted below. **Some CATA routes are shown in the map at the head of this section.** You can get the handsome **CATA** booklet with maps and lists of attractions on the various routes by writing to **CATA**, 168 Eastern Ave., Gloucester 01930, or calling **(508) 283-7916**. The bus drivers carry the **CATA** guide also. There are regular bus stops, but on non-school runs bus drivers will stop any place that it is safe to do so. **During July and August**, CATA runs a **Salt Water Trolley** (fare $1.50, reboard for 60 cents) seven days a week stopping at several of the sites we describe below. See page 142 for a list of the SWT stops. Off season **there is no CATA service on Sunday.**

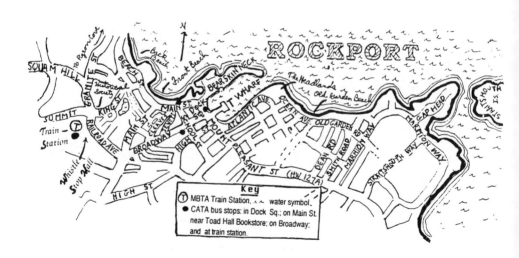

WALKS FROM THE ROCKPORT RAILROAD STATION

It's easy to fall in love with Rockport. It manages its several roles -- New England village, summer resort, tourist attraction, art colony -- with extraordinary grace. Only a short walk from the train station is the seaside village center with its gemlike church, lovely beaches, shops and clapboard and shingled houses. To get to it, turn right onto Railroad Ave. (see map on page 132) as you exit the station. You pass **Whistle Stop Mall** on your right and then come to **Five Corners**, where five streets meet. Turn left onto either Main St. or Broadway and head to the sea. Going on Broadway, you pass great white clapboard mansions, converted to guest houses and shops, and granite public buildings. Once over the first hump in the road, you will see the sea.

Broadway runs into the main street, which is called Mt. Pleasant at the point where the **T Wharf** meets it. There are public restrooms on the **T Wharf**. In the summer months, sightseeing excursions and deep sea fishing expeditions are offered here. From the T Wharf you get the best view of Rockport's "signature." **Motif No. 1,**

 a red lobster shack on neighboring **Bearskin Neck,** possibly the most painted structure in the country, because it is the traditional first assignment for Rockport's many art students.

Turning to the right as you exit the **T Wharf,** and walking by shops and houses and restaurants, you come shortly to **Dock Square** where Mt. Pleasant becomes Main St. Here a sign beckons you to **Bearskin Neck,** Rockport's most famous tourist attraction, a tongue of land curling out into the sea, once the commercial center of the fishing village that Rockport was in the 1700's. Now the tiny wooden houses have been refurbished and converted to a host of specialty stores and craft shops, exhibiting the work of local artists in glass, brass, pewter, earthenware, iron, jewelry, fabric, painting, sculpture, prints, and clothes. There are also galleries, studios, and artists' residences, as well as a legion of restaurants, food take-outs, and fish markets, supplied by the local fleets. You can get a guide to this delightful melange by writing to the **Bearskin Neck Association**, Rockport 01966. Don't omit to walk to the end of the wharves where the views are superb.

One of Rockport's delights is that it has pretty beaches right in the village. Going westward from Dock Square along the shore road, which is at first Main St. and then Beach St., you come to the small but pleasant **Front** and **Back Beaches** with

rest rooms, benches, and, sometimes, lifeguards. The indentation of the shore here is called **Sandy Bay,** which was Rockport's name before it separated from Gloucester in 1840. Arriving as you do afoot, that parking at these beaches is reserved for residents bothers you not at all.

There is another beach not far from the Village, **Old Garden Beach. The walk to it is one of Rockport's treats.** You start along Atlantic Ave. (see map on page 132), which branches off Mt. Pleasant a little beyond the T Wharf. On Atlantic, you pass shingled cottages of various eclectic styles, perched beside the water, a charming street. Soon a footpath leads you to the **Headlands**, a park atop huge boulder cliffs with wonderful views of **Sandy Bay**. You may want to go no further. To continue to the beach go along the cliff paths to a short gravel path leading out to Ocean Ave, which joins Old Garden Road. A little way along the road is **Old Garden Beach** with a small seaside park with benches above it. The beach is less than a mile from the Village. A little further along Old Garden Road, a sign on a path screened from a great estate by high bushes announces that "No Horseback Riding is Permitted". This is the entrance to a lovely walk on seaside cliffs past an enclave of summer estates. You come out on Marmion Way. A little further on, a road branching to the left off Marmion leads to Gap Head opposite Straitsmouth Island. Here you are about 1 and 1/4 miles from the Village.

Where, you may be wondering, is horseback riding permitted? In the South Woods, occupying the regions between Highways 127 and 127A (see map on page 129), are bridle paths, also used by hikers, and old abandoned roads. The aforementioned map put out by the Rockport Chamber of Commerce shows these trails and old roads leading out from streets near the Village.

On the western side of Highway 127 is the 2,000 acre **Dogtown Reservation**, a wilderness, rich in bird and plant species and wildlife, growing over the remains of a farming village abandoned in the 1830's. The area is of great interest to archaeologists, who sift through the ruins looking for clues to the Dogtowners' lifestyle. It is also of interest to geologists because it is traversed by a terminal moraine of the ice age glacier and has many odd rock formations strewn about. Some of the trails through it are described in the *AMC MASSACHUSETTS AND RHODE ISLAND TRAIL GUIDE.* **A word of caution.** It is very easy to get lost among the profusion of meandering paths which peter out. The **Briar Swamp** path described in the AMC guide starts near the Rockport train station. It is one of the oddities of our car-dominated age that the AMC guide starts its description of this trail with "park your car

in the railroad station parking lot." There is not a word of the possibility that you might arrive by train! **Don't attempt walks in Dogtown without a good map.**

Rockport Village itself, aside from the smorgasbord on **Bearskin Neck,** has a number of good stores and interesting places to browse in. Notable is the **Toad Hall Bookstore** at 51 Main, in the handsome old granite bank building. It is run by a non-profit organization, which donates all its profits to support ecological causes. At 12 Main St., in an 18th century tavern, the **Rockport Art Association** has galleries, with exhibits and bulletins announcing the many cultural events that it sponsors. On Beach St. opposite the beaches, is the **First Parish Burying Ground**, where Rockport's first settlers are buried. Visible from Main St., in another striking granite building, on Cleaves and Jewett, is the **Public Library.**

At 40 King St., which branches off Beach St., at King's intersection with Granite St., is the **Sandy Bay Historical Society,** with exhibits on local history, featuring especially the granite quarrying years. In the nineteenth century, before the days of reinforced concrete, granite for public buildings was quarried in many places along the New England coast. The thriving granite industry was an example of how New Englanders could turn what seemed a liability -- a superabundance of rock -- into an asset. Today water-filled quarries are ubiquitous on the Cape and add to its scenic beauty. The **Historical Society** building was the home of granite master Levi Sewall, who built it in 1832 with stone from his own quarries.

If you continue from the **Historical Society** along Granite, toward its intersection with Beach (after which Granite becomes the shore road), you see to the left, good examples of the area's steep boulder cliffs. Squam Hill Road, rising steeply from Granite, is one of the entrance roads to **Dogtown.** Further along, after Granite becomes the shore road, you pass the long **Granite Pier,** at which "stone sloops" -- sailing vessels designed to carry the granite -- were once loaded. Now the pier is a picnic ground and viewing spot for sailing races. The abandoned quarry on the landward side of the street, now a scenic small lake, is a good exhibit of the area's striking orange granite as is the sturdily built former home of the **Rockport Granite Company** (now a private residence). Walking along the shore road you will pass gallery after gallery and many artists' residences and accommodations. It is a walk of about 11/2 miles along the shore road from the Village to the Pigeon Cove Post Office.

There is a **CATA** route from the Village passing by Pigeon Cove and continuing around the peninsula to Gloucester. You can hail the bus anywhere along its route and get off anywhere to explore. Salt marshes, woods, beaches, rocky oceanside

outlooks are on or near the bus route. About 3 miles from the Village the bus passes by Gott Ave. A 1/2 mile walk along Gott leads to the **Halibut Point Reservation**, a park with superb views of the Maine and New Hampshire coasts. (It is one of the stops of the summer Salt Water Trolley.) On the way to the park, you pass the **Old Gott House**, built about 1702 by one of Rockport's earliest settlers.

WALKS FROM THE GLOUCESTER TRAIN STATION

Getting off the train at Gloucester, you may be somewhat disappointed at the unprepossessing nature of your immediate surroundings, a car park near a supermarket. But the **famous harbor**, a pleasant downtown of **shops, historic houses, and museums** on crooked streets, and **parks, beaches, and a great seaside promenade** are actually all close by, a few short blocks away. To head downtown and to the harbor, walk on Railroad Ave past the parking lot, and then with

A Gloucester Schooner
19th Century

the supermarket on your left, turn left onto Prospect, and then right onto Pleasant, and the prospect does become pleasanter.

A short way down Pleasant at No. 27, in a sea captain's mansion built in 1804, is the **Cape Ann Historical Society Museum**, famed because it contains the largest collection of **Fitz Hugh Lane** paintings anywhere. Virtually unappreciated during his lifetime, Lane, a Gloucester native, is now **ranked among the greatest of our nineteenth century marine painters.** In addition to the Lane collection, the **Museum** has rooms of period furnishings, numerous exhibits on Gloucester's early history, such as the letters of marque signed by George Washington giving Gloucester privateers license to prey on British shipping, and also a research library. Modest fee.

Near the Historical Society, on Dale Ave., one block west of Pleasant, is the striking, many-turreted **City Hall** (with restrooms), built in 1870, with a sea-green dome atop a very high brownstone clock tower. It is **one of the most distinctive landmarks as you approach Gloucester by the sea**. You will also see it as you walk to the Museum from the train station. Across the street from **City Hall**, with front at 88 Middle, is the **Public Library**, a fine one with a charming park beside it. Nearby on Middle, are several houses built before the Revolution. The most interesting is the **Sargent-Murray-Gilman House** at 49 Middle, with grounds extending to Main Street, built in 1768 for **Winthrop Sargent,** a wealthy merchant. Although the Sargent family has included such distinguished lights as John Singer Sargent, the painter, and Francis Sargent, a recent state governor, the most notable inhabitants of this house were Winthrop Sargent's **daughter Judith**, who wrote essays advocating equal rights for both sexes, and her husband **Reverend John Murray**. Murray, an immigrant from Scotland, **founded the Universalist Church in this country**. In 1782, by refusing to pay his parish taxes to support the local Congregational Church, he initiated a court case which led to the complete separation of church and state in Massachusetts. Up until then Congregationalism had held a preferred position in the state constitution. In summer, the **House** is open to the public on specified days each week. Modest fee.

The church that Murray founded, the **Independent Christian Church**, the country's **Mother Universalist Church**, rises nearby at the corner of Church and Middle. Its tall white tower, topped with a red dome, is another of Gloucester's distinctive landmarks. Ecumenism clearly reigns now in Gloucester. In the neighborhood, are the **Trinitarian Congregational Church,** organized in 1642, the one that Murray refused to support, and **Temple Ahavath Achim**, a Jewish synagogue, and several blocks eastward, at 142 Prospect, is the Roman Catholic **Church of Our Lady of Good Voyage**, whose

twin blue towers are outstanding signals to the approaching sea voyager. "**Our Lady**", built in 1914, serves Gloucester's Portuguese community and adds a graceful touch of the Azores to the town. The large Portuguese population in Massachusetts sea ports dates back to the mid-nineteenth century, when Yankee sea captains recruited Portuguese seamen to fill in for crew members who had jumped ship. More recently, Reverend Sun Myung Moon's Unification Church has become a presence in Gloucester with the purchase of several residences and waterfront businesses.

The Historic Gloucester folder, obtainable from the Chamber of Commerce and other information centers, contains more description of Gloucester's many historic houses. The pleasant Main St. **business district** with its variety of stores, housed in 19th century buildings, is only a block down from the above mentioned Middle Street houses. At 112 Main St., near the stores, is the local bus **Waiting Station**, where you can catch all the buses that go to Gloucester neighborhoods and ones that go to Rockport.

Only a block away from the business district, along Rogers St., is the busy many piered Waterfront on the western rim of the **Inner Harbor**. The harborside of Rogers St. is an unfortunate clutter of parking lots. But there is a fine place from which to savor the wharf and water action -- the hillside park that you'll see as you walk down Pleasant to Rogers from Main. In the park, at the top of the hill, is the **Fitz Hugh Lane House** (see page 137), built in 1849 of the local orange tinted granite. From its upper story, the not yet famous painter, paralyzed in his lower limbs since childhood, devoted himself to capturing **Gloucester Harbor**, then filled with two masted schooners. After his death, this sturdily built house was used as a jail. Today it is a **Visitors Welcoming Center** providing information folders and rest rooms.

As you face the water, in front of you is **Rocky Neck** protruding out of East Gloucester to shelter the **Inner Harbor**, and beside it is **Ten Pound Island** where **Winslow Homer** boarded with the lightkeeper during his Gloucester period. To the left is the great **Fish Pier** with its processing plants, and to the right is the **Gloucester House Restaurant** on the car-infested **Seven Seas Wharf**. You can get closer to the water, down below, across the Harbor Loop Road (see map on page 136), at the **Solomon Jacobs Park** beside the **Coast Guard Station**. The Park is named after one of Gloucester's most adventurous sea captains.

West of the Gloucester House, along Rogers St., at **St. Peter's Plaza**, is another pleasant park with benches for close-up dockside views. The above mentioned parks

are the result of a long struggle by the people of Gloucester to reserve places for the public to enjoy the doings of the fishing fleets. It is clear, as you look at the clutter of cars all about you, that encouraging bicycling on Cape Ann would be a boon, liberating acres of valuable waterfront.

Westward from Rogers, beyond the Commercial St. cut-off, a short road leads to **Pavilion Beach,** and from it, a short walk westward along the sand (to avoid the traffic on Main St.) leads to Stacy Boulevard, where a **broad sea side promenade,** with benches and green strip, extends all the way to the drawbridge over the **Annisquam Canal,** beside which there are more benches for scene-savoring. Here the views of the **Outer Harbor,** all the way to **Eastern Point** are quite grand. **This is Gloucester at its best.** You can also get to Stacy Boulevard more directly from the train station by going south along Washington from Railroad Ave. (see map on page 136) until Middle and then turning right. On the way to the **Canal,** on Stacy Blvd., you pass the famous **Fisherman Statue** honoring "they that go down to the sea in ships." Every year, in late June and early July, **St. Peter's Festival** is celebrated in this vicinity, from **St. Peter's Plaza** to the **Fisherman Statue,** with processions, concerts, sports events, dancing, and culminating in the **"Blessing of the Fleet."**

THEY THAT GO DOWN TO THE SEA IN SHIPS

The **Annisquam Canal,** dug in 1642 for small vessels, but subsequently enlarged, probably the nation's oldest canal, joins Massachusetts Bay to Ipswich Bay, via the tidal marshes of the Annisquam River. West of the **Canal,** the promenade leads past tennis courts to a charming footpath entering **Stage Fort Park,** a lovely seaside park with a **Visitors Welcoming Center, (800) 649-6839,** open fields for frolic and frisbee, picnic tables, a handsome Romanesque concession building, and most notable of all, **paths along huge boulder cliffs,** providing more outstanding views of the **Outer Harbor,** and enclosing two pocket beaches. This is more of the best of Gloucester. The **Stage Fort** is historically notable too. The earliest fishing settlement sponsored by the Puritans was planted here in 1623. As a plaque explains, "from that time, the fisheries, the oldest industry in the Commonwealth, have been uninterruptedly pursued from this port." In the name of the Park, "stage" refers to the primitive wharves built by the first settlers, and "fort" refers to the many forts built here since the 1600's to protect the Harbor, remnants of which still remain.

Cruises and whale watches leave from the **Seven Seas Wharf**, at Rogers and Porter Streets, **call (508) 283 - 1776,** and from **Rose's Wharf**, on Main St., on the east side of the Harbor, **call (508) 283 - 5110.** In season there are **CATA shuttle boats from the Harbor Loop to Rocky Neck** (see page 141 for more on Rocky Neck).

Grand as is the **Stage Fort Park,** its beaches are not Gloucester's favorites. The local favorite is the beautiful white sanded **Good Harbor Beach**, to which you can get from either Gloucester or Rockport by taking the Salt Water Trolley (in season) or the **Red Rte CATA bus**, which goes from Gloucester's waiting station on Main St. to **Rocky Neck** and then loops around by the **Bass Rocks** and then goes to Rockport via Thatcher Rd. past the **Beach** (see map at the head of this section). The Salt Water Trolley will let you off near the lovely footbridge to the beach. Unfortunately, because of traffic, the walk from the Business District (about 2 miles) is not pleasant.

The walk to the **Stage Fort** described above is not long, less than a mile, I should say. There are things of interest all the way from the train station. Should you want a longer walk, combining woodland terrain with the grand seaside walk through the **Stage Fort** and Stacy Blvd., it is possible to continue into the **Ravenswood Park**, whose eastern edge is near the western end of the **Stage Fort. Ravenswood** is a beautiful 500 acre forested area with magnolia swamps, groves of deciduous and evergreen trees, glacial swamps and ponds, and high ledges providing excellent views. It is traversed by a system of well marked car free trails described in the *AMC MASSACHUSETTS AND RHODE ISLAND TRAIL GUIDE.* The main entrance to Ravenswood is on Western Ave. about 3/4 mile beyond where Hesperus branches off from it. At the main entrance, **a large map of the Park's trails is posted**. You can use the Orange Rte **CATA** bus to Magnolia, which makes a loop with a branch along Western Ave., to take you to the main entrance. And with a good map, you should be able to find trails through the park to take you back to the vicinity of the **Stage Fort.**

On Hesperus Road about 1 3/4 miles from the Stage Fort, is **Hammond Castle**, bequeathed to the public by John Hammond, an inventor of remote control radio devices. Hammond built for himself a composite of the castles that he had

admired in Europe. He had pieces of Medieval and Renaissance castles transported and reassembled here on the Gloucester shore. The large halls and beautiful grounds frequently host concerts, art lessons, and other cultural events. Open to the public, year round. **Call (508) 283-2080 for hours.** Fee. **Hammond Castle** is also on the route of the Orange Rte. **CATA** bus to Magnolia. (See map on page 129.)

With Rocky Neck As Base. The boat from Boston lands at **Rocky Neck**, the home of a year-round fishing community and a mostly summer-only art colony, about 60 acres of rocks and sand sheltering the Inner Harbor, crowded with residences, galleries, shops, restaurants, and rimmed by wharves piled with fishing gear. The tiny galleries, often the homes and studios of artists, exude a special charm, with porches overhanging the boat-filled harbor, and steps leading down to boat landings.

You can also get to **Rocky Neck** by the local **CATA** bus from **either Gloucester or Rockport**. The **CATA Red Rte** (and in season the Salt Water Trolley) goes between the two towns with a loop passing by the **Bass Rocks** and **Rocky Neck**. **You can catch the bus at the Gloucester Waiting Station or on Broadway in Rockport.** In season, you can catch the Salt Water Trolley on the Harbor Loop or any of the stops listed on page 142. **Since off-season service is infrequent, it's best to have a schedule in hand.** The bus enters and leaves Rocky Neck along the Causeway, where there is a pleasant park with benches, affording fine views of the Inner Harbor in one direction and of the Outer Harbor in the other. **You can also get to Rocky Neck,** in season, **from the Harbor Loop by the water shuttle.** It is only 1/4 mile across the Harbor from the **Fitz Hugh Lane House to Rocky Neck**. Because of traffic and narrow sidewalks, the 2 mile walk around the Harbor rim from the Business District is not pleasant.

Rocky Neck can be used as a base for pleasant walks about the East Gloucester peninsula, which was a much painted cow pasture during Winslow Homer's day, and is now residential, but still offers some lovely walks. One possibility is a sea-side walk of about 11/2 miles to the **Beau Port Mansion**, in the **Eastern Point** enclave. Beau Port was built at the turn of the century by Henry Sleeper, a wealthy architect and interior designer. He gave free play to his imagination in creating about thirty rooms expressing various moods and themes -- Jacobean, Revere, Franklin, Mariner's, Plymouth Kitchen, Chinese Hall, Golden Step, and others. A guided tour of some of these is given from May to the end of October. The Mansion belongs to the **SPNEA** (see page 36). Call **(508) 283-0800** for fee and schedule information. But even when Beau Port isn't open, this sea side walk is wonderful. In fact it's best when the traffic is least. Going southward from Rocky Neck along Eastern Point Road, you have grand views to your right of **Ten Pound Island** and the **Outer Harbor**. You pass **Niles Beach** and enter the Eastern Point private enclave of large estates, one of which is Beau Port. You keep bearing right at various road branches, and eventually you come to it. It will be on your right by the sea. On the way to it, you pass near **Niles Pond**, a fine place for bird-watching especially during the fall and spring migrations. **In summer, entrance to the enclave is permitted only on weekdays.**

Another walk with Rocky Neck as base is to go across the East Gloucester Peninsula to the opposite shore where great orange-tinted boulders, the **Bass Rocks,** are pounded by the sea. You can climb down to cool your feet in rockweed-lined tidal pools while savoring the superb views. (When I took this walk some years ago, I went along Ledge Road to Popples to Marble.) The cross peninsula walk is about one mile. The most pleasant part, aside from lingering on the Bass Rocks, is the climb along Ledge Road, surrounded by orchards and estates amid lovely vistas. You can if you wish continue your walk by going northward along Atlantic Rd., alongside of the Bass Rocks, then detour to the scenic outlooks of Bass Road, then to Nautilus Road, from which you can cross on a footbridge to the beautiful **Good Harbor Beach,** Cape Ann's favorite, with restrooms, refreshments, and life guards. The **Red Rte. CATA bus passes by Good Harbor Beach** and so does the Salt Water Trolley (see below for SWT stops). If you attempt any of these walks in summer, **be sure to take along plenty of liquids (juices, water) to prevent dehydration**. You will encounter little shade along the road by the Bass Rocks and no roadside stands.

Scenic, curving Atlantic Road, in the past, attracted heavy traffic making progress quite dangerous for hikers, runners, and bicyclists as motorists rounded curves out of control or parked in chains on the seaside, leaving no room for others. The Salt Water Trolley (SWT) route was CATA's creative answer to the problem. Let's hope that it succeeds in helping all to enjoy safely, and to the fullest measure, this magnificent oceanside scenery, and the other sites we've described. The basic fare, as mentioned, is $1.50. You can get off anywhere and then reboard for only 60 cents. The stops are: Harbor Loop (near the Jodrey Fish Pier), North Shore Art Association (on East Main on the way to Rocky Neck), Rocky Neck, Niles Beach, Bass Rocks, Footbridge to Good Harbor Beach, Long Beach, Dock Sq. in Rockport, Front and Back Beaches, Halibut Point State Park, Annisquam Village, Gloucester Train Station, St. Peter's Plaza, Seven Seas Wharf, and back to the Harbor Loop. (This paragraph was written in the summer of 1996.)

FEASTING IN CAPE ANN

Excellent seafood, scrumptiously prepared from fish fresh off the boat and served in dining rooms overlooking the harbor is Cape Ann's hallmark. **In Gloucester,** a longtime favorite, the **Gloucester House on the Seven Seas Wharf** (Porter and Rogers Streets) serves food at moderate prices at tables outside on the wharf. Lunches from $5.95 to $9.95, and dinners from $9.95 to $14.50. **The $9.95 lunch includes a hot boiled lobster, baked beans, and cole slaw.** Call **(508) 283-1812.** Nearby, at 25 Rogers, **McT's Lobster House and Tavern** also offers fresh sea food and a waterfront view at reasonable prices. Call **(508) 282-0950.** A block up from the Waterfront, on Main St., are little cafes offering less elegance, but delicious, fresh seafood at low prices. In **Rocky Neck,** several harborside restaurants strung along Rocky Neck Ave. offer seafood and lovely views. Just look at the menus posted on the windows (or ask to see them if they are not) and choose. I've always had good luck even when coming in the off season.

Rockport too offers a tremendous choice of fine eateries. I mention a few. In Dock Sq., at the entrance to **Bearskin Neck, The Greenery, (508) 546-9593,** a combined cafe and restaurant, offers wonderful salads, seafood, and water views, at low and moderate prices. The **Peg Leg,** 18 Beach St., opposite the beaches, gets good ratings for its elegance, the quality of its meals, and prices in the moderate to expensive range. Call **(508) 546-3038. Bearskin Neck overflows** with food temptations, including little shacks where you can get strudel, ice cream, sandwiches, subs, and a variety of delicacies, and also markets where you can get cooked fresh Rockport lobster and crabmeat for your picnics. There are several harborside restaurants offering full meals at reasonable prices. I should explain that Rockport is "dry," and has been ever since 1856, when a group of temperance-minded citizens raided the local taverns, axed open their "likker" kegs and poured their contents out into the streets. The **Hannah Jumper Restaurant, (508) 546-3600** on the Tuna Wharf of Bearskin Neck **is named after the Rockport woman who led the temperance crusade.** The prices are moderate to expensive. As you expect, "likker" is not served here, but the menu says "You are invited to bring your own favorite alcoholic beverages." What would Hannah Jumper have said? I suspect that she wouldn't have minded. She was mostly concerned about the welfare of the families of local men who arrived home drunk after having dissipated their wages at the taverns. That Hannah Jumper and her co-axers were tried but not convicted, and temperance has reigned here ever since, indicates that her views were widely shared in the community. On your way to the **Headlands,** you pass her house (not open to the public), a blue shuttered cottage at the corner of Atlantic and Mt. Pleasant.

LODGING IN CAPE ANN

Rockport is chock full of lodgings -- guest houses, hotels, inns -- suitable for car-free visitors, located near the Village and train station, some run by artists. I passed many as I explored afoot, walking between the train station and the Village, and along the shore road to Pigeon Cove. For more information call the **Rockport Chamber of Commerce, (508) 546-6575.** Most of the lodgings in Gloucester seem to be oriented toward motorists. However, the **Cape Ann Chamber of Commerce, call (508) 283-1601,** lists several guesthouses and inns with promising locations near **Good Harbor Beach**, the **Bass Rocks**, and the **CATA bus route.** I sighted two of them, the **Gray Manor Inn,** 14 Atlantic Road, **(508) 283-5409,** and the **Williams Guest House,** 136 Bass Ave., **(508) 283-4931,** on a walk alongside of the Bass Rocks to Good Harbor Beach.

MANCHESTER, BRIEFLY

On the way to Rockport, the train stops near a supremely pretty sailboat-filled harbor as the conductor announces **"Manchester, Manchester."** You mentally file it away as a place to explore in the future. It turns out to be a great idea. Manchester's two main attractions open to the public are the harborside **Masconomo Park**, just about 50 feet from the train stop, and **Singing Beach, one of the North Shore's best**, with gorgeous white sand enclosed by rocks. To get to the Beach, which is about 1/2 mile from the train stop, walk along Beach St. to it (see map). In summer, **Singing Beach** has lifeguards, restrooms, and an outstanding snack counter featuring nutritious as well as delicious foods -- fruit juices, yogurts, whole wheat bread sandwiches. On the way to the Beach, a fish market on Beach St., near the park, supplies cooked lobster and crabmeat. A supermarket and restaurants near the train stop also provide feasts. A walk uphill from the station, brings you to a jewel-like town with a public library, historical society (open occasionally), and some 19th century great mansions. **All in all, a fine time can be had in this charming town by the sea.**

Chapter 4
TO RHODE ISLAND CAR-FREE

PROVIDENCE,

NEWPORT,

and around the Bay with

RIPTA

TRANSPORTATION SUMMARY

To Providence, take **Amtrak train or Commuter T train** from **South Station** near the South Station T stop on the Red Line or **Bonanza Bus** from **South Station Bus Terminal** near South Station Red Line T stop.

To Newport, take **RIPTA** bus from Providence, or **Bonanza Bus** from the **South Station Bus Terminal** near the Red Line T stop.

Explore **Narragansett Bay on RIPTA** starting from either Providence or Newport.

TO RHODE ISLAND CAR - FREE

Providence, Newport, and around Narragansett Bay with RIPTA

INTRODUCTION

To hold forth a lively experiment that a
flourishing and civil state may stand, yea and
best be maintained, ...among English spirits
with a full liberty in religious commitments.

From the Royal Charter of 1663 for Rhode Island and the
Providence Plantations

In this chapter, we shall take car-free daytrips from Boston to **Providence** and
Newport, Rhode Island, by bus or train, and shall travel around **Narragansett Bay**
with the aid of **RIPTA (Rhode Island Public Transit Authority)**. But, of course, there
are many accommodations for overnight stays, too.

Some History and Geography

Rhode Island is our smallest state, with a land area of about 1,084 square miles,
only about 50 miles long and 20 wide. You certainly could walk or bicycle across it, if
only the cars didn't get in the way. **Narragansett Bay**, the State's most prominent
geographical feature, almost cuts it in two and multiplies its shoreline. Tiny Rhode
Island has over 400 miles of sea shore with hosts of lovely beaches and sheltered
harbors, and interesting wetlands. A popular summer resort for over 200 years
offering exquisite water pleasures, it is also one of the Nation's most productive
industrial areas. These two extremes coexist compatibly in this small state.

Rhode Island's first European settlers were Roger Williams (1603 - 1684) and
his followers, **who were banished from the Massachusetts Bay Colony in 1636** for
having "dyvulged dyvers newe and dangerous opinions against the aucthoritie of
magistrates." Williams, then a minister in Salem (see Chapter 3), **asserted that civil
magistrates had no right to inflict punishment for violations of religious codes** and
espoused full "libertie of conscience," ideas now cornerstones of our Constitution,
but advanced for the time. After fleeing Salem to escape deportation back to England,
Williams founded a settlement at the head of a great bay on land purchased from the
Narragansett Indians. He named it the **Providence Plantations, in thanks for "God's
merciful Providence."**

Other persecuted groups were soon attracted to the area. With Williams' help, nearby **Portsmouth and Newport** were founded in the late 1630's by followers of **Anne Hutchinson**, who had been banished from the Bay Colony, after a trial that shook John Winthrop's Boston. (See page 18, where we encountered her statue in front of the Massachusetts State House.) More about Anne Hutchinson on pages 185, 186. **Our country's first Quaker and Jewish communities were established in Newport in the 1650's.** (See pages 180, 181, 185, 186.) **Williams himself founded the first Baptist congregation on this continent.** However, he soon left the Baptist Church to become a "Seeker" after truth in all religions. But the Church thrived without him and broke into several vigorous subsects.

Massachusetts and Connecticut Puritans regarded the situation in Rhode Island as chaotic, and, indeed, the "lively experiment" sometimes was. Early Rhode Island was beset with controversy, and, with no strong central authority, it was difficult to get public works, like public schools, started, or to control private enterprise for the public good. Rhode Island was still struggling with these problems after it entered Statehood. But the little Colony led its neighbors to religious tolerance, without which Massachusetts could not have made its graceful spring into its 19th century golden age.

Rhode Island is not really an island, but attached firmly to Connecticut on the west and Massachusetts on the north and east. The name is a shortened form of the full official name of the Colony as given in the Royal Charter of 1663 -- *Rhode Island and the Providence Plantations.* In those days, "Rhode Island" referred only to Aquidneck Island, shared by Newport, Middletown, and Portsmouth, which reminded explorer Verrazano of the Isle of Rhodes in the Mediterranean.

In the 18th century, Rhode Island moved closer to the New England mainstream. On the one hand, the Puritans themselves became far more liberal, and on the other, Rhode Island took to the sea trade with flare. Fortunes were made in manufacturing rum from West Indies molasses. But sadly, Rhode Island was most deeply involved of all New England in the slave trade. In the crucial years before the Revolution, the British crackdown on molasses smuggling elicited violent protests in Rhode Island, which led to attacks on His Majesty's customs officers and revenue schooners. We shall say more of these as we walk along the streets of Providence and Newport. The Adamses, Samuel and John, and John Hancock are the most famous instigators of the Revolutionary drama. But we'll see that they had a very strong supporting cast in Rhode Island.

In the 19th century, as in the rest of New England, fortunes made by Rhode Islanders in the sea trade were reinvested in founding textile factories, railroads, and other   commercial and industrial enterprises. Rhode Islanders claim that the country's entry into the Industrial Revolution began here, in Pawtucket, where in 1793, Samuel Slater built the country's first water-powered spinning machines, after breaking into the treasury of England's most carefully guarded trade secrets. Today, the great variety of products of the Providence-Pawtucket area includes textiles, textile machinery and precision machinery of all kinds, electrical and electronic equipment, and metal, rubber, and plastic products. An early offshoot of the metal working industry was jewelry manufacture. Providence is one of the world's great jewelry centers.

Threading through the state's history is a tale of rivalry of two cities, Providence and Newport. Before the Revolution, Newport's position at the mouth of Narragansett Bay gave it a decisive advantage in the sea trade. As its prosperity attracted intellectuals and artisans, it became the Colony's cultural center. Its larger population gave it an early lead in politics, too. Most of the early Governors of the Colony came from Newport. But during the Revolution, Newport was bled by the British occupation. Much of its population fled. As the backdoor to Boston, Providence was heavily guarded and remained untouched by the War. Newport never regained its former prominence. The War of 1812 and the advent of railroads destroyed its maritime trade. Providence then surged into the lead in commerce, industry, and population. **In 1900, when the present State House was built, Providence became the official State Capital.** Up until then, the General Assembly (or Legislature) had rotated its sessions among five sites, including Providence and Newport. In the meantime, Newport, spared from heavy industry, became one of the world's superb playgrounds. **Visits to both cities are fascinating because they have retained so much of their past.**

Today, the State has about one million residents in its one thousand square miles, the second highest population density in the country. About 200,000 live in Providence, but just about everybody commutes to the Providence area for work. So the entire state forms one metropolis. Despite the presence of so many people and so much industry in one small state, there are many charming rural areas with farm estates and single family homes, many old and of historic interest, tucked in among woods, meadows, ponds, and lakes, and along the shore. The villages have fine churches and public buildings, and often picturesque old stone mills by streams at

their outskirts. **The beauty and charm of rural Rhode Island catch the visitor completely by surprise.**

Through the rural areas wind two-lane highways. The traffic is frequent, but often not fast. So walking is not necessarily unpleasant. Of course, there is the usual desire of many in the State's Department of Transportation to speed traffic by building 4-lane highways. But this pressure is restrained by the recognition, by some at least, that the two-lane highways are lined with treasures and the resulting destruction would be intolerable. **So we can hope that rural Rhode Island will retain its picturesque charm and courteous pace.**

Information

For information write to the **Rhode Island Department of Economic Development, Tourist Promotion Division, 7 Jackson Walkway, Providence 02903** or call **(800) 556-2484** for a copy of the annual *Guide to Rhode Island,* which includes a map, lists of services and events. Additional addresses will be given in the sections on Providence and Newport. When writing or calling, say that you are going car-free and ask for the **RIPTA (Rhode Island Public Transit Authority)** map. It's important to do this so that the tourist promotion departments realize there is a demand for it and begin to include it in their information packages. **You can also call RIPTA directly** for maps and schedules. The phone numbers are: **(401) 781-9400, or toll free (800) 662-5088, or if you are hearing impaired (TDD) 461-9400**; **when you are in Newport, the RIPTA number is (401) 847-0209.** Your public library is probably also a good source for books about Rhode Island. I found **Sheila Steinberg and Cathleen McGuigan's *RHODE ISLAND, AN HISTORICAL GUIDE,*** published in 1976, especially useful.

150

From Congdon St. Park, Roger Williams' Monument Overlooks Providence

PROVIDENCE

Providence (population, 180,000), Rhode Island's capital, the City of this little City-State, **is a delightful place where the new blends comfortably with the old.** Overshadowed by Boston, only 44 miles away, an hour's trip by bus or train, Providence deserves attention in its own right because of its colleges, museums, and many historic sites casting light on the Nation's birth and growth. **A remarkable amount of the City's past still stands** and offers those in search of history an exceptionally rich feast. Not at first sight spectacular, Providence grows on the visitor.

Information. For advance information, write to the **Greater Providence Convention and Visitor's Bureau,** 10 Dorrance St., Providence 02903 or call **(401) 274 - 1636.** Be sure to tell them that you are going car-free and ask for the **RIPTA color map.** The **RIPTA information numbers are**: **(401) 781-9400**, or toll free **(800) 662-5088**, or if you are hearing impaired **(TDD) 461-9400.** There is a **RIPTA Information Office** in **Kennedy Plaza** (see page 151 and maps on pages 152 and 153).

Getting There from Boston. To get to Providence, you can take the **AMTRAK train or a T commuter train from South Station** or you can take the **Bonanza Bus from the new South Station Bus Terminal.** The train and bus stations are both next to the **South Station stop on the T Red Line.** For **AMTRAK** schedule information call either **(617) 482-3660 or (800) USA-RAIL,** and for the **Bonanza Bus** schedule call **(800) 556-3815.** The trip takes about one hour by either train or bus.

Arriving. On the train, you glide into the center of the City with the great marble dome of the **State House** floating above you to the north and the high rises of the **business district** glistening on the south. From the train station you can easily walk to Everything, to the **College Hill District** by going along Park Row, or to **Kennedy Plaza**, and the **Business District** by going along Exchange St. (See maps on pages 152, 153.) **Kennedy Plaza**, Providence's central park, adorned with islets of greenery and statues, is the main nerve center of the **RIPTA** system. **The Bonanza Bus** from Boston brings you to the North Providence terminal, where a shuttle bus awaits to take you to the bus stop in **Kennedy Plaza**, adjacent to the **RIPTA Information Booth**, where you can get the RIPTA color map, and the individual bus schedules. **The stop for the RIPTA bus to Newport is just across the street.** Standing in Kennedy Plaza, you are only a few blocks away from the **business and shopping district** and the **College Hill Historic District** (see maps). The impressive granite building at the southwestern edge of Kennedy Plaza is **City Hall,** built in 1878 and designed in the style of the Louvre and Tuileries Palaces in Paris. (Of course, there are rest rooms.)

Some Orientation: East Bank, West Bank

To understand Providence's design and history, it helps to know that **what is now Kennedy Plaza was once covered by the Salt Cove**, where fresh water from two rivers -- the Mohassuck and Woonasquatucket -- mixed with salt water from **Narragansett Bay** carried by the tidal flow of the **Providence River**. In the 18th century, ocean going ships sailed up on the tides to today's city center. Separate villages developed on the two sides of the River, joined at first by a ferry and later by a drawbridge. Now the water is channeled by canals through the city center. But you can still see the two distinct communities, the **College Hill Historic District** on the **East Bank** of the River, and the **Weybosset Hill District**, now the **business core**, on the **West Bank. The East Bank was where Providence began**, the site of Roger Williams' settlement of 1636, and later the mercantile and residential center of the busy 18th century seaport. **The West Bank**, still mostly pasture in the 18th century, **became the financial, commercial, and government center of the industrial city of the 19th century. The reason why so much of 18th century Providence remains intact is that the industrial city did not grow over it but along side of it.** You can walk from one city to the other by crossing the canals (see maps). In the hurricane of 1938, the tides surged from their channel to flood the center city up to the second

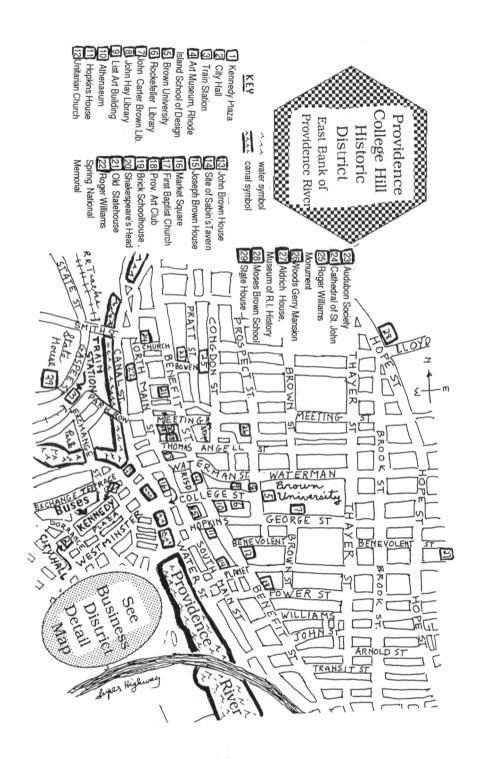

KEY

1. Kennedy Plaza
2. City Hall
3. Train Station
4. Art Museum, Rhode Island School of Design
5. Brown University
6. Rockefeller Library
7. John Carter Brown Lib.
8. John Hay Library
9. List Art Building
10. Athenaeum
11. Hopkins House
12. Unitarian Church

~~~ water symbol
≈≈≈ canal symbol

13. John Brown House
14. Site of Sabin's Tavern
15. Joseph Brown House
16. Market Square
17. First Baptist Church
18. Brick Schoolhouse,
19. Prov. Art Club
20. Shakespeare's Head
21. Old Statehouse
22. Roger Williams Spring National Memorial

23. Audubon Society
24. Cathedral of St. John
25. Roger Williams Monument
26. Woods Gerry Mansion
27. Aldrich House,
28. Moses Brown School,
29. State House
Museum of R.I. History

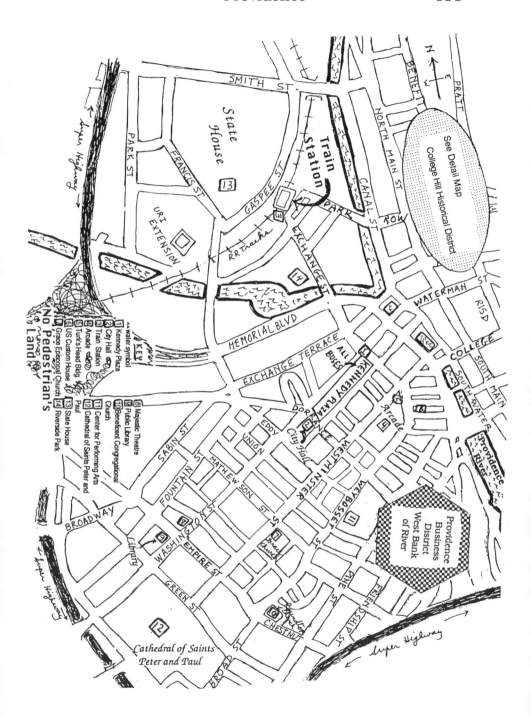

KEY

1. Kennedy Plaza
2. City Hall
3. Train Station
4. Arcade
5. Turk's Head Bldg
6. US Custom House
7. Grace Episcopal Church
8. Majestic Theatre
9. Public Library
10. Beneficent Congregational Church
11. Center for Performing Arts
12. Cathedral of Saints Peter and Paul
13. State House
14. Riverside Park

≈ water symbol

stories of buildings. A dam and watergates now protect the city. After years of hiding its canals. Providence is now. to the pleasure of both residents and visitors, celebrating its water treasures by building canal-side parks and walkways, and pedestrian bridges to link its central districts.

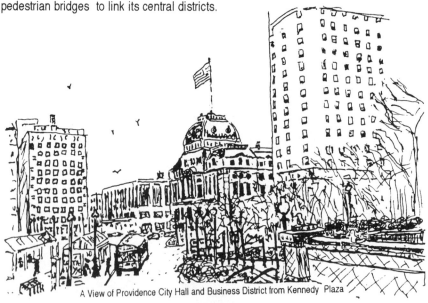

A View of Providence City Hall and Business District from Kennedy Plaza

The College Hill Historical District

I shall assume that you are in Providence's **Kennedy Plaza** after having arrived from Boston by bus or train. Let's begin our exploration by going eastward along Westminster St. (a block south of the Plaza) across the canal (see map) to the East Bank of the Providence River, to the **College Hill Historic District,** Providence's most remarkable neighborhood. **Here its offerings to those interested in history are spectacular**. The crossing is easy because the traffic is not aggressive and there are traffic lights to help you. and a new pedestrian bridge leads you to a park beside **Market Square** on the east side. We shall say more of Market Square later on our **Mile of History Walk.** The **College Hill Historic District** is so crammed with historical sites that it is worth several trips to Providence by itself. It is hard to know where to start. Here on the east side of the River were the markets. wharves. warehouses. rum distilleries. candle factories. cooper shops. shipyards. and other manufactories of the busy trading port of the 1700's. The merchants, tradesmen, artisans, and mechanics lived on the hillside. Miraculously, an enormous amount of the 18th century still stands, tucked in among the more modern buildings of the **Colleges and State Courts**. As you climb the Hill, you encounter tree-shaded streets of beautiful houses and terraced gardens straight out of the 18th century. And looking downward toward the City spread beneath you. it is not hard to imagine Providence's merchants scanning the River, watching the ships wending their way through the busy harbor traffic to and from the sea. What follows are some of the Hill's highlights.

The Colleges. Let's begin with the Hill's two colleges. **The Rhode Island School of Design**, one of the country's foremost art schools, nestles against the Hill near its bottom, its main campus being bounded by North Main, Benefit, College, and Waterman Streets. On the south side of College St., the lofty tower, arcaded entrances, and Grecian colonnades of the **State Court Buildings** harmonize beautifully with the **School of Design.** Founded in 1877 to teach textile design, the School has since expanded to embrace the complete range of fine as well as applied arts. **Open to the public** is its excellent **Museum of Art**, one of the Nation's finest small museums, **with entrances on Benefit near College St.** Its collections include treasures from ancient Greece and Rome, twenty centuries of oriental art, including a towering Buddha from 10th century Japan, an outstanding selection of French art, including works by Manet, Monet, Degas, Cezanne, and Matisse, masterpieces of older European art, American painting and contemporary art. Its Pendleton Collection of antique American furniture, china, textiles, and painting is renowned. The manner of display is generally exquisite. The Museum offers rotating exhibits, educational programs, and concerts and films, and serves the area's primary and secondary schools as a major resource for art education. The entrance fee to this remarkable museum is modest. Call **(401) 454-6500** for schedule.

Uphill along College from Benefit, you pass two modern buildings, the **List Art Building**, on the left, and the **Rockefeller Library**, on the right, both belonging to the Hill's second college, **Brown University**, the country's seventh oldest college, highly rated today, granting a Ph. D in a number of fields, with a coeducational student body of 6, 500. Continuing along College St. and crossing Prospect, you come at the crest of the Hill to the **Van Wickle Gate** to the **Main Campus**, where Brown's older buildings surround the **College Green**. Directly beyond the Gate, is the College's oldest building, **University Hall**, built in 1770, when the College was moved to Providence from its original site at Warren, where it had been founded in 1764. One of the College's goals was to train Baptist ministers, but it was also stipulated that "all members Hereof shall forever enjoy full, free, Absolute and uninterrupted Liberty of Conscience." Now used as an administration building, in 1770, when University Hall was the sole "College Edifice," it housed dormitories and classrooms. During the Revolution, from 1776 to 1782, it housed first American and then French troops.

University

Hall

Originally, the College was called Rhode Island College, but, in 1804, its name was changed in gratitude for the generous gifts of the Brown family. The four Brown brothers, Nicholas, John, Joseph, and Moses, "Nic, John, Jo, and Mo" in local parlance, were leaders in the business, politics, and culture of Colonial and Federalist Providence. **Much of the City's early history is intertwined with the story of the Browns.** Joseph took little interest in the family's multitudinous business enterprises, but devoted himself to the sciences and the arts. He studied the works of English architects and designed many of the Hill's finest buildings, including University Hall, which he modeled after Princeton's Old Nassau Hall. He was the College's first Professor of Experimental Philosophy. We'll say more about the Browns. **A walk about the Hill is like turning the pages of an 18th century romance, in which the Browns are the principal characters.** They and their friends were the leaders of this town of 4,500, which, in the crucial Revolutionary years, led the Colony of 60,000, which by its unwavering eagerness for Independence had an influence all out of proportion to its size, in pulling along larger but more divided Colonies.

You can get a map of the campus at **Faunce House** (with a theater, dining rooms, lounges) on the north side of the **Green** (facing Waterman St.). Call **(401) 863 -2378** for information. Tours of the campus are given several times each day. Some of Brown's notable collections are: **John Hay Library** on the corner of Prospect and College, holding the country's largest collection of Lincoln's manuscripts, and an extensive treasury of Rhode Island history; the **John Carter Brown Library,** on the George St. side of the Green, noted for its Americana collections, particularly early maps, books on Spanish America, Native Americans, and Colonial History; the **Annmary Brown Memorial** on Brown St., containing an art collection and exhibits describing the history of the first fifty years of printing. The main library is the relatively new **Rockefeller Library** on College and Prospect. On College, just west of the **John Hay Library**, the **List Art Building** often has exhibits of student art open to the public. Use of the above libraries is usually courteously extended to visitors who announce a serious purpose.

The two colleges provide the area with a stream of cultural events announced on the various bulletin boards, and the students and faculty support a variety of businesses that add to the area's interest. On Main and Thayer Streets, shopping districts offer bookstores, clothing stores, coffee houses, beer halls, sports supply shops, grocery stores, travel agencies, and movie theaters.

John Carter Brown Library

Meeting History on the Hill. **The Hill's historical gems are most dense on its two oldest streets, Main and Benefit,** and the little streets between them. (See map on page 152.) In the 17th century, Main was the only street: water flowed beside it, and the farms of Roger Williams' little "Towne" (see page 165) ran uphill from it. In the 18th century, it was lined with wharves and warehouses; ships could then sail up the River as far as what is now the intersection of Olney and North Main. **Starting about 1750, Benefit St.** parallel to Main St., but uphill a little way. **became the preferred place for the residences of the merchants,** whence they could watch the busy harbor doings, while distancing themselves from the clangor.

Let's walk along Providence's **Mile of History** trail, its counterpart to Boston's **Freedom Trail.** A fine guide, put out by the **Providence Preservation Society,** call **(401) 831-7440,** is entitled *BENEFIT STREET: A MILE OF HISTORY*. The path that I've chosen is a loop of about 2 miles, counting detours, going south along Benefit from College until Power, then down to Main, and north along Main to Church, and then back up to Benefit. But you can take the sites in any order that you prefer. There are parks and open houses along the way, and, especially on South and North Main Streets, places to eat. **And, of course, you need not "do" everything in one day.**

Let's start at the **Athenaeum** at the south east corner of Benefit and College, cater corner to the **School of Design.** This neo-Greek building was built in 1838, but its collections date back to a subscription library organized in 1753 that served Providence's budding intellectual life. Two of the library's founders were young **Moses Brown** and his friend and mentor **Stephen Hopkins,** of whom we shall say more below. In the 1760's a fire destroyed the collection, except for the 250 books that were "out" at the time. The pleasant interior has an Art Room with European masters. In the 19th century, two famous writers trysted in its stacks -- **Edgar Allen Poe** and **Sarah Helen Whitman,** the Helen of his "To Helen."

Continuing southward along Benefit, you see on the right, at the corner of Hopkins St., a simple clapboard house. **From 1742, until his death in 1785, this was the home of Stephen Hopkins** (1707 - 1785), **Colonial Rhode Island's greatest political figure,** its Samuel Adams and Benjamin Franklin rolled into one. A successful merchant, **he was elected Governor ten times by the Colony's General Assembly (Legislature) between the years 1754 and 1768.** Until Hopkins' political success, virtually all of the Colony's governors had come from Newport. We see here an important difference between Colonial Rhode Island and Massachusetts just before

Stephen Hopkins House

the Revolution. Under the "new" charter of 1692, Massachusetts Governors were appointed by the Crown and were apt to be at odds with the popularly elected Legislature. But, in Rhode Island, Governors were elected by the Legislature, and, like Hopkins, were apt to be staunch supporters of the cause of the people against the Crown.

Benjamin Franklin and Hopkins became friends when the two worked together, during the French-Indian War, on a prophetic defense plan calling for a union of the American Colonies, which, however, was rejected by the British. Like Franklin, a self-educated man, Hopkins did his best to uplift Providence's cultural life. **He was an early proponent of Rhode Island College, now Brown University**, and served as its first Chancellor. He was one of the founders of Providence's first newspaper. **In the crucial 1760's, his widely read articles helped shape public opinion on the rights of the Colonies.** Protesting the Stamp Act and the restrictions on New England's trade, he wrote "all laws and taxations which bind the whole (empire) must be made by the whole."

He was **Chief Justice of the Colony's Superior Court** at the time of the **Gaspee uproar** (of which we write more on page 160). He was elected by the Assembly to be one of the Colony's two delegates to the **Continental Congress, and was a signer of the Declaration of Independence**. "My hand wavers but my heart does not", he said as he signed with palsied hand. In the Congress, **he worked to establish the American Navy.** Not coincidentally, his brother, Esek, was chosen to be the Navy's first Commander-in-Chief, and his friends, the Brown brothers, got a contract to outfit two of the Navy's first 13 ships. (My source here is William McGlouglin's *RHODE ISLAND, A HISTORY.*)

The House's period furnishings include the bed that another of Hopkins' friends -- **George Washington** -- slept in while enroute to meet with Count Rochambeau at Newport to plan the Yorktown campaign in March, 1781. Currently (summer, 1996), open hours are Wed. and Sat., 1-4.

Further south at **285 Benefit** is the strikingly handsome **Unitarian Church,** built in 1816, designed by **John Holden Greene**, who was the architect of several of the Hill's loveliest Federal period buildings. The congregation traces itself back to Providence's **First Congregational Church of 1722.** Congregationalists were the overwhelming majority in the rest of New England, but in Rhode Island they were one sect of many. The church bell may be the largest ever cast by Paul Revere and Sons.

Continuing southward, you find, at the corner of Benefit and Power Streets, **Providence's most famous mansion,** the **John Brown House,** once the home of the Hill's most colorful character and successful enterpreneur, now the headquarters of the **Rhode Island Historical Society**. For open hours call **(401) 331-8575**. **John Brown was the bold leader** (lawless rogue, some would say), **who organized the burning of the Gaspee**, Rhode Island's most notorious act of defiance in the pre-Revolutionary tumult. (We say more about the burning on page 160.) He and his brother Nic owned rum distilleries, spermaceti candle factories, iron furnaces, and ships. They engaged in the West Indies molasses and African slave trade before the Revolution, and in the China Trade afterwards. During the War, they supplied and equipped the Continental Army and Navy, and launched their own fleet of privateers against British shipping.

This lavish house, designed in 1785 by John's brother, Joseph, was described by **John Quincy Adams as the "most magnificent and elegant private mansion that I have ever seen on this continent".** Great effort has gone into restoring the period furnishings and wall papers, and to assemble outstanding collections of silver and china of the period to give the visitor the impression of its former glory. This palace was a marvel in its day and still is. **Washington slept here too -- on his visit to celebrate the State's ratification of the U.S. Constitution in 1790.** Rhode Island was the last hold out of the original thirteen Colonies. John Brown had strongly urged his wavering countrymen to ratification. No doubt he was propelled by public spirit, but Alexander Hamilton's proposal that the Federal Government should assume the debts incurred by the Colonies in waging the War, for which the Brown brothers had been chief suppliers, must have pleased him, too. The darker side of John Brown was that he was in the slave trade before the Revolution, and tried to continue in it after 1788, when Rhode Island declared it illegal.

Further up Power St., at No. 66, is the handsome **Thomas Poynton Ives House,** built in 1806. This was the home of **Hope Brown Ives**, Nicholas Brown's daughter, after whom Hope St. and **Hope College** of Brown University are named. **She and her brothers, Nicholas Jr. and John Carter Brown, were major benefactors of Brown University.** This new generation of culture-supporting Browns were the grandchildren of **John Carter,** the scholarly printer of Shakespeare's Head (see page 163). Their fortune was no longer tainted by the slave trade. By their day, following the pathway of their pioneering uncle, **Moses Brown,** the family was making fortunes from its investments in textile manufacture and other industries.

John Brown House

Two blocks from the John Brown House, at the northeast corner of Planet and Main, **once stood Sabin's Tavern**, the official stop of the stagecoach from Boston, but most famous because **on the night of June 9, 1772, its southeast room was the place of assembly of the Gaspee "Partyers"**, a group of about 40 armed men, who embarked in 8 long boats at the dock opposite and rowed in the dark for about 7 miles to a point of land where the **H.M.S. Gaspee**, a British revenue schooner, lay aground, helpless until the high tide. **They evacuated the crew at gunpoint and set the ship afire. No fatalities, one wounded.**

The Gaspee had run aground earlier in the day while giving chase to the packet Hannah, whose captain rushed to Providence to inform John Brown of the ship's predicament. Brown immediately arranged for the midnight "party." He readied the boats and had a drummer walk along Main St. announcing that the Gaspee had run aground and inviting anyone who wanted to assist in getting rid of the "troublesome" vessel to come to James Sabin's House after dark.

The fire set the British aglow. A ship of the King's Navy had been destroyed!! Along side of this, tarring and feathering customs officers was mere exuberance!! **In the uproar that followed, special Royal investigators were appointed and huge rewards were offered** for the arrest of the culprits, who were to be sent to England for trial. Most remarkably, **despite the huge rewards and the openness of the "party" arrangements, no one was ever prosecuted**. We see here the extraordinary "togetherness" of Providence, then a town of 4,500, center of a county of 19,000. The "partyers" belonged to the town's leading families, all friends or relatives of Stephen Hopkins, the Chief Justice, who vowed that he would not hand anyone over to be tried in England, in violation of the basic right of the accused to be tried amidst the sympathy of neighbors. Top to bottom within this close society nearly all were agreed that the heavy duties imposed on molasses threatened their economic survival and were unjust. The King's Law was wrong and it was not wrong to evade it.

What John Adams called the "Real Revolution", the one for the minds of the people, was clearly well under way in Providence at the time of the Gaspee Affair in 1772. **And Providence was not alone**. Except in degree, the Gaspee Affair was similar to eruptions then occurring all along the New England coast, wherever the British tried to curtail molasses smuggling. "What right has the King to America?", asked Reverend Isaac Skilman in a sermon in Boston devoted to the Gaspee Affair. He answered, "He can have no more right to America than what the people by

compact invested him with, which is only the power to protect them and to defend their rights, civil and religious, and to sign as their steward such laws as the people of America consent to." (My sources for the Gaspee Affair were S.G. Arnold's *HISTORY OF RHODE ISLAND* and Alice M. Baldwin's *THE NEW ENGLAND CLERGY AND THE AMERICAN REVOLUTION.*)

The Gaspee Affair is now celebrated by a gala week of special events in early June – parades, re-enactments, sports events, feasts. Consult your Rhode Island Guide for schedule. Sad to say, Sabin's House was demolished in 1891. A plaque in the parking lot now occupying the site commemorates the remarkable events initiated here. Fortunately, these days, a preservation consciousness prevails in the area. Nearby, old warehouses on South Main have been recycled to shops and restaurants, and you can find much good board and entertainment here once again.

The names of Planet and Transit Streets celebrate the enthusiastic search for knowledge of the Hill's leading intellectuals, Stephen Hopkins, Jabez Bowen, and Joseph Brown, who set up a telescope at the corner of Benefit and Transit to watch the transit of the planet Venus in 1769. Their telescope is now part of Brown University's historic memorabilia.

Going northward along South Main from the Sabin Tavern site, you pass the Old Stone Bank, with its impressive gilded dome, built in 1898, and then, **at 50 South Main, you come to the handsome mansion that Joseph Brown built for himself in 1774**. Continuing northward you pass the **State Court Buildings** and arrive, near the intersection of South Main and College Streets, at **Market Square, the civic and commercial center of early Providence.** (This is the first of the Hill's major historic sites that you encounter if you go to the Hill along Westminster from Kennedy PLAZA.) In the 18th century, a drawbridge to this point allowed farmers to bring their produce to the Market from the West Bank.

The centerpiece of Market Square is the Market House, completed in 1775, designed by Joseph Brown and Stephen Hopkins. Now enclosed, the first floor was originally open so that farmers could drive their teams in. A plaque indicates that on March 2, 1775, Providence arranged a great tea burning "party" here to protest the tax on tea and to proclaim their solidarity with Boston, which had at this time been under martial law with its port closed for 10 months (since May, 1774, when the Intolerable Acts had been enacted). During those months tremendous activity was going on in Rhode Island, paralleling that in Massachusetts. Subscriptions were raised to help beleaguered Boston, troops were organized and trained, munitions were assembled and stored, cattle and produce were gathered to feed troops in the event of the outbreak of war, and Providence's Brown brothers turned from making anchors and chains to guns and cannons. The center of these preparations was in Providence because a British customs contingent was stationed at Newport. **Throughout the conflict that soon followed, the Market Place was used as a barracks and for mustering troops.** On the night of April 19th, 1775, when news was received in Providence of the Battle of Lexington, troops began to assemble here. **One thousand men departed the next day toward the scene of strife.** Today the Market House is owned by the Rhode Island School of Design.

A little north of the Market Place, at 75 North Main St., **with steeple soaring to 180 feet,** is another Providence gem, **the Baptist Meeting House**, designed by Joseph Brown after the style of St. Martins in the Fields in London, and completed in 1775. **This is the oldest surviving church in the City. Its congregation dates back to 1639, when Roger Williams founded it.** It is the Mother of all Baptist Churches in America. Traditionally, every year, part of the graduation ceremonies of Brown University (which is non-sectarian) is held here. While the Church seats about 1,400, the congregation of 1775 numbered only about 300. So its design was truly an act of faith! Open to the public, Mon.-Fri., 10 - 3.30. Sat. 9 - 12. Tour Sun. at 12.

North of the Meeting House, a short detour from Main onto Thomas St. brings you to the **Providence Art Club** at No. 11, where works of local artists are exhibited. The house, built in 1789, was once the **home of the Dodge brothers, Nehemiah and Seril, who founded Rhode Island's silversmithing industry.**

Further north, on the block of Meeting St. between North Main and Benefit, are two significant historic sites. At No. 24 is the **Brick School House,** built in 1769, and used both as a school and meeting place in the tumultuous years before the

Revolution. **In an especially significant Town Meeting, on May 17, 1774,*** shortly after the port of Boston was closed in reprisal for the Tea Party, Providencers adopted a resolution expressing sympathy for Boston and recommending that trade with Great Britain be stopped until the port was opened. Then they approved a second resolution instructing the town's delegates to the Assembly **"to use their influence at the approaching General Assembly for promoting a CONGRESS,** as soon as may be, of the Representatives of the several colonies and provinces of North America, for establishing the firmest Union, and adopting such measures as to them shall appear most effectual (for this) purpose." A call for a Congress of all thirteen Colonies, a strong, unequivocal backup for the call that John Hancock had made two months earlier.

But that is not all. **At the same meeting, the citizens voted to petition the Assembly to end slavery in the Colony** because **"personal liberty is an essential part of the natural rights of mankind."** Discussions of their own inalienable rights had made Providencers aware of injustice to others. One of the leaders of the Hill's anti-slavery movement at this time, who helped push through this resolution, was **Moses Brown,** youngest brother of slave-trader. John Brown. We can imagine the family rows.

All of the above resolutions were adopted at the next meeting of the General Assembly in Newport. Stephen Hopkins and Samuel Ward were elected as Rhode Island's delegates to the Congress. The **Brick School House** is now occupied by the **Providence Preservation Society,** whose good works have saved many of the Hill's houses from decay and demolition. A number of excellent brochures are on sale here. For information about guided tours call **(401) 831-7440.**

Nearby, at 21 Meeting St., is Shakespeare's Head, built in 1722, now occupied by the **Junior League,** once the home and place of business of **John Carter,** a printer trained by Benjamin Franklin. **Here, from 1762 on, Carter and Sarah Goddard published Providence's first newspaper,** *THE PROVIDENCE GAZETTE AND COUNTRY JOURNAL,* a powerful voice of dissent in the pre-Revolutionary years. Carter was also the local postmaster. So Shakespeare's Head was a busy place of coming and going and socializing of the literately inclined. Today, the public is invited to enjoy the garden.

---

* It is not clear from the sources where this momentous pre-Revolutionary Town Meeting took place, whether at the School House or the Old State House (see page 164) or some other milieu.

On North Main north of Meeting St., with grounds extending to Benefit, is another jewel, the **Old State House, built in 1762**, now the home of the **State Historical Preservation Society. From 1762 until 1900**, when the present State House was built, **the General Assembly (Legislature) met here whenever it was holding its sessions in Providence. After the "shot fired round the world" in April 1775, this was the headquarters from which the General Assembly conducted Rhode Island's share of the war effort** -- defense of the Colony and collaboration with Massachusetts and Connecticut forces and the Continental Congress. **The most dramatic act of the Assembly took place on May 4, 1776, when by a vote of 60 to 6 it renounced Rhode Island's allegiance to the British Crown.** At the time, the Continental Congress in Philadelphia was still agonizing over the question of Independence. (See Chapter 2 pages 96 to 99.) Two months later Rhode Island rejoiced in the Declaration of Independence of all thirteen Colonies. The joy was short lived. **In December 1776, Newport was invaded and occupied by a large British force, and refugees poured into Providence,** which was saved from starvation that winter only by provisions from Connecticut. Other excitements that have occurred in this grand old house were **the post-War visits of Washington, Jefferson, Lafayette, and John Adams.** Open Mon. - Fri., 8.30 to 4.30.

A little further north, between North Main and Canal Streets, we switch into the 17th century as we come to Roger Williams' Spring, now a **National Memorial** with Visitors Center offering exhibits, and rest rooms. Call **(401) 521-7266.** A stone's throw from the Spring was Williams' house, the center of the settlement that he had founded in 1636, in the "Cause of Libertie of Conscience." Like the Massachusetts Puritans, who had expelled him, Williams believed in government by compact or consent of the people. He wrote

> The foundation of civil power lies in the
> people; and it is evident that such
> governments as are by them erected have
> no more power, nor for longer time, than
> the people consenting shall betrust to them.

(My sources here and in the paragraphs that follow are Alice M. Baldwin's *NEW ENGLAND CLERGY AND THE   AMERICAN REVOLUTION* and William McLoughlin's *RHODE ISLAND*.)

Over one hundred and thirty years later, these ideas would animate the Gaspee Partyers, and **would be echoed in the Declaration of Independence. Like the Puritans and Pilgrims, Providence's early settlers entered into a compact, but with the difference that theirs was intended to extend only to Civil Matters.** An extremely devout man, Williams believed that the Civil Power had to be rigorously separated from the Religious because God wanted only voluntary allegiance. As he put it, "Forced worship stinks in God's nostrils."

But it was not always easy to separate the Civil from the Religious. In Providence's early days, before a civil code had been established, the settlement was beset with controversies. A typical case was that of Joshua Verin, who had come with Williams from Salem. His wife Ann, a pious woman, attended the frequent religious services -- prayers, Bible reading, giving testimony, and so on -- that were held next door in the Williams house. Verin became very annoyed, and insisted that she was spending too much time away from the home and was thereby breaking the Lord's Commandment on the subjection of wives to husbands. When he tried forcibly to keep her from going next door to pray, her screams were heard all over the little village. **The case was brought before the Town Meeting, which voted that Ann's "Libertie of Conscience" was coequal with Joshua's** and that he had no right to restrain her from attending prayer meetings. Much displeased, Verin took his wife and goods back to Salem.

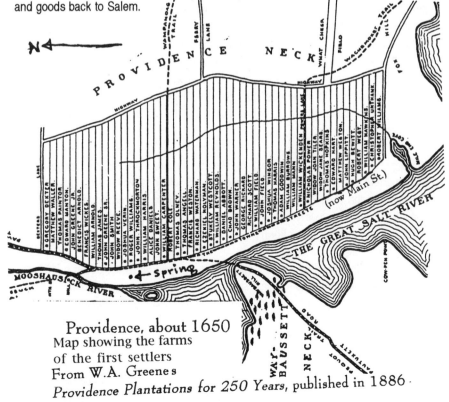

Providence, about 1650
Map showing the farms
of the first settlers
From W.A. Greenes
Providence Plantations for 250 Years, published in 1886.

Although Williams was a "Seeker" after truth in all religions, he was very critical of some. **At age 70, he rowed the 18 miles from Providence to Newport to debate the Quaker leader George Fox**. In addition to his philosophical searches, Williams spent much time studying the language and the culture of the Native Americans, and published in 1643 his *KEY INTO THE LANGUAGE OF AMERICA,* once famous and used widely. He loved and respected the Native Americans, and they in turn loved and respected him. **It is said that they would not sell him the land for the Providence Plantations, but insisted on giving it to him as a gift.**

Opposite the Park, at 271 North Main, is the **Cathedral of St. John, built in 1810** to replace King's Chapel, built in 1722, Providence's first Episcopal Church. Today, this is the **headquarters of the Episcopal Diocese of Rhode Island.** The graveyard behind the church, reached through its rectory, has headstones dating back to the early 1700's. Climbing along Church St. back to Benefit, you come to **88 Benefit**, built in 1780's and **occupied in the 19th century by Sarah Helen Whitman**, a poet and member of the Hill's literary circle.

Continuing southward along Benefit, you come to No. 109, an elegant Federalist house designed by John Holden Greene in 1809 for Sullivan Dorr, a merchant and manufacturer. **Dorr's son Thomas, a champion of the poor and disenfranchised, was the leader of Dorr's Rebellion of 1842**, aimed at removing the property restriction on suffrage. He was elected Governor in an extra-legal election, arranged by his party, in which all males over 21 were allowed to vote. The Rebellion was not bloody. As the rebels attempted to capture the Armory (at 176 Benefit), their two cannons, old pieces captured from British General Burgoyne in 1777, refused to fire. Dorr was imprisoned for awhile but released because of poor health. Full suffrage for males did not come to Rhode Island until 1888. (Full suffrage for males had come at the beginning of the 19th century in Massachusetts and Connecticut.)

Nearby at 40 Bowen, just west of Benefit, in an 18th century house, is the headquarters of the **Rhode Island Audubon Society**, which maintains 33 nature preserves in the state, with a primary goal of education on conservation and proper use of natural resources. The building is open from 9-5, Mon.-Fri., and houses an **outstanding natural history library**

A detour to climb up to Congdon St. brings you (see map on p. 152) **to a park with gorgeous views**. A giant statue of Roger Williams gazes out beneath a huge stone arch at the city that he founded. (See picture on page 150.) The great Seeker after Truth is buried here. The nation's Constitution is also his monument.

Other Hill Highlights. Continuing uphill along Meeting St. until Prospect at the crest of the Hill, you come to the **Woods-Gerry Mansion** at 62 Prospect, built in 1860 in the Italianate style. **The School of Design uses the House for galleries and offices. Sculpture is exhibited on the hillside. Lovely!** Open Mon. - Fri., 8.30 - 4.30, Sat., Sun., 1- 4. Free. Closed on weekends during the summer. On the grounds once stood one of the extensive system of signal beacons that stretched from Cambridge to New London to warn of the movements of British troops. The beacon here, a kettle of tar mounted on a tall post, was tended by Joseph Brown. It is said that the light could be seen in Cambridge 40 miles away.

East of the Brown Campus, at 110 Benevolent, between Hope and Cooke Streets, is the **Aldrich House,** built in 1822, now owned by the **Rhode Island Historical Society**, and housing the **Museum of Rhode Island History**. Call **(401) 331-8575** for information on schedule. Among the notables of the Aldrich family was Nelson Aldrich, a U.S. Senator from 1881 to 1911, author of the Aldrich Plan, upon which our Federal Reserve System is based. A master of detail, he worked out legislation -- on tariffs, railroad rates, and so on -- to satisfy various business interests, and amassed a personal fortune in ways that we would consider unethical today. His daughter Abby married oil baron John D. Rockefeller, Jr. The benefactions of the two families are highly visible in the Hill's colleges.

At 257 Hope St., is the **Moses Brown School**, now a "prep" school, originally a Quaker "Boarding School," spreading over 43 acres **donated by Moses Brown, youngest of the Brown brothers.** Moses left the family's Baptist religion to become a Quaker early in life. He also shunned the family business because he was opposed to the slave trade. Along with Reverend Samuel Hopkins, the Congregational minister of Newport, he was the leader of the eventually successful movement to banish the slave trade from Rhode Island. At one point, he sued his brother John for engaging in the slave trade illegally. The jury, awed by John's prominence, refused to convict him. Like his brothers, Moses was a shrewd business man, and prospered on his own. **After the Revolution**, during which he adhered to Quaker pacifism, **he decided the time was ripe to enter the area of textile manufacture, which had been most jealously guarded by the Mother Country during the Colonial period**. Whether at work or play, whether rallying or rioting or tarring and feathering or rowing for miles to burn His Majesty's ships, Americans had steadily enriched English textile manufacturers, except, of course, during the brief periods of boycotts. After several attempts to set up water-powered textile machinery, Moses Brown and his partner William Almy encountered success in the person of **Samuel Slater,** a gifted mechanic, trained in the English mills, blessed with a photographic memory. We shall continue this story when we take a **RIPTA** bus to visit the **Slater Mill** in Pawtucket.

At 121 Hope St., near Power St. on the southern slope of the Hill, is the **Rhode Island Historical Society's Library**, with artifacts, exhibits, and an extensive collection on the State's history. Call **(401) 331-8575.**

There are many other notable places on the Hill, but I'll let you explore on your own.

The State House
However you approach Providence, its most distinctive landmark is the gleaming marble State House, set on a knoll north of the railroad station. It has the largest self-supporting dome in the Western Hemisphere, second only to St. Peter's in Rome. From College Hill, Smith Street, on the north border of the Roger Williams Spring National Memorial, offers a pleasant route to it. And from the Business District, a pleasant route is to go up Exchange St. to the railroad station, pass through the station, and cross Gaspee St. to the State House. (See maps on pages 152, 153.)

The **State House**, designed in 1900 by **McKim, Mead, and White,** soars above the City. Atop its dome is Independent Man, a representation of the spirit of Roger Williams. On the lawns, from which you have superb views, are statues of Rhode Island natives, **Nathaniel Greene, the Revolutionary War General, who rescued the campaign in the South**, and **Commodore Oliver Hazard Perry, hero of the Battle of Lake Erie in 1813**, and originator of two of America's favorite quotes, " We have met the enemy and he is ours," and "Don't give up the ship."

Providence   169

Inside, in the **Governor's Reception Hall**, hangs a full length portrait of George Washington by another native son, **Gilbert Stuart.** The Legislative Chambers and the offices of legislators are located here, while the various State bureaucracies are scattered about the City. Portraits of famous Rhode Islanders and historic memorabilia adorn the walls and halls. **Enshrined in the Senate Lobby is the original Charter of 1663, granted by Charles II, from which the quotation on page 146 was taken.** The Charter specified the Colony's borders, and just in time, too, because Massachusetts and Connecticut were always claiming pieces of it. The Charter also specified the form of government -- how the Town Meetings would elect delegates to the Assembly, and how the Assembly would elect the Governor and other officers, and so on. **It granted Rhode Island a large degree of autonomy**. Massachusetts' original charter had been revoked because the British considered the Bay Colony too aggressive. But Rhode Island was not considered a threat and **managed to hold on to this Charter until Statehood. Because its officials were elected and not Crown-appointed, there was much rapport between them and the people,** even during the Colonial era. For example, after the first Royal stamp distributor was driven out of Newport, the Colony simply ignored the Stamp Act. Governor Samuel Ward claimed that he was not authorized to appoint anyone else to the job! Another extraordinary show of togetherness occurred during the French-Indian War when the British imposed a blockade on the French Sugar Islands, and consequently the outlook for Rhode Island's 33 rum distilleries seemed very bleak. However, the British allowed one exception to the blockade; they permitted passage of flag-of-truce ships carrying French prisoners of war to be exchanged. Governor Stephen Hopkins obligingly authorized flag-of-truce voyages in which prisoners were carried to the French Islands one or two at a time to prolong the process as much as possible. Sometimes there were *no* prisoners aboard the truce ships. Perhaps this is when the name "Rogue's Island" was coined.

Several blocks north of the State House, at 97 Admiral St., is the **Esek Hopkins House, built around 1740**, owned by the State and open by appointment. Call **(401) 421-3300. Esek Hopkins**, brother of Stephen, and one of John Brown's slave-ship masters, **was the first Commander-in-Chief of the American Navy**. His actions, however, were the subject of controversy in Congress, and his tenure was short; he was appointed in November, 1775, suspended in March, 1777, and dismissed in January, 1778. Unlike his brother Stephen, who sparkled at everything he did, Esek seems to have been a tragi-comic character who attracted mishaps. But much of the trouble was not his fault. He had difficulty recruiting crews because seamen preferred to serve on privateers, on which they shared in the "prizes" and enjoyed laxer discipline. Eventually, Congress prohibited enlistments on privateers and merchant ships until the Navy's quota was filled, but too late to help poor Hopkins. Another of his problems was John Brown, who diverted resources and labor earmarked for preparing Navy ships to readying his own privateers.

The Business Core, Briefly

Now let's walk westward from Kennedy Plaza into Providence's Business Core, on the West Bank of the almost invisible Providence River. The Business District is very compact, dense with all the stores, restaurants, bars, banks, offices, and so on that you expect in the government, financial, commercial, and industrial center for a population of 1,000,000. I've already mentioned City Hall, the impressive gray granite building, at the southwestern edge of Kennedy Plaza. Westminster St., a block south of City Hall, is the main street, crowded with office workers and students from Johnson and Wales University during the day. Looking upward you can see turn-of-the century elegance in the stone ornament above the twentieth century facades. At the corner of Westminster and Mathewson, is Grace Episcopal Church designed in 1846 by Richard Upjohn, most famous as the architect of New York's Trinity Church, which he created in 1847.

The Arcade, running between Weybosett and Westminster Streets, with Greek temple facades on both streets is unique, a nineteenth century shopping mall. Built in 1828, to attract shoppers away from the East Bank markets, today it is a mini-Quincy Market, with three levels of specialty stores and eateries opening onto balconies with their original cast iron railings. A visit here is a must! Unbelievably, this one of its kind building was once scheduled for demolition. Fortunately, the "renewal" funds ran out, and, by the time money was available, the winds of Preservation had begun to blow through Providence.

Fitting neatly into the sharp corner where Weybosset and Westminster meet is the multi-storied Turks Head Building, built in 1913, with a giant turbaned head sculptured in granite protruding from the fourth floor like a ship's figurehead. It is a scaled up model of the figurehead that adorned a little shop that once occupied this corner in the late nineteenth century. The handsome graystone at 24 Weybosset, now housing offices, was built in 1855 as the U.S. Customs House. Its high and dry

Providence Arcade, about 1828

position would surprise you if you didn't already know that the Providence River once sloshed at its doorstep. **The construction of the U.S.Custom House here signifies that, by 1855, Providence's center of commerce had shifted to the West Bank Weybosset District.** Earlier, in 1790, shortly after Rhode Island had ratified the Constitution and joined the Union, a U.S. Custom House had been built on the East Bank, then the commercial center. Further along Weybosset, at No. 220, is the **Providence Performing Arts Center, call (401) 421-2787**, which hosts a variety entertainment events.

At 201 Washington, just north of Westminster, is a marvelously ornate building with green and gold terra cotta moldings, the former **Majestic Theatre,** a movie palace built in 1916. **Now it is the Lederer Theatre, home of Providence's widely acclaimed Trinity Square Repertory Company**, whose home season runs from October to May. Call **(401) 351-4242**. On Washington and Empire, a block west of the theatre, is the **Providence Public Library,** a fine one with a collection of over seven hundred thousand volumes, eight neighborhood branches, and many outreach services. Of course, there are restrooms.

The oldest church in the Business Core is the Beneficent Congregational Church on Weybosset, called the Roundtop Church because of its gilded dome, built in 1809, but redesigned in 1836, when the dome was added. Its building marked the beginning of the West Bank as a fashionable place of residence. Near the church, **Abbot Park** is a tiny oasis of greenery with tree-shaded benches and a fountain, protected forever by the deed of its donor, Daniel Abbot, "for the use of the publick." Going uphill along Westminster, you come to **Cathedral Square**, dominated by the

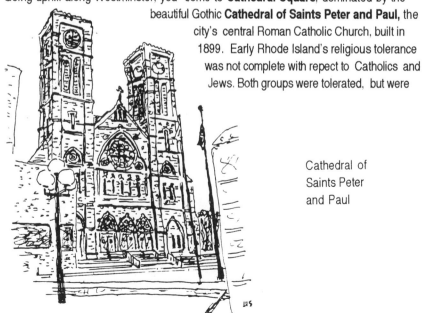

beautiful Gothic **Cathedral of Saints Peter and Paul,** the city's central Roman Catholic Church, built in 1899. Early Rhode Island's religious tolerance was not complete with repect to Catholics and Jews. Both groups were tolerated, but were

Cathedral of
Saints Peter
and Paul

denied suffrage by the Colony's early laws. When Rhode Island joined the Union, the religious restriction on suffrage was removed. but a property restriction remained (see remarks on Dorr's rebellion above), which was large enough to deny the vote to the waves of Roman Catholic immigrants arriving to work in the mills. **This church symbolizes a complete turnaround in status for Roman Catholics in the State,** their growing numbers, affluence, and political power. Today Roman Catholics are the overwhelming majority in the State. The surrounding plaza in three levels, bordered by offices and residences, a part of a recent urban renewal program, was designed by I. M. Pei.

Taking RIPTA to other Providence Highlights.

Providence has many attractions, easily reached by taking a **RIPTA** bus from Kennedy Plaza. Below I mention just a few.

Federal Hill. Providence's Little Italy. Providence has a large population of Italian ancestry, and a genuine Old Country Italian neighborhood on Federal Hill, along and near Atwell's Ave., complete with ristorantes, grocerias, pizzerias, the real thing. It is just west of the Business Core. However, you are separated from it by a confusing spaghetti of traffic. So take the **Atwell's Ave.-Academy RIPTA bus no. 26** to it. You can, if you wish, go the length of the line once and then get off the bus on the way back to browse.

Roger Williams Park. RIPTA bus no. 20 going along Elmwood Ave. from the center of town will take you past the entrance to this lovely park, with landscaped gardens, trees, and shrubs spread over 430 acres of rolling hills overlooking several lily-padded miniature lakes. Basically delightful, but unfortunately the paved roads traversing the grounds tempt hotrodders to speed through. The land was donated by Betsy Williams, a descendant of Providence's founder, Roger Williams. Her cottage, built in 1772, stands on the grounds, which also harbor a **Zoo, Museum of Natural History, and a Planetarium.** The **Casino,** built in 1897, is now the home of a **Children's Theatre.** Summer concerts are performed in the neo-Greek **Temple of Music. This is Providence's favorite family park. Call (401) 785-9450.**

Slater Mill in Pawtucket. Take RIPTA bus no. 99 to it from Kennedy Plaza and ask the driver when to get off. **Built in 1793, this was the first successful water-operated cotton-spinning mill in America**, a harbinger of the U.S. entry into the Industrial Revolution. **Samuel Slater**, who had worked for seven years in the Derbyshire

spinning mills, and had mastered the intricacies of the Awkright machinery, **was the Prometheus who brought England's most treasured trade secrets to America**. His financial backers were **Moses Brown** and **William Almy**. Slater contacted Brown and Almy upon hearing of their many failed attempts to start water-run spinning mills. After Slater's success, water-run cotton spinning and afterwards cloth weaving mills sprouted over New England's many fast flowing streams. **But until 1815**, when **Francis Cabot Lowell's consortium** in Massachusetts started their large scale cloth making operations (see pages 102-107), **Rhode Island led the Nation in textile manufacture**. Afterwards, it was second only to Massachusetts.

    In addition to the Slater Mill, the grounds include the Wilkinson Mill, a water-powered iron-working shop designed to supply parts for the Slater Mill. Also on the grounds, stands the **Sylvanus Brown House**, which housed workers. What is astonishing is the prettiness of the building and grounds. You are reminded that water power was not polluting. There is no dirty grayness here; instead there are twinkling bright clapboard buildings and tree shaded grounds by a picturesque waterfall, all in contrast with the factories surrounded by treeless deserts that you pass on the bus route from Providence. **But even though the outdoor scene is pretty, it is well to remember how difficult the working conditions were inside the mills,** long hours, noise, and cotton-dust filled air. **And Samuel Slater was notorious for employing child labor.** In Rhode Island, sad to say, working conditions were generally worse than in Massachusetts, and slower to improve, with fewer safeguards for children. **But eventually, here too, the formation of labor unions led to improved conditions.**

    Exhibits explore life in the 1800's with emphasis on the technology of the day. Guided tours of the mills with demonstrations of early spinning techniques and operation of water powered machines are given from Memorial to Labor Day daily except Monday, and on weekends during the winter months. Call **(401) 725-8638** for more information. Fee.

Eating in Providence
    Of course, you are not going to starve in Providence. There is plenty of good food in all price ranges. A detailed restaurant guide would take many pages. I'll just point out the districts where you should look. The **Business Core** is chock full of eating places for the many office workers who pour out at lunch time. The **Arcade** has plenty of eateries, with juices, soups, salads, sandwiches, pizza, pasta, quiche, Chinese food, cheese cake, bagels, croissants, French bread, espresso, cappuccino,

and so on. At 36 Weybosset, in the 𝕰quitable 𝕭uilding, the **Custom House Tavern** offers good food at reasonable prices. Among the many other fine lunch places in the Business Core are the **Back Stage Deli** and **Choices**, both on Westminster, and offering great salads and breads and steamed vegetables at low prices. On my last visit to Providence, a companion and I had delicious lunches at moderate prices at the **Union Station Brewery**, just off Exchange Terrace. You descend steps between two buildings to it. From the nearby parking lot, a tunnel leads under Memorial Drive to the new **Waterplace Park,** where office workers relax and picnic in warm weather. In the **College Hill** district, restaurants and sidewalk cafes abound on **North and South Main Streets**. Further uphill **on Thayer Street** are several coffee houses and beer parlors. I had an excellent meal at a sandwich shop there serving natural food concoctions, sprout and cheese salads, pita pocket sandwiches, herbal teas, and wonderful desserts at low prices. **I was delighted also that several patrons stopped to express approval of my "Car-free is Carefree" button.** Parking is restricted in the areas adjacent to Brown University and RISD, and there is a consciousness here of the devastation that unfettered car use would wreak upon the Hill. It goes without saying that you will find several moderately priced good Italian restaurants in the **Federal Hill, Little Italy** district, also grocerias where you can buy the finest ingredients for your own cookery.

Lodgings

Although we have been considering Providence as a daytrip from Boston, there are many lodgings in all price ranges, within walking distance of downtown or a **RIPTA** bus stop, beginning with the **Biltmore Hotel**, in the upper price range, and in the center of everything. However, since all the places that we describe in this chapter, are served by RIPTA buses, we shall treat the entire area as one compact, connected district and shall postpone listing lodgings until the end of the chapter. You can stay anywhere and visit the other places. The possibilities include the **Youth Hostel** at the **University of Rhode Island** in Kingston (U.R.I.), and **campgrounds near Galilee**, as well as the sumptuousness of the Biltmore, all easily reached by public transit.

NEWPORT

Newport (population, 38,000) is several fascinating places rolled into one.
There is **Colonial Newport, where 400 buildings pre-dating the Revolution, more than in any other city, survive on narrow streets**, miraculously saved from widenings and bulldozers. There is **Newport of the "Gilded Age,"** with **palatial mansions** built in the 1890's by New York and Philadelphia's wealthiest families, **now museums open to the public**, thanks to the **Preservation Society of Newport County,** who began acquiring them as they were being abandoned in the 1930's due to the combined impacts of the Depression and Income Tax. **Then there is today's tourist mecca, the Newport of music festivals and tennis tournaments, the yachting capital of marinas and yacht clubs**, formerly host to the America's Cup Race. The docks that once were piled high with privateer's booty and witnessed the tragedy of slave auctions are now crowded with galleries, craft shops, boutiques, restaurants, taverns, food stores, all bubbling over with visitors. **The pineapple**, once displayed by Colonial warehouse men to entice the townspeople to inspect their exotic wares, **is now Newport's official welcome symbol**, rendered artistically in glass, stone, water color, oils, posters, post cards, everywhere. **And then there is the Newport of pounding surfs, and beautiful white beaches, of rocky tidal pools and wild-flower meadows, of sea-side cliffs commanding gorgeous views**, the exquisite, natural Newport that attracted all those rich people in the first place.

Then there is Newport, the present day city of year-round residents, the fishermen, the boat builders and repairers, the trades and crafts people who run the shops and restaurants, the workers of local industries, the many, including artists, writers, and retirees from all walks of life, who have come to stay in Newport because it is such a terrific place. From the 1940's to the mid-1970's, Newport was a U.S. Naval Base, and the Navy was the area's major employer. In 1974, when the Navy closed many of its installations, massive unemployment resulted, which has now to a large extent been solved by intensified tourist promotion. So underneath the resort, there is a real city, gallantly caring and coping. It has a charm all its own. **You meet the real city by taking RIPTA buses. They are fun!!**

Information. The packet of material supplied by the Rhode Island Department of Economic Development (see address on page 149) will undoubtedly contain much information about Newport. But in addition you may find it advantageous to write to the **Newport County Convention and Visitor's Bureau, 23 America's Cup Ave., Newport, R.I. 02840**. or call **(401) 849-8048,** for maps, etc. Upon arrival in Newport,

you will find that the Visitors Bureau, with its extensive array of information literature and visitor services, forms part of the **Gateway Transportation and Visitors Center** (see map on page 178) and **adjoins the Bonanza and Ripta bus station, where there are restrooms.** It is near **Washington Sq., the docks,** and **Everything.** Bus and walking tours leave from here as do RIPTA buses. **It is a terrifically convenient set-up for visitors.** For Newport events information call **(401) 848-2000.**

Getting To Newport. From Boston, you can take a **Bonanza Bus** to Newport **from the new South Station Bus Terminal** near the South Station T stop on the Red Line. Call **(800) 556-3815** for Bonanza Bus schedule. There are several buses a day. The trip takes about 1 hour and 30 minutes. **From Providence,** there are almost hourly RIPTA buses to Newport from Kennedy Plaza. **Call (401) 781-9400 for schedule information, or (800) 662-5088,** or, if you are hearing impaired, **(TDD) 461-9400** The trip takes about 55 minutes. **The final bus stop for both the Bonanza Bus from Boston and the RIPTA bus from Providence is Gateway Center at 23 America's Cup Ave.** (see last paragraph), which has rest rooms and is just a few blocks from **Washington Sq. and the Heart of Everything**. The RIPTA route is a pleasant introduction to the picturesque towns and parks lining the east side of the Bay. The Bonanza route from Boston will give you intriguing glimpses of Fall River, Massachusetts, and Portsmouth, and Middletown, Rhode Island. From the Gateway Center terminal, RIPTA buses depart for a loop in Newport and nearby Middletown.

Orientation. The Newport peninsula is at the southwestern tip of **Aquidneck Island,** which Newport shares with Middletown and Portsmouth. Newport is shaped like a boot, with tip pointing into Narragansett Bay, toward Conanicut Island, and sheltering a beautiful harbor at the ankle of the boot. **Colonial Newport adjoins the Harbor** on the western side (Narragansett Bay side) of the peninsula. Its main streets were **Thames**, on the waterfront, and **Spring** one block away. A gentle slope led uphill from **Long Wharf** to **Washington Square,** the town's center. **The palaces of the Gilded Age** are located about 3/4 of a mile east of **Colonial Newport**, on the cliffs on the eastern side of the peninsula with views toward Middletown and the ocean. The palaces face Bellevue Ave., **and at their rear is the famous Cliff Walk, Newport's greatest attraction.** On the shore, sandy beaches alternate with surf pounded rocks.

Getting about on the Newport Peninsula. Walking is the ideal way, with an occasional assist from the local RIPTA bus, or a taxi, or a shuttle boat. It is possible to rent a bicycle, too, at several places, including **Ten Speed Spokes,** located at the

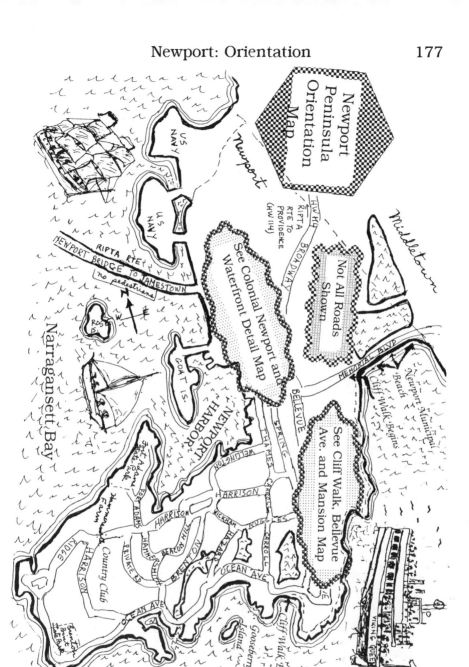

corner of Elm St. and America's Cup Ave, a block north of the Gateway Center bus terminal, call **(401) 847-5609**. Bicycling is actually an old Newport tradition. The **League of American Wheelmen** was organized here in the 1880's. However, in season, traffic conditions can make cycling difficult. In season, the RIPTA local bus offers frequent and extensive service about the peninsula. Call **847-0209** for Newport RIPTA information. Off season service is less frequent and less extensive

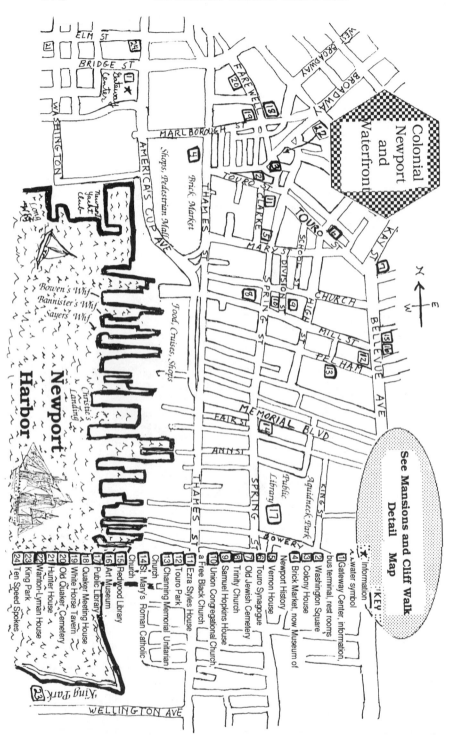

Colonial Newport and Waterfront

See Mansions and Cliff Walk Detail Map

KEY
✱ Information
💧 water symbol
🚌 bus terminal, rest rooms

1 Gateway Center, information,
2 Washington Square
3 Colony House
4 Brick Market, now Museum of Newport History
5 Vernon House
6 Touro Synagogue
7 Old Jewish Cemetery
8 Trinity Church
9 Samuel Hopkins House
10 Union Congregational Church; a Free Black Church
11 Ezra Styles House
12 Touro Park
13 Channing Memorial Unitarian Church
14 St. Mary's Roman Catholic Church
15 Redwood Library
16 Public Library
17 Art Museum
18 Quaker Meeting House
19 White Horse Tavern
20 Old Quaker Cemetery
21 Hunter House
22 Wanton-Lyman House
23 King Park
24 Ten Speed Spokes

Newport Harbor

Bowen's Whf
Bannister's Whf
Sayers Whf

Food, Cruises, Shops

Christie's Landing

Shops, Pedestrian Mall

Brick Market

Newport Yacht Club

Long Whf

MARLBOROUGH

THAMES

TOURO

MARY ST

DIVISION ST

SPRING ST

CHURCH

MILL ST

PELHAM

MEMORIAL BLVD

FAIR ST

ANN ST

SPRING

BOWERY

THAMES ST

KING ST

Aquidneck Park

Public Library

BELLEVUE AVE

KAY ST

BROADWAY

FAREWELL

ELM ST

BRIDGE ST

WASHINGTON

AMERICA'S CUP AVE

HIGH ST

SCHOOL ST

CLARKE ST

King Park

WELLINGTON AVE

Colonial Newport

Colonial Newport is intertwined with today's Business Core and wharfside tourist bazaars. We can take it all in together. At the center of the Colonial town was the **Parade Ground** now **Washington Square, just a few blocks from the Gateway Center bus station**. At the eastern end of the Square is the **Colony House,** designed by Richard Munday in 1739. This was the seat of the Colony's government during the Newport sessions of the General Assembly. **From its balcony, in September, 1776, the Declaration of Independence was read to a joyous populace**. But the euphoria soon evaporated as the British occupied the town in December setting off a huge exodus to Providence. The British stayed for three years, departing in October, 1779 to pursue the campaign in the South. In July, 1780, the French arrived, and with them some of the town's former population and gaiety returned. The Colony House was used as a barracks by the British and a hospital by the French. **Upon the sudden death of French Admiral de Ternay, the first Catholic mass in Rhode Island was held here.** It has since been restored to its pre-Revolution form. Guided tours are given by appointment; call **(401) 846-2980, or (401) 277-6790.**

Colony
House

Toward the Harbor side of Washington Square, on Thames St., is the **Brick Market,** built in 1760, designed by Newporter **Peter Harrison**, who also designed **Boston's King's Chapel** and **Cambridge's Christ Church** (see Chapter 1). This striking brick building with heroic Ionic columns served as a temple of commerce and symbol of Newport's pre-revolutionary affluence. At the time, Newport had a fleet of 200 vessels engaged in foreign trade, and 400 in the coastal trade. In commerce, it was ahead of New York, and behind only Boston. With a population of 9,000, it was fifth in the Colonies. The town had about 900 residences and 400 warehouses. But the British ravaged Newport, destroying 500 buildings for firewood. The town never recovered its former commercial pre-eminence.

Today the Brick Market houses the Museum of Newport History, call (401) 846-0813, and adjoins a mall with shops and galleries. Crossing through the mall you come to America's Cup Ave, which borders the Waterfront. (See map on page 178.) The wharves are bee hives of tourist enticements, with more galleries, shops, and restaurants, all with a water view.

Washington Sq. itself was the scene of vigorous, New England style popular demonstrations against the Stamp and Sugar Acts, burnings in effigy, and so on. But most memorable is the occasion for which it was named. **It was here in March, 1781 that Washington experienced what must have one of the most extraordinary moments of his military career.** He had come to Newport to meet with Count de Rochambeau to plan the campaign in the South. He, whose army was hungry and in shreds and tatters, stood here as he was saluted by arrays of French troops in gleaming attire. Washington himself was resplendent in the uniform of a marshal of France, which signified that these troops were under his command. He spent only a few days in Newport, because he was eager to return to his American troops. The French fleet and troops departed soon after to head southward. The ensuing collaboration of the Americans and French resulted in the surrender of Cornwallis at Yorktown in October, 1781, the effective end of the War.

Rochambeau's headquarters, where he and Washington worked on the Yorktown campaign, **were at the stately Vernon House, built in 1773 and still standing at the corner of Clarke and Mary Streets** about one block from Washington Square.

Touro Street forms the southern border of Washington Square. **At 72 Touro,** two blocks east of the Square, is the **Touro Synagogue, the oldest synagogue in North**

Touro
Synagogue

America, built in 1759. Attracted by Rhode Island's reputation for tolerance, Jews from Holland and Portugal began to arrive in Newport in the 1650's. They made key contributions to its maritime trade and industry. For 100 years they worshipped in their homes. Then under the leadership of Isaac de Touro, this synagogue was built. **Among its treasures is a Torah dating back to 1658, brought from Amsterdam.**

The Synagogue survived the Revolution undamaged, and after the War was used as the seat of the General Assembly while the Colony House was being repaired. **On his post-War visit to Rhode Island in 1790** (see pages 159 and 164), **George Washington assured the congregation that the new Nation would "give to bigotry no sanction, to persecution no assistance."** It was a poignant moment for the Jewish community. Although Jews had previously been tolerated in the Rhode Island Colony, they had been denied full citizenship. Earlier in 1684, the Rhode Island General Assembly had offered them only "as good protection here as any *stranger* residing among us." They were admitted to full citizenship with voting rights only after the Revolution.

The building was designed by Peter Harrison, and is considered his masterpiece. The exterior has an elegant simplicity, and the interior is airy and graceful. It is said that Jefferson, who accompanied Washington on his 1790 visit to Rhode Island, was influenced by this building in his plans for Monticello. Open: mid-June to Labor Day, Mon.-Fri., 10-6; Labor Day to mid-June, Sun. 2-4. Open Saturday year-round for services only. Call **(401) 847-4794** for guided tour information.

A little further eastward, near where Touro meets Bellevue Ave., **is the old Jewish cemetery,** with inscriptions in Hebrew, English, Portuguese, Spanish, and Latin. The **Newport National Bank building** on the north side of Washington Square was the home of one of the Synagogue's members, **Abraham Rodriguez Rivera,** a merchant, who introduced the art of spermaceti candle making to the Colony, destined to become one of its most important enterprises. A staunch Patriot, Rivera fled the town during the British occupation.

Trinity Church, the most beautiful of Newport's early churches, rises on Spring St., between Church and Mill Streets. It was built in 1725, and designed by Richard Munday, with an exterior resembling Boston's North Church, and an elegant interior, more evidence of the flourishing of the arts in Newport before the Revolution. **Dean (later Bishop) Berkeley**, one of England's most celebrated scholars and churchmen, preached here during his three-year stay in Newport, from 1729 to 1732.

He greatly stimulated Newport's intellectual life, and was in turn impressed with its examples of religious tolerance. He wrote to his friends in England, "Here are four sorts of Anabaptists, besides Presbyterians, Quakers, Independents, and those of no profession at all. Notwithstanding so many differences, here are fewer quarrels about religion than elsewhere..."

This Anglican church was attended by the town's Tories in the troubled years before the Revolution. **Two of its parishioners, Thomas Moffat and Martin Howard, were burned in effigy on the Parade Ground in front of the Colony House for defending the Stamp Act.** However, two more recent Royalist visitors -- Queen Elizabeth II, and the Archbishop of Canterbury, who came in 1976 -- were handsomely treated. The Church is open daily from mid-June until Labor Day. It has box pews, a one of its kind wine-glass pulpit, and an organ, tried and tested by Handel himself, a gift of Bishop Berkeley. Members of the Church's early congregations are buried in the graveyard beside it, as is Admiral de Ternay, and the Berkeleys' infant daughter. The park adjoining offers benches and lovely Harbor views.

The building of Trinity Church and the presence of Bishop Berkeley were **part of the works of the Society for the Propagation of Gospel,** based in London, to foster the Anglican Church in the New World. **New England's Congregationalists monitored the doings of the Society anxiously,** especially after the 1760's when it seemed likely that the Anglicans might establish an American Episcopate. **As might be expected, Newport's two Congregational Churches were breeders of Patriots. They were also the center of the Colony's anti-slavery movement. Samuel Hopkins,** minister of the First Congregational Church, **fearlessly denounced slavery and the slave trade to a congregation studded with slave owners and slave traders.** But eventually his congregation resolved that slavery was contrary to the Lord's Gospel. A dedicated scholar and theologian, Hopkins appears as the saintly hero in THE MINISTER'S WOOING by Harriet Beecher Stowe. **His home was at 46 Division,** which runs off Mary. Opposite, at 49 Division, is the **Union Congregational Church, built in 1834, Newport's first Free Black church.**

Entrance, Union Congregational Church

At 14 Clarke St., is the former home of Hopkins' colleague, **Ezra Stiles,** minister of the **Second Congregational Church**, another towering scholar. The Meeting House that Stiles preached in, built in 1735, stands across the street from his home. Stiles encouraged the spirit of tolerance that was budding within the Puritan-founded churches, and had the friendliest of relations with the Jewish rabbi and the ministers of Newport's many churches, all except the Anglicans, whose activities he watched warily. In deference to his enormous learning, the Baptist ministers asked him to help them set up Rhode Island College (now Brown University). In the years before the War, **his sermons on the limits of the King's power and religious freedom were widely distributed to New England's Congregational ministers.** In December 1776, Newport's Congregationalists fled before the British occupation. In exile, Stiles continued to preach, and served as **President of Yale University** from 1778 to 1795.

At the corner of Pelham and Spring St., is the **United Congregational Church**, built in 1855, whose congregation is a reunion of ones tracing back to Hopkins and Stiles. On Pelham near Bellevue is the **Channing Memorial Unitarian Church,** built in 1888, named in honor of Newport native **William Ellery Channing** (1780 - 1842), **the great apostle of Unitarianism. With him we see the blossoming of Puritanism into liberalism,** theological and social. As a young man, Channing had attended Hopkins' church and was greatly influenced by the minister's devotion to systematic theological constructions. After graduating from Harvard and serving in various ministries, in 1803, he became the pastor of Boston's **Federal St. Church**, where he served until his death. Like his Puritan ancestors, Channing upheld the role of reason, but, unlike them, came to the conclusion that Christ was a great moral teacher and not divine, and that the Bible was a book whose meaning was to be sought in the same manner as that of other books. His eloquent writings and sermons influenced droves of Congregational Churches to convert to Unitarianism, and others to break into Unitarian and Trinitarian fragments. Channing was also a supporter of advanced political and social causes, including William Lloyd Garrison's Abolition Movement when it was still unpopular. He is honored in Boston by a statue in the **Public Garden**, opposite the **Arlington St. Church** (see page 39). Here in his native town, he is honored by this church and a statue opposite it in **Touro Park**, which fronts on Bellevue between Pelham and Mill St. **Julia Ward Howe** (1819-1910), editor of an

Channing Statue and Viking Tower in Touro Park

anti-slavery newspaper, leader in the woman's suffrage movement, and author of *THE BATTLE HYMN OF THE REPUBLIC*, was a member of this church during her years of summer residence in Newport.

In **Touro Park,** you will see also the **Old Stone Tower,** which was for a long time the subject of wild speculations, including a poem by Longfellow, that it might have been built by the Vikings on one of their early visits to the New England coast. Recent archaeological studies indicate it is actually a remnant of an old stone mill built by **Governor Benedict Arnold,** the great grandfather of the notorious traitor. The Arnolds were among the first settlers in Roger Williams "towne". (See map on page 165.)

On Memorial Blvd., near Spring St, is **St. Mary's Roman Catholic Church,** built in 1848, for **Rhode Island's oldest Roman Catholic parish.** Here **Jacqueline Bouvier** married **John F. Kennedy.** then U.S. Senator from Massachusetts.

At 50 Bellevue, adjoining lovely gardens, is the Redwood Library, built in 1748 in the style of a Roman Temple, to "promote Knowledge and Virtue by Free Conversation," one of the country's oldest libraries, a witness to the vigorous cultural life of 18th century Newport, and another of architect Peter Harrison's great achievements. The Library's collection includes portraits of Newport citizens by **Gilbert Stuart** and other early Rhode Island painters. Among its many treasures is **a map of Newport in 1758 by Ezra Stiles.** Open Mon.-Sat., 10 - 5. (The Redwood, although open to the public, is not a public library. **Newport Public Library** is located on Spring St., in Aquidneck Park, just south of Memorial Blvd.) Near the Redwood Library, at 76 Bellevue, in a Victorian building, is the **Newport Art Museum, call (401) 848-8200,** with a permanent collection of 19th and 20th century American art. Fee.

So far the places we have visited have all been south of Washington Square. To the north are many fascinating sites, too. At the intersection of Farewell and Malborough Streets. about two blocks from the Square. is **the country's oldest**

Redwood
Library

surviving Quaker Meeting House, built in 1700, with enlargements added in 1808 and 1818. The congregation dates back to 1657, when Newport's first boatload of Quakers landed. They found ready converts among the town's first families. The Coddingtons, Coggeshalls, Eastons, and Dyers, all became dedicated Quakers. In the **Quaker graveyard** opposite 35 Farewell Street lie **William Coddington, Nicholas Easton, and John Coggeshall,** all founders of Newport and among the Colony's first governors. **All had fled from Boston after Anne Hutchinson's trial.** Here we come to one of the most intriguing stories of early New England. Anne Hutchinson's.

   The Hutchinsons, Anne and William, were wealthy, pious Puritans, residents of "old" Boston in Lincolnshire, who had followed their favorite minister. John Cotton (grandfather of Cotton Mather), to the "new" Boston in 1634. **In John Winthrop's diary, Anne Hutchinson is described as "a woman of ready wit and bold spirit."** Eighty years later, **Cotton Mather would call her "an American Jezebel,"** in his *HISTORY OF NEW ENGLAND.* The mother of 15 (fifteen!) children, she possessed extraordinary intelligence and was a charismatic leader. Had Cambridge University and the Puritan ministry been open to her, she might have become the most brilliant of theologians. As it was, she won immediate popularity in Boston, at first, for her skills in nursing and experience as a mother and midwife. In her house, where the **Corner Bookstore** now stands (see Freedom Trail, pages 21, 22), she conducted Monday morning meetings with the women, in which she commented on the sermons preached the previous day by the pastors of the Boston Meeting House. But soon her audience included the women's husbands and families. Theological discussion was apparently the Puritans' favorite leisure-time activity. Of most intense interest was the subject of Salvation. According to Hutchinson, Salvation depended upon God's special grace rather than on the "works" -- good deeds, Bible study, prayers, soul searching, and other human efforts -- favored by the majority of "orthodox" Puritan ministers. Her appeal was immense. A newcomer to Boston was greeted with

> Come along with me, I'll bring you to a woman that preaches better Gospell than any of your black-coates that have been at the Ninniversity, a Woman of another kind of spirit, who hath many Revelations.

(My sources on Anne Hutchinson are McGlouglin's *RHODE ISLAND,* Battis' *SAINTS AND SECTARIES,* and Augur's *AMERICAN JEZEBEL.*)

   Of course, such words were regarded as insults by scholarly Puritan ministers, who had left promising careers in England to preach in the "Wildernesse," and build their ideal Church-State on "good works" rather than revelations. **As Hutchinson's popularity spread, her supporters were soon challenging John**

Winthrop and the orthodox ministers for political and religious leadership of the Bay Colony, which were then intertwined. The upshot of Winthrop's attempt to retain power was that she was charged with troubling "the peace of the Commonwealth" and speaking "divers things prejudiced to the honor of the churches and ministers." In her trial, her accusers were also her judges. Hutchinson courageously stood her ground, parrying Scriptural citation with citation. A great drama. But the end of the unfair battle was inevitable. **She was excommunicated from the Church and banished from the Colony.**

In 1638 nineteen Boston families accompanied the Hutchinsons in their exile to Rhode Island, where, with Roger Williams' help, they purchased land on Aquidneck Island. The Hutchinsons settled in Portsmouth, and others led by William Coddington founded Newport. After her husband's death in 1642, Anne Hutchinson and 6 of her children moved to Long Island, where they were killed in an Indian massacre. **Among Anne's best friends in Boston was Mary Dyer.** The Dyers, William and Mary, were part of the exodus to Rhode Island. Like many Hutchinson followers, Mary Dyer converted to the Quaker religion, whose concept of individual "Inner Light" seemed not far from Hutchinson's "special grace." The Quaker religion must also have appealed to Mary Dyer because it recognized the right of women to be preachers. As a dedicated Quaker, Mary Dyer returned to Massachusetts to preach her faith. She was expelled from the Bay Colony twice. **On her third return, in 1660, she was hanged on Boston Common**. Her husband was then Secretary of the Rhode Island Colony.

The statues of Anne Hutchinson and Mary Dyer in front of the Massachusetts Statehouse (see Freedom Trail, page 18) are expressions of regret by the Commonwealth for the sorry treatment that they received. Over the years, much has been written about the Hutchinson affair, the so-called Antinomian Controversy, from many different angles. A notable attempt to set the record straight was written by her descendant, **Thomas Hutchinson,** who was Royal Governor of the Bay Colony at the time of the Boston Tea Party.

Statue of
Anne Hutchinson,
Garden,
Massachusetts Statehouse

The White Horse Tavern opposite the Quaker Meeting House may be the country's oldest continuously operated tavern. It was built in 1663 by William Mayes, who is said to have been a pirate!! It is a favorite restaurant today.

Further north at Farewell and Warren is the **Burial Ground** with more early settlers and interesting headstones. It is divided into "free" and "slave" parts. Newport had the largest slave population in all New England; about 15% of its population at the time of the Revolution were slaves. A monument in the "free" section is dedicated to **Samuel Ward, who was elected Colonial Governor three times and was chosen, along with Stephen Hopkins, to serve in the Continental Congress.** He died in Philadelphia in March 1776. His replacement **William Ellery**, grandfather of William Ellery Channing, arrived in Philadelphia in time to win immortality as a signer of the **Declaration of Independence**. The park near the cemetery is dedicated to Ellery.

Samuel Ward's granddaughter, **Julia Ward Howe,** a Newport summer resident, is most famous for her anti-slavery work. But she was also a leader in the world peace movement. In 1871 she proposed an International Women's Peace Congress. She wrote "Why do not the mothers of mankind interfere in these matters to prevent the waste of that human life of which they alone bear and know the cost." **Institution of Mother's Day** as a national holiday ensued from her efforts.

The PSNC maintains several distinguished Colonial houses in Newport, including the **Hunter House at 54 Washington**, which French Admiral de Ternay chose as his headquarters. Call **(401) 847-1000** for open hours and fee information. At **17 Broadway, the Wanton-Lyman house,** built around 1690, and subsequently enlarged by a series of prominent residents, is maintained by the **Historical Society,** which conducts educational programs on its grounds. Call **(401) 846-0813.**

Obviously I have mentioned only a few of Newport's 400 surviving Colonial houses, but enough I hope to get you walking about and peering at the plaques which you will see nearly everywhere. Steinberg and McGuigan's *RHODE ISLAND* has much more information on Newport's Colonial Houses.

Hunter
House

The Harbor

South of the Gateway Center, on the west side of America's Cup Ave and Thames St., the **Harbor teems with tourist temptations**, shops, galleries, restaurants, and bars. This was the heart of the busy seaport of Colonial days, when Newport had 900 residences and an astonishing 400 warehouses and 22 rum distilleries. In the pre-Revolutionary ferment, Newporters aroused the wrath of His Majesty's customs officers by refusing to provision his revenue schooners sent to patrol the Bay during the crackdown on molasses smuggling. But today Newport merchants are eager to provide the necessities, and more, for the many foreign cruise ships visiting the Harbor, including those of Her Majesty, Elizabeth II. Especially busy is the area between **Bannister's and Bowen's Wharves**. Here, amid the galleries and eateries, the visitor is also offered a number of sea adventures, including guided tours of the Harbor and Narragansett Bay aboard motor vessels and sight-sailing ships, fishing expeditions, whale watches, and sailing lessons. Signs here and further south on Thames advertise boat charters and sailing schools.

South of Bannister's and Bowen's is Sayer's Wharf, from which the **Old Port Marine Company** offers **from about mid-May to mid-October passenger boat service to Fort Adams Park** (see below), which is three miles away by land but only one by sea. During weekdays, the service is hourly from 8 A.M. until 10 P.M. and on weekends there is service until 1 A.M. Call **(401) 847-9109** for more information. This service allows you to attend the many events, concerts, etc. held at the Park, and allows you to catch (in summer) the ferry to **Block Island** (of which we write more in Vol. 2), which starts at 9 A.M. from Providence and docks at about 11 A.M. at Fort Adams Park to pick up more passengers. Old Port Marine also offers tours of the Harbor and Bay aboard the *Motor Vessel Amazing Grace.*

The Newport Mansions

About 3/4 miles east of Colonial Newport, strung out along Bellevue Ave., are several magnificent estates, in the style of European palaces and castles. The fabulously wealthy spent enormous sums at the turn of the century trying to outdo each other in the conspicuous construction of these summer homes. Not even in Europe will you find so many elegant castles in so small a region. The furthest is only about 3 miles from the center of town, and most are closer. **How should you get to them? Walking is the best way. And the best way to walk to the more distant ones is via the beautiful Cliff Walk** (see page 191 and map on page 190), which passes by their back yards. Or if you prefer, the RIPTA loop bus can assist you.

Several of these mansions have been restored to their original elegance and **are open to the public from spring until fall** thanks to the efforts of the **Preservation Society of Newport County.   Call (401) 847-1000** for information on fees and schedules, or write to the **PSNC, 118 Mill St., Newport 02840** for their brochure on the mansions. In July, the mansions form exquisite back drops for the concerts of the **Newport Music Festival,** which features a galaxy of international stars performing a range of music and dance from classical to modern. For more information **write to Newport Music Festival, POB 3300, Newport, R.I. 02840-0992.**

Brief Descriptions of PSNC Mansions (in order of their appearance along Bellevue as you walk south from the Redwood Library). **Kingscote** (built in 1839), the oldest and the smallest, on the west side of Bellevue, is a Victorian "cottage" designed by **Richard Upjohn**, architect of New York's **Trinity Church**, for George Jones of Savannah, Georgia. **The Elms** (built in 1901), on the west side of Bellevue, the estate of coal magnate E.J. Berwind, designed by **Horace Trumbauer** after the 18th century Chateau d' Asnieres near Paris, has lovely gardens with labeled trees. **Chateau-sur-Mer** (built in 1852), on the east side of Bellevue, is a lavish palace designed for China Trade merchant William Wetmore by **Richard Morris Hunt**. A special feature is a children's toy museum. **The Breakers** (built in 1895), a magnificent colossus on

Marble
House

Newport Cliff Walk and Mansion Map

Key

- ∿∿∿ Water Symbol
- - - - Cliff Walk Path
- 1 Kingscote
- 2 The Elms
- 3 Salve Regina University
- 4 Chateau sur Mer
- 5 The Breakers
- 6 Rosecliff
- 7 The Marble House

Ochre Point (walk east along Ruggles from Bellevue to it), designed for Cornelius Vanderbilt by **Richard Morris Hunt** after the style of a 16th century Italian palazzo, features a children's playhouse. **Rosecliff** (built in 1902), on the east side of Bellevue, was designed for Mrs. Hermann Oerlich by **Stanford White** after the Grand Trianon at Versailles. It served as the backdrop for the movie, *THE GREAT GATSBY*, based on Scott Fitzgerald's novel. **The Marble House** (built in 1892), on the east side of Bellevue, designed for William Vanderbilt by **Richard Morris Hunt**, is the most sumptuous of the palaces, with a gorgeous interior in marble of many colors. All the original furnishings are intact.

The Cliff Walk

The Cliff Walk is exquisite. As you walk along it, the grounds of the great estates are on one side, and on the other, the surf explodes against the rocks 100 feet beneath you, and you have a continuum of gorgeous views, and the fragrance of wild roses. **If you have time for just one thing, this is it.** You will want to come back again and again in every season of the year. The walk begins at the Cliff Walk Manor on Memorial Drive at the western end of the **Newport Municipal Beach**, about one mile from Washington Square, and continues for about 3 miles to Bailey's Beach. At several points, the walk intersects city streets leading to Bellevue Ave., so you can detour to visit the mansions whose entrances are on Bellevue. At Narragansett Ave., you encounter the **Forty Steps** descending to the sea on one side and ascending to the street on the other. Nearby spreads the beautiful campus of **Salve Regina University.** At Ochre Point, is the **Breakers Mansion**. And, if you walk along Ruggles to Bellevue and turn left, you soon come to **Rosecliff** and the **Marble House. This wonderful walk is the gift of the City of Newport to you.** At various times, the owners of the great estates tried to block the path. Fortunately, the courts upheld the right of the public to access to the sea. Also fortunate are the recent projects, sponsored by the National Park Service, the State, and City, restoring portions of the bank that had begun to erode. Be prepared to retreat should the path appear dangerous.

Cliff Walk

Beaches and Parks

Newport Municipal Beach. This beautiful beach on Memorial Drive stretches for 3/4 of a mile beside the Causeway between Newport and Middletown. You see it from the Cliff Walk. The best way of getting there is by walking. It is about one mile from Washington Square, and the walk is pleasant with sidewalks all the way. You can also take a RIPTA bus which passes it on the way to Middletown. During the season, from Memorial to Labor Day, services include a concession stand serving wine as well as soft drinks, lifeguards from 9 to 6, rentals of surfboards and other beach equipment, an amusement park, rest rooms and a bath house (fee). Coming as you do car-free, you won't have to worry about the parking situation. (See map on p. 177.)

King's Park. This Park on Wellington Ave. about a mile from Washington Sq. has a small beach and terrific harbor views. Just walk south along Thames St. and turn right when you get to Wellington. (See maps on pages 177, 178.) The RIPTA local bus can be used to give you an assist. In season it is furnished with benches and picnic tables, lifeguards and free bath houses, and a snack bar across the street. Of course, you can also pick up some wonderful food along the way on Thames St. A statue of Rochambeau reminds you that this was where the French landed in July 1780.

Gooseberry Beach. This beautiful beach shares a cove with Hazard Beach, also beautiful but not open to the public. It's off Ocean Drive. To get to it take the RIPTA bus to the corner of Caroll and Ruggles, and then walk south along Caroll to it (about 1/2 mile from Ruggles). (See map on p.177.) There are rest rooms (fee) and a small concession stand. Sand dunes and wild roses and tiny **Gooseberry Island** just opposite make this an exquisite little beach. Coming as you do car-free, you need not worry that the parking lot is reserved for Newport residents.

Fort Adams State Park. In season, you can take the passenger boat from Old Port Marine (see page 188) on Sayer's Wharf (call **(401) 847-9109**) **to this terrific Park,** sprawling on 23 acres, with benches, picnic tables, beaches attended by lifeguards, restrooms, and concession building. (See map on p. 177.) Dominating the grounds are heavy granite barracks and gun emplacements, survivors of an ancient fort, built in 1799. The former mule stables serve as changing rooms for bathers. Pleasant seaside walkways offer superb views of Jamestown and Newport Harbor. The **Museum of Yachting** is housed in a brick building on the waterfront. The outdoor theatre at the northernmost point of the Park hosts rock and jazz concerts. The **Block**

Island Ferry stops at Fort Adams Park at about 11 A.M., from mid-June to Labor Day, on its way from Providence to Block Island (about which we write more in Vol. 2).

Hammersmith Farm. Almost next door to Fort Adams Park is a real farm with cows, plowed fields, and meadows. This lovely seaside estate also has a 28 room "cottage" and Olmsted-designed gardens. The property once belonged to the Auchincloss family, **in-laws of President John F. Kennedy**, who used it as his summer White House. Open May to October, 10-5, fee.

Food in Newport

There's plenty of good food in Newport in all price ranges, in food stores, sandwich shops, restaurants, wharfside cafes, ice cream parlors, delicatessens, taverns, everywhere. Just look at the menus in the windows, and choose your price range. The Mall near the Brick Market has ice cream parlors and delicatessens. **Yesterday's** on Washington Sq. has live music in the evenings and moderate to expensive food. Good salads. **In the Bannister and Bowen Wharf area, The Black Pearl's** outdoor cafe is very popular for chowders at lunch and drinks in the evening; the **Cooke House** is praised for its continental cuisine, moderate to expensive; and the **Bistro** also gets much acclaim for its French cuisine. **Christie's** at Hammet's Wharf is very popular, too, with excellent luncheon specials. The historic **White Horse Tavern**, at the corner of Farewell and Marlborough has a reputation for delicious food and elegant service, expensive. Further south on Marlborough, the **Mudville Pub** serves good food at moderate prices. At 103 Bellevue, opposite the Art Museum, **Griswold's Pub**, offers pleasant open air service and Mexican-American food at moderate prices. **Muriel's** at the corner of Spring and Touro, near the movies, offers delicious Italian food at moderate prices. Also popular for Italian cuisine, are **Salas'** an old favorite, on Thames, near Memorial Blvd (inexpensive), and **Puerini's** at 24 Memorial Blvd, just west of Bellevue (moderate). After walking along the Cliff Walk, I enjoyed eating at the **Cliff Walk Manor Restaurant**, at 117 Memorial Blvd, at the Walk's entrance. The food and service were pleasant, and the view was superb. Moderate to expensive.

Lodgings in Newport

Newport is chock full of lodgings, from hotels to bed and breakfast inns, in all price ranges. At the end of the chapter, I shall give more clues.

FORTY
STEPS
CLIFF
WALK

AROUND NARRAGANSETT BAY WITH RIPTA

Roughly speaking, Providence, Newport, and the **University of Rhode Island campus in Kingston (URI)** form a triangle joined by **RIPTA routes which encircle Narragansett Bay.** See the map on page 195. We have already described Providence and Newport. We begin this section by describing the URI campus briefly, and then go on to some of the highlights of the routes joining the **URI to Galilee** (see below) **and Newport.** And then finally, **we shall take a RIPTA bus from Newport to Providence.** For RIPTA information call **(401) 781-9400, or toll free (800) 662-5088,** or if you are hearing impaired, **(TDD) 461-9400.** A fine map of the RIPTA system can be obtained at the RIPTA Information Booth in Kennedy Plaza, or you can ask to have one mailed to you when you call RIPTA information.

The URI Campus in Kingston

The URI's main campus spreads over 1200 acres in Kingston. It was founded by the State in 1892 as an agricultural college, but is now a multiversity with departments in the arts, sciences, engineering, nursing, and pharmacy, offering

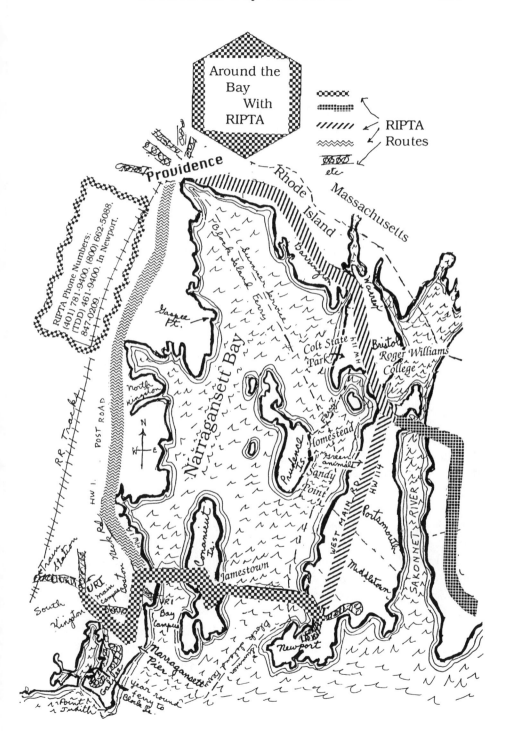

Around the
Bay
With
RIPTA

RIPTA
Routes

etc

Providence

Rhode Island

Massachusetts

RIPTA Phone Numbers:
(401) 781-9400. (800) 662-5088.
(TDD) 461-9400. In Newport.
847-0209.

Gaspee
Pt.

Warren

Barrington

Colt State
Park

Bristol
Roger Williams
College

Narragansett Bay

North
Kingston

Homestead

Green
animals

Sandy
Point

Prudence

Portsmouth

RR. Tracks

POST ROAD

HW 1

main campus

Conanicut
Is.

Jamestown

Middletown

WEST MAIN RD

HW 114

SAKONNET RIVER

Train
Station

URI

South
Kingston

URI
Bay
Campus

Narragansett
Pier

year
round
ferry to
Block Is.

Newport

Point
Judith

general education and career training to about 11,000 undergraduate and graduate students. The campus sits in an attractive rural area, home to some of Rhode Island's few remaining working farms.

RIPTA buses from Providence (no. 66) and Newport (no. 64 or 69) take you directly to the **Memorial Union Building, the center of student activity and also the Waiting Station for the RIPTA buses to Galilee** (see page 197). It is also possible to take an AMTRAK train from Boston or Providence to the Kingston train station, about one and one half miles west of the campus. You can walk to the campus, or take a RIPTA bus, or a taxi.

The campus climbs up and down hills covered with shaded walks and orchards of flowering trees and shrubs. Most striking are the older buildings constructed of the area's beautiful granite, gray warmed with rose and topaz tints. The **Memorial Union is an ideal place to wait for a bus.** It has restrooms, a bookstore and other shops, and cafeterias leading out to inviting open-air decks, with tables and chairs. At the Information Desk, you can get a map of the campus and also pick up a copy of the student newspaper, *THE GOOD FIVE-CENT CIGAR (just what the country needs).* **The RIPTA bus schedules are posted outside where the bus stops.** For information on the campus' many cultural events, including art exhibits, concerts, theatre productions, films, and lectures, call **(401) 792-2056.** Some special places are: the **Fine Arts Center,** housing galleries and a theatre; the **botanical garden** with nearby greenhouses; the **Watson House,** a late 18th century farmhouse run as a museum with period furnishings; the **geological collections in Green Hall;** collections of **textiles and costumes in Quinn House.**

Near the Campus on Kingston Rd. (SR 108) is a notable assembly of Colonial and Federalist buildings. I mention a few. **The South County Art Center** at 1319 Kingston Rd. was once the Helme House built in 1760. At 1309 is the **Caleb Wescott Tavern,** built in 1774. Nearby on Potter Lane, the **Elisha Potter** farm house was built in 1809. At 1313 Kingston Rd. is the **School House,** built in 1759. The **Kingston Inn** at 1320 was built in 1755 and run by the Potter family. The **Kingston Free Library** at 1329 was built in 1775 as the County Courthouse. For more information on these and other Kingston historical sites, see Steinberg and McGuigan's *RHODE ISLAND.*

West of the Campus, roads lead from Kingston Rd. into the **Great Swamp Natural Area,** in which the **Audubon Society** maintains a series of nature trails. (If you walk from the train station to the Campus, you will pass these entrance roads.) In 1675, the

Great Swamp was the scene of a battle of **King Phillip's War**, which was to spread throughout New England, the last anguished uprising of the coastal Indians, who perceived how little land remained to them. The battle was not fought by Rhode Islanders, who had difficulty in organizing themselves for such an undertaking, but by Massachusetts and Connecticut forces. **At this time, Providence was burned to the ground and its settlers fled to Newport.** The outbreak of the war was the greatest sorrow to Roger Williams, who had hoped to maintain the best relations with the Indians. He unfortunately had no control over the actions of other settlers. The war was an explosion over an accumulation of grievances and misunderstandings. **At the western edge of the Campus, beyond the athletic fields, is the URI Youth Hostel,** of which we say more under *Lodgings.*

Taking RIPTA From the URI to Galilee

Galilee, the year-round port of departure for **Block Island** (see Vol. 2), is a small fishing village with a very busy harbor. **There are several RIPTA buses a day from the URI which bring you right to the ferry dock.** Catching and processing fish is obviously Galilee's main business. But in recent years several tourist enterprises have sprouted here. The Harbor is crowded with "head" fishing boats on which for a fee you can go out on a day's, or half-day's, fishing expedition. The **Tuna Tournament** is an annual event. Near the docks are food take-outs, a grocery store, and restaurants with a harbor view. A short walk from the dock through the Village brings you to a white sanded beach, with life guards and concession stand in season. The beach extends for miles, southward to the **Point Judith Light** (about 2 miles away), and northward to **Scarboro Beach**. It is a lovely place for a walk beside the waves in any season.

About a fifteen minute walk from the dock (my companion and I hiked through the tidal marshes to it to avoid the road) is the **Fisherman's Memorial Park Campground.** (In the warm weather, have mosquito repellent or netting along.) **An entrance to the Park is on the Point Judith Road, along the bus route from URI,** and so you can get to it directly from the bus. On the way back to URI from Galilee, the bus goes along Ocean Drive past the beautiful and very popular **Scarboro Beach**. RIPTA buses will stop just about anywhere on their route so you will have no trouble getting off to explore.

Opposite the dock in Galilee is a State Department of Environmental Management Office, where you can get literature including a recreational map showing public beaches, trails, and natural areas.

Highlights on the RIPTA Route from the URI to Newport

The RIPTA route from the URI to Newport has everything. You go past farms in Kingston, then to the shore and past the beaches of Narragansett Pier, and then over the bridge to Conanicut Island with its sheep pastures and pretty marinas, and then you get spectacular views of the Bay as you cross the bridge to Newport. And all the while you are in a very sociable company of students and retirees and jostling school children. This wonderful service is approximately hourly on weekdays.

Starting from the URI, here are some highlights. As the bus goes along Kingston Road (SR 108) to the shore, it passes the **Museum of Primitive Culture** (ask the driver where to get off)* with artifacts of primitive cultures from around the world. **Call (401) 783-5711** for information on open hours and fee. The bus reaches the shore at **Narragansett Pier,** at the intersection of the Kingston and Boston Neck Roads. **This is one of the State's most popular beaches** with concession stands, lifeguards, bath houses, and surf board rentals in season. **The intriguing fieldstone towers joined by an archway spanning Ocean Drive** are relics of Narragansett Pier's former glory when trainloads of wealthy New Yorkers came to stay at great Victorian hotels overlooking the sea. The towers were part of the **Towers Casino Entertainment Hall**, built in 1884 by McKim, Mead, and White. They now house the **Narragansett Chamber of Commerce**, and you can drop in for maps and literature. Most of the old hotels were destroyed in a "renewal" project. The **Town Hall** is a few blocks west of the Beach. The name Narragansett Pier is itself a relic of the days when ocean going liners could dock at a long pier extending outward from the shore. **The RIPTA bus stop is across the street from the Beach.** There is also direct RIPTA service to Narragansett Pier from Providence (bus 14).

*On my last visit, I discovered that **not all** buses between Newport and URI take this scenic route by the Museum of Primitive Culture, and along the shore by Narragansett Pier Beach. Some go directly from the URI Bay Campus (see next page) along SR 138 to the main URI campus.

From Narragansett Pier, the bus heads northward along the Boston Neck Road. The Narragansett Bay Campus of the URI is on South Ferry Road, which intersects the Boston Neck Road about 4 miles north of Narragansett Pier. The bus route loops through the 165 acre shoreside campus. It is the headquarters of the URI Graduate School of Oceanography, the Marine Advisory Service, and the University's ocean-going research vessel, the Endeavor. The campus also houses several Federal marine laboratories and the State's atomic research reactor.

On Boston Neck Road, less than a mile north of South Ferry, is the Silas Casey Farm, open about three days a week from June to October. Fee. Call (401) 227-3956. This farm was the 18th century plantation of a prosperous shipowner and gentleman farmer, and is still a working farm today. Exhibits on the farm present a vivid picture of the life of the landed gentry in 18th century Rhode Island. But it should be explained that Rhode Island's South County farms were not typical of the rest of New England, where the overwhelming majority of farms were run by individual families with few hired hands. Here in Rhode Island's rich southlands, sad to say, slave-run farms were frequent.

Less than a mile north of the Casey Farm, Snuff Mill Road runs westward from the Boston Neck Road. The name refers to the snuff mill operated by Scottish immigrant John Stuart, the first in New England. Stuart's son, Gilbert, the widely acclaimed portrait painter, was born in 1756 in the simple house by the mill, now a National Historic Landmark. The Stuart house and mill is about one mile west of the bus route.

A little north of Snuff Mill Road, the bus turns eastward to cross over the Jamestown bridge to Conanicut Island. This elongated island, about 6 miles north to south, and one mile east to west, is no longer an island as auto traffic pours through it, crossing the Bay on two bridges which have replaced the ferries that ran up until the 1960's. Yet a rural air still lingers. There are sheep pastures, nature preserves, and charming villages. The bus route between Jamestown Bridge on the west and Newport Bridge on the east zig-zags so as to pass through the most populated sectors of Jamestown. It heads east along Eldred, then south along the North Road, on which it passes an old windmill and the Quaker Meeting House, and the Marshmeadows Nature Preserve; then it turns eastward on Narragansett Ave., Jamestown's main street, and goes to Jamestown Harbor before heading northward along the rim of the Harbor to Newport Bridge. The park overlooking the sail-filled harbor, facing Newport, is a good place to get off the bus to undertake an exploration of Jamestown. Across the street are hotels and restaurants in the Victorian seaside style. **Berthed at the south side of the Harbor is a former ferry boat,** now converted to a restaurant and inn. When I was there some years ago, a hardware store near the Harbor rented bicycles in season. **As long as you stay off the roads linking the two bridges, bicycling about Conanicut Island should be fun.** Also on Narragansett Ave. is the **Jamestown Museum,** open mid-June to September, fee. The historical exhibits include one on the old ferry system formerly connecting Jamestown to the mainland. Everyone that I spoke to, without exception, expressed regret on the passing of the ferries. (One of these will be encountered in Volume 2 in the shape of a harborside restaurant in Portland, Maine.)

The bus crosses Newport Bridge (on which pedestrians are not allowed) and takes you on a tour of Newport's charming northern neighborhoods, before bringing you to the Gateway terminal on America's Cup Ave., where the last of the jovial party of passengers -- retirees, students, artists -- disperses.

From Newport to Providence by RIPTA
Now let's go to Providence from Newport. RIPTA provides approximately hourly service. Once you get out of the carpark desert north of Newport, this route is a good indicator of Rhode Island's close-together charm. You glimpse lovely small farm estates overlooking the Bay and country villages with tree-shaded main streets a block or two from marinas on the water. The bus goes along SR 114, which is called the **West Main Road** in Middletown and Portsmouth, and becomes **Hope St.** in Bristol. Below we give some highlights.

On the Prescott Farm, at 2009 West Main Rd., near the Middletown-Portsmouth border, is an assembly of Colonial buildings brought here from other sites by the PSNC, including **an operating windmill** that grinds cornmeal sold at the adjacent **Country Store** (originally the Earle-Hicks House built in 1715), and the **Prescott Guardhouse,** used as a guardhouse during the British occupation of Newport, and now run as a museum of early settler furnishings. **Call (401) 847-6230 or (401) 847-2071 for information on fee and open hours.** The land once belonged to Henry Overing, a Loyalist. **British General Richard Prescott** was accustomed to make nocturnal trysts in Overing's house. One night in July, 1777, he was surprised and kidnapped and rowed to Providence by a group of American soldiers under Colonel William Barton, who had been informed of the General's habits. This feat did not affect the balance of power. Newport remained secure in British hands. But it helped boost morale in Providence, where Barton was awarded a bonus by the General Assembly.

As for Prescott, he apparently didn't suffer much during his captivity. A few days after the event, some British soldiers under a flag of truce brought him his purse, wardrobe, wigs, hair powder, and perfumes. (My source here was Richman's *RHODE ISLAND.*)

The **Green Animals**, on Corey Lane, which runs off to the west from SR 114, is a famous **topiary display of animals sculptured from trees and shrubs**, started by Thomas Brayton around 1880. The grounds include formal flower beds, fruit and vegetable gardens, a gift shop, and a **children's Victorian Toy Museum**. Open from May to September. Fee. **It is run by the PSNC** and you can get combination tickets for this and other PSNC sites. **Call (401) 847-1000.**

About one mile north of Corey Lane, at the junction of SR 24 and SR 114, are a flagpole and plaque commemorating the gallant role of **the First Rhode Island Regiment in the Battle of Rhode Island in August 1778.** The soldiers of the First Regiment were blacks who had been promised their freedom if they would enlist in the Continental Army. This particular campaign had been begun in hopes of wresting Newport from the British. **It was to be a great historic occasion**, the first collaboration of the Americans and French. Earlier in the year, upon hearing of the French Alliance, Washington had declared a day of rejoicing for the "glorious news". Now the Alliance was to bear its first fruits. The grand plan was that the French under Admiral D' Estaing would give battle to the British Navy at Newport while American land troops under General Sullivan would take the town. Unfortunately, the campaign was a fiasco because D' Estaing withdrew at a crucial juncture to repair his ships in Boston, leaving the Americans without sea support. They retreated to Providence, with the First Regiment valiantly guarding the Army's rear from the onslaught of the Hessians.

A footnote to the affair is that John Brown, annoyed that his privateers still had to run past the British batteries at Newport, wrote a scolding letter to General Nathaniel Greene, in which he declared his disgust with the Sullivan-D' Estaing expedition. Greene angrily replied that "those that have been at home making their fortune and living in the lap of luxury" should be ashamed to make "sport of officers who have stood between them and ruin."

You get terrific views as the bus continues northward over the **Mount Hope Bridge** and into **Bristol**. On the right you catch sight of a sign announcing **Roger Williams College** and on the left, by the shore of the Bay, is **Colt State Park**, with lovely paths and seaside horseback riding. Hope St. in Bristol is lovely with many

Colonial and Federal buildings. In the 18th century, Bristol was Newport's rival as the Colony's slave-trade center. Like John Brown, members of Bristol's wealthy **De Wolfe family** continued in the slave trade after it was banned. The **Linden Mansion** on Hope and Wardwell Streets, built in 1810 for the De Wolfe family, is the town's main showpiece. Open during the warm months. Call **(401) 253-0390** for hours and fees.

Bristol's Church St., which crosses Hope, leads to the dock for the Prudence Island ferry, which runs year-round. If you take the 10 AM ferry in the morning, you will have time for a few hours walk exploring the Island before coming back on the afternoon ferry. **Call (401) 245-7411** for schedule information. On Prudence Island, the ferry stops at **Homestead** and at **Sandy Point**, where there is a light house, and also the **Prudence Island Inn.** The Island is pleasantly rural. About three miles north of Homestead, at the northern tip of the Island, is the **North Prudence State Wildlife Management Area. At the southern tip of the Island**, about three miles from Sandy Point, is the **new 640 acre South Prudence Bay Island Park**. After it was abandoned by the Navy, thanks to a swell of citizen opposition, the area escaped development by the Federal Government as a liquid gas terminal.

A little out of town, bus passes the **Blithewold Estate**, with 33 acres of landscaped gardens overlooking the Bay, once the summer home of coal magnate Augustus Van Wickle, a Brown University graduate and benefactor. The mansion and grounds are open to the public during the warm months. Call **(401) 253-2707** for open hours and fees.

After Bristol, the bus makes its way through **Barrington's main street** past its **very handsome Town Hall**. And soon after going through a highway melange, you are in Providence proceeding past the cafes on South and North Main to Kennedy Plaza.

Along the bus route through Bristol and Barrington, you will catch sight of an enclosed sea-side bicycle path which crosses the road at several points. Cyclists are hoping that eventually the path will be extended to Providence and Newport.

LODGING IN RHODE ISLAND

Almost all of the following are taken from the **Rhode Island Visitors Guide**. See page 149 for the directions on how to get it. The prices, which I got by phone inquiries, are only to give you a rough idea. Prices vary with season, furnishings, services, etc.

In Providence

Biltmore Hotel, Kennedy Plaza, (401) 0700. An ideal location: near the financial district; a few blocks from College Hill; and near all RIPTA buses. Doubles run from $99 on week ends (including breakfast for two) and $114 on week days (no breakfast).

Old Court, Bed and Breakfast, 144 Benefit St., (401) 751-2002. Another terrific location, right in the midst of The Mile of History Trail on College Hill, and, because Central Providence is so compact, a short walk to the Business District and Kennedy Plaza. Doubles run from $115 (week day) to $135 (week end) from March to October and about $15 less in off season.

In Newport

Hotel Viking, One Bellevue, (401) 847-3300. This is the grand dame of Newport hotels. It was built by the owners of the mansions to house the overflow of their summer guests. The location is the best possible, a walk of a few blocks from: the Harbor; the Brick Market; the Gateway Center; the Touro Synagogue; Trinity Church; Touro Park; the Redwood Library. The Old Jewish Cemetery is a hundred feet away. And the nearest mansion, the Elms, is about 1/2 mile away, and a pleasant walk of a mile will bring you to the entrance to the Cliff Walk and the Municipal Beach. The interior is charming. Doubles run from $139 in season; after Labor Day the rates go down to $99 per double; and by October they go down to $79 with two buffet breakfasts included. In winter the rates for a double go down still further. (But then many attractions are closed.)

The Cliff Walk Manor, 82 Memorial Blvd, (401) 847-1300. Open only from March to December. A beautiful cliff-side location at the entrance to the Cliff Walk and

overlooking the Municipal Beach. A pleasant walk of about a mile to Colonial Newport. Doubles run from $110 (no view, week day in September) to $185 (a room with a view on a summer weekend).

The Guide lists numerous bed and breakfast accommodations in Newport. I give just two below, both near the Viking Hotel.

Yankee Peddler Inn, 113 Touro St., (401) 846-1323. Doubles begin at $75 in September and are higher in summer.

Hydrangea House Inn, 16 Bellevue, (401) 846-4435. Doubles begin at $90 from May to October but range from $55 up in the off season.

On RIPTA Around the Bay Routes

Dutch Inn by the Sea, Great Island Road, Galilee, (401) 789-9341. This Inn has a strategic location near the RIPTA bus stop, the beach, and the dock for the ferry to Block Island. Rates are $75 for a double week days and $95 for a double week ends.

URI Youth Hostel, at the edge of the URI Campus (see pages 194-197), (401) 789-3929. Dormitory arrangements, but for under $20 a person you can use the URI, which is the terminal of RIPTA routes to Providence, Newport, and the Galilee dock of the ferry for Block Island, as your base to explore RI by public transportation.

Fisherman Memorial Park Campground. As pointed out on page 197, the RIPTA bus going along the Point Judith Rd. between Galilee and the URI Kingston Campus passes by the entrance to this Campground. With a light tent and plenty of mosquito repellent, you can camp here, and use this as your base to explore: Block Island; the beaches near Galilee; the URI; and Newport.

CHAPTER 5
TO PORTSMOUTH, NH CAR-FREE

Athenaeum in Market Sq.

In which we daytrip to Portsmouth, NH car-free traveling by Greyhound Bus from Boston's South Station and disembarking in historic Market Square, where we are close to Everything.

PORTSMOUTH, NH CAR-FREE
RAMBLES ABOUT STRAWBERY BANKE

Some Attractions Near Market Square, and Longer Walks from Market Square

INTRODUCTION

New Hampshire has only 18 miles of sea shore, but it was along the coast that its first English settlements were planted in the 1620's. **Of these, the most important was the one on the Piscataqua River called Strawbery Banke** by its first settlers because of the profusion of the delicious fruit that greeted them as they scrambled ashore after their long ocean crossing. Later, in 1653, the townsfolk decided that the name was too frivolous, and petitioned the Massachusetts General Court to change it to Portsmouth. **Portsmouth became the chief town of the New Hampshire Colony and seat of its government, home of the Royal Governors, and meeting place of the popularly elected Assembly.** As capital of one of the original thirteen Colonies, Portsmouth had at the time of the Revolution a larger influence on the course of the Nation than it would ever have again.

Today's charming sea town, population 25,000. whose major employer is a U.S. Navy Yard located on one of the many River islands, **preserves a remarkable amount of its Colonial past,** the palaces of the crown-appointed Governors and the homes of the Patriots who drove the last of them into exile. Its historical sites and museums, lovely riverside parks, lively marketplaces, boat cruises, Theatre by the Sea, and excellent restaurants make Portsmouth a delightful place for many visits.

Information. Many have written lovingly of Portsmouth. Three of the best older guides are: C.S. Gurney's *PORTSMOUTH, HISTORIC AND PICTURESQUE*, published about 1900, containing many photos as well as an informative text; *RAMBLES ABOUT PORTSMOUTH*, by C.W. Brewster, alias *THE RAMBLER*, dating from 1869, and full of historic anecdote; *AN OLD TOWN BY THE SEA*, written in the 1890's by Thomas Bailey Aldrich, who also wrote *THE STORY OF A BAD BOY*, once a children's favorite, based upon his boyhood in Portsmouth. These books are apt to be in New England public libraries, but probably not in bookstores. For more up-to-date information on today's attractions and services, you can write ahead to the **Greater Portsmouth Chamber of Commerce, 500 Market St., Portsmouth, NH 03801 or call (603) 436-PORT.**

Getting There from Boston. Not so long ago, there were several buses a day from Boston taking you directly to **Portsmouth's Market Square, the center of everything**. Now alas, there are just a few going to Market Square, although many taking you to the Pease International Terminal, miles away from the center of town, from which you would have to take a taxi to Market Square. **Greyhound Bus Line (call (617) 526-1810 or (800) 231-2222) offers a few trips a day to Market Square from its Boston terminal in South Station** (on the T Red Line). Of these, probably the one leaving at 12 noon, and arriving in Market Square at 1.30 gives you the most convenient possibility for a day trip to Portsmouth. The latest return Greyhound bus from Market Square to Boston is 6 PM. The timing does allow for a pleasant visit, in which you can visit some of the historical sites. For a longer trip, the **C and J Trailways, call (800) 258-7111,** offers about 16 trips daily from the South Station Bus Terminal, **but these are regrettably to the Pease Terminal.** Going to Portsmouth by Greyhound from Portland (see Vol. 2) allows a longer daytrip, to and from Market Square, so I include some of the longer walks. **One of my hopes is that by raising a Car-Free consciousness, we can reverse the deplorable trend to moving bus terminals out to the highway** and **preserve the elegance of in-town arrivals.**

North Church in Market Square

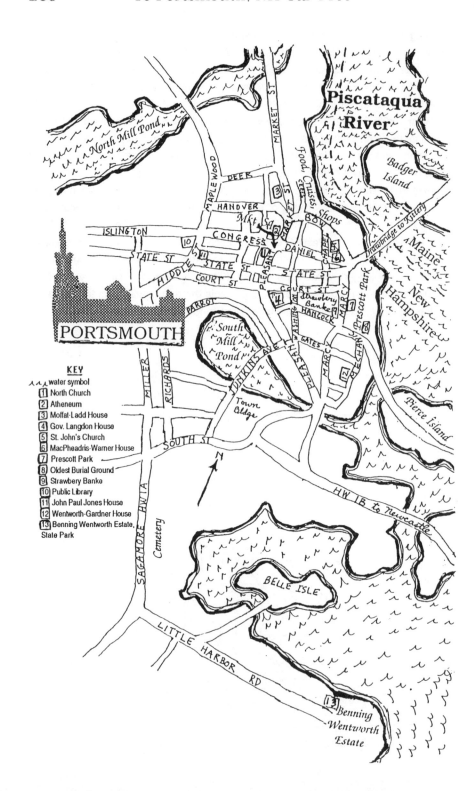

HISTORY NEAR MARKET SQUARE

The Greyhound bus swings off the highway onto Market St., past docks, salt piles, brick warehouses, Colonial mansions, and comes to a stop in brick-paved **Market Square,** opposite the **North Church,** the town's center near everything -- shops, historic sites, and the swiftly flowing Piscataqua with its profusion of islets and bridges. **Portsmouth presents a banquet for history buffs.** All the following are within a few blocks of Market Square. Later we shall take walks to more distant sites.

Let's start with the **North Church in Market Square**, built in 1854, for a congregation organized in the 1600's. It is a symbol of the Puritan heritage and the Congregational Way, which were dominant in New Hampshire at the time of the Revolution, when Congregational Churches were reckoned as centers of sedition by the Royalist rulers of the Colony. This church was no exception. A plaque announces that two **of its parishioners, John Langdon and William Whipple, were signers of the Declaration of Independence**. We shall say more about them when we visit their homes. The ministers of this church were also noted for their fiery defense of the people's rights versus the power of the Crown. **Reverend Samuel Langdon**, who preached here from 1747 until 1774, when he left to become **President of Harvard,** was chosen to head the College, it is said, less for his scholarship than for his patriotic zeal. It was he who led the Army's prayers on Cambridge Common on the night before the Battle of Bunker Hill. **And it was he who greeted Washington on behalf of the College when the Virginian arrived in Cambridge to take command of the Continental Army.** One of Langdon's successors was **Ezra Stiles** (whom we met in Newport), who preached here after fleeing from Newport.

If you go south from Market Square along Pleasant St., you come at No. 143 to the magnificent **Governor Langdon House**, built in 1784, one of Portsmouth's showpieces, **declared to be the City's finest by George Washington** upon his visit in 1787. Managed by the SPNEA (see page 36). Open from June 1 to October 15. **Call (603) 436-3205** for open hours and fees.

John Langdon rose from clerk and cabin boy and other lowly jobs to make his fortune in the sea trade. **An ardent Patriot, he was elected to the Continental Congress,** and, as already mentioned, **was a signer of the Declaration of Independence**. After the War, **he was a framer of the U.S. Constitution, U.S. Senator, and five times Governor of the State.** In 1777, during the darkest time of the War, at a meeting of the New Hampshire Assembly in Exeter, he pledged his personal fortune to equip General Stark's troops for the crucial Battle of Bennington, the prelude to British General Burgoyne's defeat at Saratoga. We note that the New Hampshire

Patriots had at this time moved their government to Exeter because of their fear of the strong Royalist faction in Portsmouth.

In the Continental Congress, Langdon worked on the Navy Committee, and it was undoubtedly due to his suggestion that Portsmouth received the commission to build several ships for the embryo Navy, including the *RANGER,* which was commanded by **John Paul Jones** (see page 214). **Snug beyond the many Piscataqua islands, the Portsmouth shipyards were never attacked by the British Navy.**

Across the street and a little south from the Governor Langdon House is the lovely **Haven Park** with a view of the **South Mill Pond**, a gift of the family of the **Reverend Samuel Haven**, another of Portsmouth's patriotic Congregational ministers. Haven preached at the South Church, now Unitarian. A sign in the Park tells you that, during the War, Haven supervised the manufacture of saltpetre (potassium nitrate - KNO_3) to supply the Continental Army's need for gunpowder. Of course, no one in those days knew the chemical formula of saltpetre, but Haven, a Harvard graduate, was able to find a usable recipe in one of his natural science books. He boiled manure rich soil in water (which gave the necessary nitrate, NO_3) and passed the resulting solution through fireplace ash (for potassium, K), and, Lo and Behold, it worked.

So far we have mentioned only the Patriot side of Portsmouth, which was numerically dominant. **Now about its powerful Royalist faction.** If you continue south on Pleasant St. from Haven Park, you come at the corner of Washington to No. 346, **the Governor John Wentworth House**, built in 1769, now part of the Mark Hunking Wentworth Home for the Chronically Invalid (not open to the public). This was the home of the last of New Hampshire's Royal Governors, driven into exile in 1775. **John Wentworth** was amiable and able. Among his accomplishments was bringing **Dartmouth College** to New Hampshire. But he lived in troubled times, and it was his duty to enforce the hated taxes and trade regulations. **He aroused popular ire when he dissolved the Colony's Assembly after it had voted for a Committee of Correspondence to collaborate with those in other Colonies in opposing the British tax acts.** The rage against him boiled over when the Patriots learned that he had secretly arranged for Portsmouth carpenters to go to Boston to build barracks for the British troops stationed there after the Boston Tea Party. Still preserved in the interior of this house are the marks of mob violence. As the crowd was battering the front door, the Governor and his family fled out of the back door, boarded a boat in the Mill Pond and rowed to New Castle (see page 218) for protection.

John Wentworth was the last of three Wentworth Crown-appointed Governors, all natives of New Hampshire, which was unusual since Crown-appointed Governors were apt to be natives of England. His predecessor was his uncle, **Benning Wentworth, the first Royal Governor appointed after New Hampshire was made a Crown Colony by edict of George II in 1741**. Benning was one of the 16 children of **Lieutenant-Governor John Wentworth** (the grandfather of the above mentioned John), who served as New Hampshire's head from 1717 to 1730, when the Colony was still under the nominal rule of the Massachusetts Governor. It should be noted that although most of the large, powerful Wentworth clan were Royalists, a notable exception sailing against the family stream, was **Hunking Wentworth**, brother of Benning and uncle of Governor John, **an ardent Patriot, who at age 78 was chosen to head Portsmouth's Committee of Safety, the rebel government.**

Portsmouth's Royalists were apt to attend the Church of England services in the **Queen's Chapel,** which burned down and was replaced in 1808 on the same site, at the corner of Chapel and Bow Streets, by **St. John's Episcopalian Church**. St John's has some of the original furnishings and equipment of the Queen's Chapel, including the Bibles, silver altar vessels, and mahogany chairs, which were gifts of Queen Caroline, wife of George II, after whom the Chapel was named. **In its belfry rings a bell which was part of the spoils of war brought home in 1745** by the New Hampshire troops from the **amazing Louisburg Campaign** (of which we write more on page 221). If you go to St. John's from Market Square by walking along Market and then Bow Street, you can enjoy on the way the charming scenes of 19th century warehouses overlooking the River. They were once crowded with rum and molasses and spice, but are now recycled to a host of stores specializing in local crafts and foreign imports. Some of the best restaurants in the State are located in the little dockside cobbled lanes which lead off Bow. At No. 125 is the home of the **Theatre by the Sea**, Portsmouth's excellent repertory theatre.

Walking on Bow St., you will see, on the right, St. John's rising on its hill. At eye level from the street, under the churchyard cemetery, you will see carved in stone the name Wentworth. **Benning Wentworth, his father John, and others of Colonial Portsmouth's high and mighty are buried here.**

If you walk along Chapel St. from St. John's to Daniel St., and turn left, you will come to another of Portsmouth's major show pieces, the MacPheadris-Warner House, open seasonally to the public, fee. We quote the description in Thomas Bailey

St. John's
as seen from
Bow St.

Aldrich's *OLD TOWN BY THE SEA.* "It was built in 1718 by **Captain Archibald MacPheadris, a Scotch man, a wealthy merchant and member of the King's Council.** He was the chief projector of one of the earliest iron-works established in America. Captain MacPheadris married **Sarah Wentworth, one of the sixteen children of (Lieutenant) Governor John Wentworth,** and died leaving a daughter **Mary (later Mary Warren),** whose portrait with that of her mother, painted by Copley, still hangs in the parlor of his house. The interior is rich in paneling and wood carvings .... The halls are wide with handsome staircases. The principal rooms ... have large open chimney places adorned with the quaintest of Dutch tiles. In one of the parlors is a choice store of family relics -- china, silver, costumes, old clocks, and the like. At the head of the staircase are pictures of two Indians life size -- probably portraits of chiefs with whom Captain MacPheadris had dealings, for the captain was engaged in the fur as well as the iron business." **Uncovered accidentally by workmen in the 1860's were about 500 square feet of the walls with "sketches in color, landscapes, views of unknown cities, Biblical scenes, and modern figures among which was a lady at a spinning wheel."** Aldrich goes on to say that the painter of these pictures is a mystery. However, fans of Kenneth Roberts, who read his *NORTHWEST PASSAGE,* will encounter these pictures again as the work of Roberts' fictional hero, Langdon Towne. Mystery solved! Swinging back to reality, in 1762, a lightning rod was installed, the first in all New Hampshire. It is said that Ben Franklin himself came to see that the job was done properly.

If you continue along Daniel St. from the MacPheadris-Warner House and turn right to pass under the bridge, then going past the waterside Pier II Restaurant, and the lobster pounds near it, you arrive at the beautiful **Prescott Park** on the River. **You can also get to the Park more directly from Market Square by going along State St.**, which is one block away from Market Square, to Marcy St., once called Water St., which borders on the Park. The Park has trees, gardens, benches, walkways, sculpture, and rest rooms. In the Park, **Sheafes Warehouse**, built in 1705, is now a nautical museum open in the warm season, free. Concerts, performances of the Theatre by the Sea, art festivals, and boat cruises are part of the summer happenings. At the eastern edge of the Park is the **Point of Graves Cemetery**, Portsmouth's oldest, dating back to 1671 with stones bearing good examples of skull and crossbones art.

Across Marcy St. from Prescott Park is a major attraction, the **Strawberry Bank Historic Neighborhood**, 10 acres bounded by Court, Marcy, Hancock, and Washington Streets, **with gardens, 35 historic buildings, 85 exhibit rooms, 5 furnished period houses, archaeological excavations in progress, craft shops, gift shops, and a coffee shop.** In the houses, which range from the 17th to the 19th century, some on their original sites, others transported to the area, **craftspersons**

rent workspace and sell products of their own design made with tools, materials, and techniques of Colonial days. You can watch cabinet making, boat building, blacksmithing, leatherworking, spinning, weaving, potmaking, and much more. There are special exhibits on restorations in progress, Portsmouth history, early furniture, archaeological tools, etc. There is an art gallery run by the New Hampshire Art Association. There are hosts of educational programs and activities, including fife and drum parades, plays, dances, and concerts. In short, a very rich smorgasbord. And the houses all have their stories. **Prudence Penhallow's "Penny Shop"** in the Deacon Penhallow House was once patronized by **John Paul Jones;** at 386 Court St. is the **Nutter House** built by **Thomas Bailey Aldrich's grandfather**, and the setting for his STORY OF A BAD BOY; being restored is **John Stavers' tavern**, first called the 𝕰𝖆𝖗𝖑 𝖔𝖋 𝕳𝖆𝖑𝖎𝖋𝖆𝖝 when it was a hangout for Tories, but later renamed 𝖂𝖎𝖑𝖑𝖎𝖆𝖒 𝕻𝖎𝖙𝖙 to avoid the wrath of Patriots. And so on. Strawbery Banke is open from May through October. **Call (603) 436-8010** for information on hours, fees, and special events.

South of Strawbery Banke on Marcy and Hunking Streets, is the **Old South Meeting House**, now a Children's Museum. From its grounds, Reverend Haven dug manure to manufacture saltpetre for the Continental Army. See page 210.

Strawbery Banke is aptly named, for it is located on what were the very berry strewn meadows that so refreshed the first colonists. The RAMBLER tells us that the Great House, built in 1631 by the first settlers, who were financed by John Mason, New Hampshire's original proprietor, stood at what is now the corner of Marcy and Court Streets at the northeastern edge of the present day Strawbery Banke Preservation Project. **Strawbery Banke, which is run by a non-profit guild, was Portsmouth's answer to the threat of urban renewal of the 1960's**. Another growing problem, although seemingly more benign, is the covetousness of various "Colonial Villages" and the antiquarian departments of museums around the country. Thus the **parsonage of Reverend Samuel Langdon** (see page 209) was transported to Sturbridge Village, and the magnificent **Wentworth-Gardner House** was acquired by New York's Metropolitan Museum of Art with the goal of re-erecting it in Central Park! But the latter, however, was recovered, and still stands, elegant and debonair, on its original site, east of Prescott Park on Mechanic Street, in the midst of busy fishmarkets and wharves piled high with lobster traps. The scene is utterly charming, but the

Wentworth-Gardner
House On Mechanic St.

mansion, built in 1760 for Thomas Wentworth, brother of Governor John, looks beleaguered. Open May to October, fee.

Another of the grand mansions signifying Portsmouth's Colonial splendor is the **Moffat-Ladd House** on Market St., built in 1763, by Captain John Moffat. You pass it on the left as you walk from Market Square toward the cruise boat docks. Behind it are lovely Colonial gardens. Captain Moffat's son-in-law, **William Whipple, a signer of the Declaration of Independence,** lived here after his marrriage to Catherine Moffat and until his death in 1785. In addition to serving in the Continental Congress, **Whipple was commander of the First New Hampshire Brigade in the Battles of Bennington and Saratoga,** and was the chief negotiator for the Americans of the terms of Burgoyne's surrender at Saratoga. Before the War, Whipple had been the master of ships bearing, as the RAMBLER puts it, "that dark living freight, (the) blemish (of which) has not been obliterated by the fame which shines round his name." Whipple, however, tried to redeem himself by freeing his own slaves on the eve of the battles against Burgoyne so that they would have some liberty to fight for, which they did quite ably. The House is open from May to October, fee.

At the corner of Congress and Middle is the **Public Library,** and a block away at the intersection of Middle and State is the **John Paul Jones House,** built in 1758 by a Captain Purcell, whose widow took in boarders, the most famous of whom was **John Paul Jones.** The Scotsman lived here for only two years while impatiently supervising the finishing touches on his ship-to-be the RANGER then being built in the Portsmouth shipyards. The House is now the headquarters of the **Historical Society** and is run as a museum with early furniture, portraits, porcelain, and silver, and documents significant in early Portsmouth history, including an original of the famous recruiting poster signed by John Hancock as President of the Continental Congress inviting "gentlemen" to come to Portsmouth to enlist as members of the RANGER's crew. On November 1, 1777, the RANGER, bearing the newly designed American flag, sailed out of Portsmouth Harbor. **Call (603) 436-8420.** Open from May to October. Fee.

In Market Square, a few steps from the bus stop, is the **Athenaeum** (see title page), a private subscription library organized in 1817, housing rare imprints of the Colonial period. It is open to the public only on Thursday afternoons, 1-5, and is well worth a visit if you are there at the right time. The front room overflows with memorabilia including paintings, maps, ship models, documents, photos, and there is a 25 minute recording explaining the significance of various items. Free.

We have barely tapped into Portsmouth's gold, but enough has been said to get you peering at the house plaques. Almost any walk that you can devise in the vicinity of Market Square is apt to be a necklace of gems.

Benning Wentworth House
in Little Harbor

LONGER WALKS

The following walks were suggested by Thomas Bailey Aldrich and the *Rambler*. Of course, TBA and R didn't have to contend with today's auto traffic. Nevertheless, despite having to walk facing traffic in places, I enjoyed them all, and hope you do, too.

Walk No. 1. To the Benning Wentworth House (alias the Wentworth-Coolidge House) in Little Harbor. Now let's go to Benning Wentworth's House in Little Harbor, his residence and meeting place of his Council during his long tenure as Governor of the Colony. It is a mostly pleasant walk of about 2 and 1/2 miles from Market Square. I suggest that you first cross the South Mill Pond on Junkins (see map on page 208) and turn right onto South St., and then left onto Sagamore and then left again onto Little Harbor Rd., where after about 3/4 miles you will see signs directing you to the grounds, which will be on the left side of the road. An alternative to walking along the sidewalk on Sagamore, which is near car traffic, is to walk to Little Harbor Road through the greenery of the lovely cemetery which parallels Sagamore Road. The cemetery overlooks an inlet of the tortuous Piscataqua.

On Little Harbor Road, you are out of the compact part of Portsmouth in an area of great estates and religious retreats. **Bordering the road are pine groves, a very appropriate theme for our walk, because the Wentworth fortunes were based on the great white pines that once covered New Hampshire, part of the Great Belt of Pines from Nova Scotia to New Jersey.** The tall trees that you pass on the way to Little Harbor are mere striplings compared to the majestic evergreens that once grew here, many of which had lower branches 100 feet from the ground and measured over 7 feet at the base. With masts from these Titans powering the ships of the Royal Navy, Britain enjoyed an advantage over her European rivals, and was willing to pay top prices to secure the supply. The efforts made to bring the giants to the sea were legendary. They were usually cut in times of deep snow, with smaller trees and shrubs arranged to cushion the fall. And then according to one contemporary description: "When the trees are fallen, they yoke seventy or eighty pair of oxen and drag them along the snow, and when they have once effected this, they never stop on any account whatever till they arrive at the water's side." (Taken from L. H. Gipson's *THE BRITISH EMPIRE BEFORE THE REVOLUTION, VOLUME III.*)

By the early part of the 18th century, the pine forests near the Piscataqua were nearly exhausted, and New Hampshire business interests were losing lucrative mast contracts to Maine. The Wentworths and their colleagues hit upon a long range solution to the problem. Through their agents at the British Court, they succeeded in enlarging New Hampshire's territory westward to and beyond the upper Connecticut Valley at the expense of Massachusetts. **They also managed to get New Hampshire declared a separate Royal Colony with its own Governor**, namely Benning Wentworth. As Governor, Benning was a skilled steward of New Hampshire's lumber interests, and his own family's. **By extensive land grants, he encouraged the settlement of over 200 new towns in western New Hampshire and Vermont**, where foresters kept the supply of lumber moving to fill New Hampshire contracts. Benning also enriched himself directly by retaining 500 acres of each town grant.

But the picture we get from historians of Benning Wentworth as a shrewd businessman and power broker **is not nearly as famous as his portrayal in Longfellow's poem *LADY WENTWORTH*** as a lonely, elderly, eccentric widower, who startled all of Portsmouth by marrying his pretty, young housekeeper, Martha Hilton, in a surprise ceremony at a dinner party including the Reverend Arthur Brown of Queen's Chapel. The Reverend and other guests were all unaware of what was about to occur. As Longfellow tells it, when the guests were assembled over the dinner table, Martha glided into the room, exquisitely dressed, and the Governor, rising from his seat,

> Played with his ruffles, then looked down,
> And said unto the Reverend Brown
> "This is my birthday; it shall likewise be
> My wedding day; and you shall marry me!"

"To whom, Your Excellency?" asked the Reverend. "To this lady," replied the Governor taking Martha Hilton by the hand. "As the chief magistrate of New Hampshire, I command you to marry me!" It was a delicious triumph for Martha, whom we first meet in the poem as a scantily clad ragamuffin being chided by Dame Stavers, who ran the 𝕰𝖆𝖗𝖑 𝖔𝖋 𝕳𝖆𝖑𝖎𝖋𝖆𝖝 𝕴𝖓𝖓 (see page 213) with her husband John.

Longfellow also gives a description of Benning's house in Little Harbor

> It was a pleasant mansion, an abode
> Near and yet hidden from the great high-road
> Sequestered among trees, a noble pile
> Baronial and Colonial in its style.
> Within unwonted splendors met the eye
> Panels and floors of oak, and tapestry,
> Carved chimney pieces, where on brazen dogs,
> Reveled and roared the Christmas logs;
> Doors opening into the darkness unawares
> Mysterious passages and flights of stairs
> And on the walls in heavy gilded frames
> The ancestral Wentworths with Old-Scripture names.

The grounds overlooking the water are very lovely, just right for a picnic after your walk. And you can see across to **New Castle,** the destination of our next walk, where the now (1995) unoccupied **Wentworth-by-the-Sea** dominates the landscape. How you wish the Park Service would provide row boats so that you could row yourself over to explore New Castle. But the Park Service hasn't dreamt of such an idea yet.

Marry me to this lady!

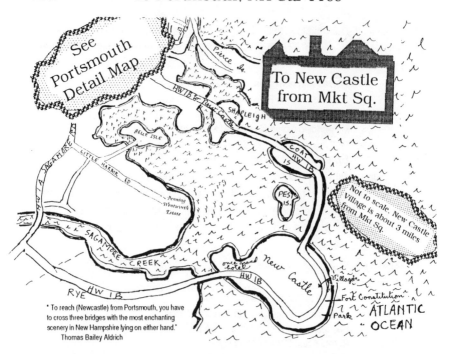

To New Castle
from Mkt Sq.

* To reach (Newcastle) from Portsmouth, you have
to cross three bridges with the most enchanting
scenery in New Hampshire lying on either hand."
Thomas Bailey Aldrich

**Walk No. 2 To New Castle. From Prescott Park, the River vista is a charming one
of numerous islets linked by bridges and causeways.** Getting from here to there
among them is a game that you can't lose. Even if you don't get "there," you are apt to
get to some place that also has its pleasures. My favorite "there" among the islets is to
New Castle, an old town, once part of Portsmouth, about three miles from Market
Square. New Castle is one of New England's marvels, reminiscent of Marblehead
(see Chapter 3, *A NORTH SHORE SAMPLER*) because its main street is lined with 18th
century houses, with hardly any later interspersals, another Colonial village, a real
one, and not a reconstruction, just as it was THEN.

A pleasant way to go to New Castle is to go from Market Square to Prescott
Park, walk through the Park, and then take a loop onto the picturesque Mechanic
Street with its lobster docks and fish markets, past the Wentworth-Gardner House (see
page 213) and then back to Marcy and then to the left along New Castle Ave.
(Highway 1b), and now you are on your way. **There are three bridges to New Castle,
and the scenery is delightful on all of them:** water and islets on both sides of you,
lobster persons tending their traps beneath you, and fisherpersons trying their luck
beside you. The first two bridges have narrow sidewalks for gazing, but the third, a
causeway built upon the rocks, has no shoulder, unfortunately, for pedestrians.
Fortunately, the traffic is relatively scarce, and there are some joggers to slow it down.

When you cross the third bridge into New Castle limits. you may be disappointed at first because the neighborhood you have entered, while attractive, looks like innumerable others, with new homes everywhere. But don't give up. Keep walking along the main road, and after you turn the bend by the school house, you will see it, the **Old Town,** with simple Colonial houses densely set, facing each other on both sides of the unwidened street. And one block away, on the waterside street, are more ancient houses, each with its backyard reaching to the sea. There is a General Store on the main street where you can purchase juices and other refreshment.

If you continue along the main road (Highway 1b) past the center of the Old Town, you come to a sign directing you to the left to the site of **Fort Constitution**, known as **Fort William and Mary** in Colonial days, one of the guardians of the entrance to Portsmouth Harbor. This is the fort to which Governor John Wentworth and his family fled (see pp. 210, 211). **This fort was also the scene of what is generally regarded as New Hampshire's climax moment in the pre-Revolutionary ferment.** On December 14, 1774, when Boston was beleaguered and suffering from the yoke of the Intolerable Acts, inflicted in retaliation for the Tea Party, **Paul Revere** rode into Portsmouth with a message for its Committee of Safety from the Committee in Boston to the effect that the´British were about to send additional troops to buttress the garrison at Fort William and Mary, and that no more gunpowder was to be exported from England to America. Adding the two pieces of news together, Portsmouth Patriots decided that if they were to get any gunpowder they had better do so quickly. **The very next day on December 15, 1774, 400 Patriots from Portsmouth and New Castle,** under the leadership of John Sullivan (later General) and John Langdon (see pp. 209, 210), **sailed to the Fort in gundalows and laid siege to it.** The Fort's commander realizing that he was outnumbered, fired a single shot above the crowd and surrendered. The gunpowder, munitions, and cannons captured here were stored in Durham and Exeter, **and later were taken to Bunker Hill.** (My source is Ralph May's *EARLY PORTSMOUTH HISTORY.* In case you are wondering, a gundalow is a flatbottomed sailing boat with pivoting mast for scooting under bridges. You will find examples in Strawbery Banke.)

Returning to the main road (Highway 1b) and continuing, in about 1/4 mile you will see on the left the entrance to **New Castle Common**, a lovely park, with a beach, ball fields, tennis courts, rest rooms (open seasonally), and beautiful ocean views. This is our first peek at the ocean. In Portsmouth, you are about two miles from the ocean, three as the River wiggles. The many islands block the view to the sea when you are in the town's center.

About a mile further, on the main road, about 4 miles from Market Square, you come to the once magnificent, turn of the century, **Wentworth by the Sea Hotel**. Not so long ago, this hotel, a gleaming colossus, offered its guests exquisite service and many sea side pleasures, boats, swimming, golf, tennis, luxurious halls, and dining rooms. It was **President Theodore Roosevelt's** choice for the formal signing of the **Treaty of Portsmouth in 1905**, which ended the Russo-Japanese War. Several Presidents were guests. From here you can retrace your steps back to Portsmouth, or you can continue on Highway 1b and go back to Market Square via Sagamore Rd. (See maps on pp. 218 and 208.)

Walk No. 3. To Lady Pepperell's House in Kittery. There are several bridges to Kittery, Maine across the River from Portsmouth. Most are not intended for pedestrians. But the drawbridge beside the Pier II Restaurant has a sidewalk, and you can cross to Kittery, Maine. The bridge takes you across Badger Island, where the *RANGER* was built. On the bridge you get lovely views of the Piscataqua shores, and a closer look at the Navy shipyards, which are really on the Kittery side of the River. On the opposite side, after turning right at the first light onto Government Street, you enter a cosy, pleasant shoreside neighborhood. There is not as much traffic on this street as there is on Walker street, which runs parallel to it, and leads into the Navy yard. You turn to the left as the street turns and cross Walker onto Wentworth, then Whipple (HW 103) and finally you are led to the bridge to **Kittery Point**. Crossing Spruce Creek on the bridge, and continuing on Pepperell Road, after a bend in the road you will find it, the **Lady Pepperell House**, on the right side of the road, near a peaceful, ancient shoreside cemetery, with the graves of the families of some of Portsmouth's early settlers and great shipbuilders of the nineteenth century.

Lady Pepperell House

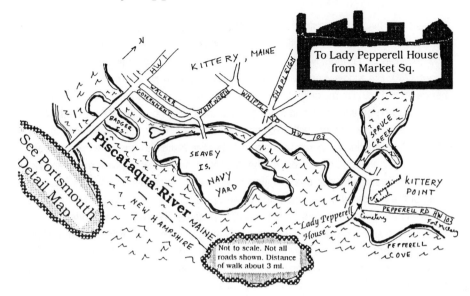

The House was the home of the widow of Sir William Pepperell, who led the New England land forces in 1745 against the French fortress at Louisburg on Cape Breton, Nova Scotia. The campaign was organized by Governor William Shirley with the consent of the Massachusetts General Court. The cause was a popular one in all of coastal New England because French warships and privateers, under protection of the fortress, constantly threatened the fishing and merchant fleets. But despite the cause's popularity, many doubted whether the goal could be achieved. "Fortified towns are hard nuts to crack and your teeth are not used to them" wrote Ben Franklin to his brother in Boston, whence the expedition set sail amid much fanfare and the blessing of the celebrated evangelist, the Reverend George Whitefield: "Despair not with Christ as Leader." It is said that prodigious quantities of rum as well as wind and prayer propelled the Great Adventure.

To the astonishment of the doubters, the New Englanders triumphed! The New World Gibraltar crumbled. The victory is now perceived as a critical turning point in Colonial consciousness, which hastened the Revolution, as it dawned upon Americans that they could be a match for much vaunted European power.

Also remarkable is that William Pepperell (1696-1759), Colonial Kittery's wealthiest landowner, shipowner, and merchant, had had little military experience prior to the campaign. But he was a man of shrewd common sense, and a natural leader, well liked by the many with whom he had business dealings. His appointment to head the land forces attracted many Maine and New Hampshire volunteers. He used part of his fortune to help finance the campaign. For the victory, he was knighted and received in London with great acclaim. The Lady Pepperell House was built about 1760. His widow, **Lady Mary Hirst Pepperell**, lived here from about 1765 until her death in 1789. On my only trip to the House it was closed. But my companion and I enjoyed sitting on the porch and looking out at the Cove, now called **Pepperell Cove**, and once a busy harbor, with wharves, warehouses, and rum distilleries. In the nearby Congregational Church built about 1729, Sir William's box pew is preserved. A lane near the church, leads to the former home of **Sir William's son-in-law, Nathaniel Sparhawk**, also one of Kittery's wealthiest merchants and sea traders. But most of the Pepperell estate, including extensive landholdings along the Maine coast up to Scarborough, was confiscated in 1778, because his heirs were Tories. If you continue along the shore road, in about 1/2 mile, you come to **Fort McClary State Memorial Park,** where you can climb up on hills and battlements to enjoy beautiful views. I estimate that you are now about 31/2 miles from Market Square. The Park has picnic tables, rest rooms, and the remnants of a series of old forts that guarded Kittery and Portsmouth, including a well preserved Blockhouse built in 1844.

OTHER PORTSMOUTH ATTRACTIONS

The twisting Piscataqua and its islets provide Portsmouth with a long waterfront. Visitors have the choice of many seaside restaurants and intriguing cruises. **Portsmouth Harbor Cruises, call (603) 436-8084,** offers from its dock on Ceres St. trips along the River as well as ocean voyages to the **Isles of Shoals**, about 9 miles from the mouth of the River, celebrated by nineteenth century poet Celia Thaxter, whose summer cottage was on Appledore. Now the Isles host a base for marine research and summer retreats of churches and organizations.

Food is fabulous in Portsmouth. There is excellent food to be had in all price ranges from take-out counters to candlelight, white cloth service restaurants, in and near Market Square. On my last trip to Portsmouth (winter, 1995), after getting off the Greyhound bus from Portland, I had an excellent lunch at the **Cafe Brioche** in the Square, at the corner of Daniel and Pleasant. At this popular place, you order soups,

Congregational Church
in Pepperell Cove
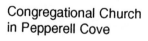

sandwiches, salads, coffees, breads, and pastries at a counter, and try to find an unoccupied table. The food is exquisite. The cheese Danish pastry that I got here was the best I ever had. Later, in the evening, my companion and I chose the **Stockpot**, a restaurant on Bow St. with a rear picture window overlooking the River. I ordered a sea food paella, moderately priced, which turned out to be superb. These are just two of an extraordinary number of fine eateries near Market Sq. It was in the off season, but most seemed to be busy. Portsmouthers apparently know that they have a very good thing. In the warm months, many tables are brought outdoors so diners can enjoy views to match the food. Shops near the Square offer goods of great variety featuring the crafts of area artists as well as foreign imports. All in all, Portsmouth is a fine place to be cast adrift in.

LOCAL PUBLIC TRANSPORTATION

Portsmouth has, in addition to taxi service, bus service to several nearby towns in Stafford and Rockingham counties, to Durham, Exeter, and others. The service to Durham, home of the **University of New Hampshire,** is almost hourly during school sessions. For information call **COAST,   (603) 862-2328,** the non-profit organization which coordinates the services of several carriers. On my latest visit (winter, 1995), I got a COAST schedule at the **Federal Tobacco Store,** which is on Hanover St., one short block from the Greyhound Bus stop in Market Sq. In summer, the **Coach Co. , (603) 474-5941,** runs the **Sea Coast Trolley** to lively **Hampton Beach** at a bargain one way fare of $1.50.

a 19ᵗʰ century view of
Portsmouth Harbor

Remarks on Restrooms (Toilets). Where Are They? In general, you can find them in public buildings of all kinds -- city and town halls, public libraries, park visitor centers, chamber of commerce information centers, in the larger museums, and so on. Food Courts of shopping malls have public rest rooms. There are also rest rooms in most restaurants, pubs, and hotel lobbies. You may feel uncomfortable about using these if you are not a patron. My advice is just go in and use them if you know where they are, and inquire politely if you don't. Now to apply these generalities to specific places we've visited. On the Freedom Trail, there are rest rooms in the Information Center on the Tremont St. side of the Boston Common between the Boylston and Park St. T stations, and in the State House on Beacon St., at the National Park Visitor Center on State St., in the Quincy Market, at the Visitor Center of the Constitution Historic Park, and at the Bunker Hill Monument Visitor Center. Not on the Trail, but near it, City Hall has, of course, rest rooms. It is important to realize that you shouldn't expect to find public rest rooms in certain ancient houses -- like the Paul Revere House or the Old South Meeting House -- not easily equipped with sturdy modern plumbing. There are no rest rooms on T buses, and except for South, North, and Back Bay Stations (see page 6), none at the downtown T stops. Not all commuter train stops have stations with rest rooms. The Lowell Station does have rest rooms. However, at Concord when you get off the train, you will have to rely on the restaurants or the Public Library, or the North Bridge Visitor Center. In Lexington, Buckman's Tavern does have rest rooms. When you get off the Red Line train at Kendall Sq./MIT, the food court adjoining the Tech Coop does have rest rooms. In Harvard Square, the Coop has rest rooms, as do several of the College buildings, like the Science Building (see page 64). In Beacon Hill, the nearby state buildings, State House, Courts, etc. make convenient rest stops. In Back Bay, the Boston Public Library is a fine stop on many counts. In Providence, the City Hall rest rooms are convenient to the Kennedy Plaza RIPTA buses. The Union Train Station, the State House, the Roger William Spring Visitor Center, the RISD Art Museum, and many Brown U. buildings open to the public all have rest rooms. In Newport, as already mentioned, the bus station at the Gateway Center has rest rooms. I haven't mentioned it, but the Court House in the park in Washington Sq. also has rest rooms. The URI Student Union is a convenient rest stop when changing buses there.

Vegetarian Food. I am pleased to say that, if your vegetarian diet includes eggs and milk products, you will have no trouble finding good food at the places listed in the various food sections. Look under Food in the Index for page numbers.

BIBLIOGRAPHY

Aldrich, Thomas Bailey, *An Old Town by the Sea*, Houghton Mifflin, Boston and NY, 1917

Arnold, Samuel G., *History of the State of Rhode Island and the Providence Plantations*, 2 v., available only in reprint, Reprint Co., 1970

Augur, Helen, *An American Jezebel: the Life of Anne Hutchinson,* Brentano's, NY, 1930

Baldwin, Alice, *The New England Clergy and the American Revolution*, Duke University Press, 1928

Bahne, Charles, *The Complete Guide to Boston's Freedom Trail*, New Towne Press, 1993

Battis, Emery John, *Saints and Sectaries: Anne Hutchinson and the Antinomian Controversy in the Massachusetts Bay Colony,* U. of North Carolina Press, 1962

Brewster, Charles W., *Rambles about Portsmouth*, 2 v., Portsmouth, NH, C. W. Brewster, 1869-1873

Car-Free In Boston, Association for Public Transportation, 1996

Clayton, Barbara, and Whitley, Kathleen, *Historic Coastal New England*, Globe Pequot, Chester, CT 1992

Dublin, Thomas, *Lowell, An Industrial City*, National Park Service, 1992

Fisher, Alan, *Country Walks Near Boston within reach by Public Transportation,* Appalachian Mountain Club, 1976

Faison, S. Lane, *The Art Museums of New England,* 3 v., David R. Godine, Boston, 1982

Foner, Eric, *Reconstruction Era : America's Unfinished Revolution, 1863-1877, Harper and Row, NY, 1988*

Franklin, Benjamin, *Autobiography of Benjamin Franklin*, Dover Thrift Imprints

Gipson, L. H., *The British Empire Before the American Revolution*, 6 v., Caxton Ltd. , 1936-54, revised edition in 2 v. , Knopf, NY, 1958-59

Harris, John, *The Boston Globe Historic Walks in Boston*, Globe Pequot, Chester, CT,1982

Hogarth, Paul, *Walking Tours of Old Boston*, Brandywine, NY, 1978

Kales, Emily and David, *All About the Boston Harbor Islands*, Hewitts Cove Publishing, Hingham, 1993

Kay, Jane Holtz, *Lost Boston*, Houghton Mifflin, Boston and NY,1980

Larcom, Lucy, *A New England Girlhood*, Houghton Mifflin, Boston and NY, 1889

Levin, Phyllis Lee, *Abigail Adams, A Biography*, Ballantine Books, NY, 1987

Longfellow, Henry W., *Collected Poetical Works*, Houghton Mifflin, Boston and NY, 1911

Massachusetts Bicentennial Commission, *Commemorative Guide to Massachusetts* (collection of illustrated essays), 1975

McDonald, Forrest, *Alexander Hamilton, A Biography*. Norton, NY, 1979

McLoughlin, William G., *Rhode Island, A History*, W.W. Norton, NY, 1986

Morison, Samuel Eliot, *Maritime History of Massachusetts*, Northeastern University, Boston, 1980 (reprint of 1961 ed.)

Murfin, James V. and others, *Guide to the Historic Places of the American Revolution*, National Park Service, 1974

Peabody, James B., *John Adams, A Biography In His Own Words*, 2 v., Newsweek, NY, 1973

Poppelius, John, and others, *What Style is It?*, Preservation Press of National Trust for Historic Preservation

Rabson, Carolyn, Editor, *Songbook of the American Revolution*, NEO Press, Peaks Island, ME, 1974

Russel, Howard S., *Indian New England before the Mayflower*, Univ. Press of NE, Hanover, NH, 1980

Shepherd, Jack, *The Adams Chronicles: Four Generations of Greatness*, Little Brown, Boston, 1975

Sherr, Lynn, and Kazickas, Jurate, *Susan B. Anthony Slept Here, A Guide to American Women's Landmarks,* Times Books, Random House, 1994

Southworth, Susan and Michael, *AIA Guide to Boston*, 2nd ed., Globe Pequot, Old Saybrook, CT, 1992

Steinberg, Sheila, and McGuigan, Cathleen, *Rhode Island, An Historical Guide*, RI Bicentennial Foundation, Providence,1976

Webber, C.H., and Nevins, W. S., *Old Naumkeag*, A.A. Smith, Boston, 1817

Whitehill, Walter M. and Kotker, Norman, *Massachusetts, A Pictorial History*, Charles Scribner and Sons, NY 1976

Willison, George, *The Pilgrim Reader* (the Pilgrim story in their own words with Willison's notes), Doubleday, Garden City, NY, 1953

Zaitzevsky, Cynthia, *Frederick Law Olmsted and the Boston Park System,* Belknap Press, Cambridge, MA., 1982

The Meaning of Terms

Colonial. This word is used to describe buildings and institutions in this country before the American Revolution. Thus colonial government refers to the government of the American Colonies before 1775. This could vary in detail depending on the Royal Charter of a Colony. See pages 3, 17, 18, 146, 147, 158, 169 for some details of the Massachusetts Bay and Rhode Island Royal Charters and their differences. In architecture, the word Colonial embraces a wide range of styles. The simple Adams Birthplace clapboard houses (pages 100-101), the Paul Revere House in Boston's North End (page 27), the rambling House of Seven Gables in Salem (page 124), and the elegant "King" Hooper Mansion in Marblehead (page 114) all qualify as Colonial houses by this definition. One feature they share is that they are all made of wood, widely available in New England. In fact, the walls of the Hooper Mansion, which aspires to look like a Georgian English manor house, are sheathed in wooden shingles carved to look like stone blocks. **Patriots.** This term is widely used to describe American Colonists who, before the Revolution, were against certain acts of the British Parliament, and who supported, in varying degrees among the 13 Colonies, more power for Colonial popularly elected legislatures and fewer restrictions from the Crown. New Englanders were early in wanting to go all the way, namely, that Colonial legislatures should be supreme. The **Sons of Liberty** were a group organized first by Samuel Adams in Boston, and later throughout the Colonies, which regularly planned demonstrations against British regulation of Colonial trade, the most famous of which was the Boston Tea Party. **Loyalists or Tories** were citizens supportive of the authority of Parliament and the Crown. Many were members of the British administration.

The House of Seven Gables

Index

(continued from page 108)

"Charlie handed in his dime at Kendall Square Station
He changed for Jamaica Plain;
 When he got there the conductor told him one more nickel
Charlie could not get off the train.

 Now all night long Charlie rides through the station
Crying what will become of me? ......

 Charlie's wife goes down to Scollay Square Station
Every day at a quarter past two
 And through the open window she hands Charlie a sandwich
As the train comes rumbling through."

The chorus goes
          "Well, did he ever return?/ No he never returned
          And his fate is still unlearned.
          He may ride forever 'neath the streets of Boston
          He's the man who never returned."

Many changes have taken place on the Boston landscape since the song was written. Scollay Square, famous for its night clubs, bars, and strip tease shows, has metamorphosed into Government Center, with City Hall Plaza and the JFK Federal Building near the T exit. And the MTA (Metropolitan Transit Authority) has become the grander MBTA (Massachusetts Bay Transit Authority). Color coding of the lines was introduced since Charlie's ill fated ride. The Jamaica Plain line is now the E Green Line, and you don't have to pay a fare when you get off at a surface stop along Huntington Ave., as when you go to the Museum of Fine Arts.

Greater Boston Convention and Visitors Bureau, (617) 536-4100 or (800) 888-5515. Street address on page 4. Web address, http://www.dvm.com/users/dvm/boston

MBTA (Massachusetts Bay Transit Authority), (617) 722-3200 or (617) 222-3200 or (800) 392-6100 or for hearing impaired (TDD) 722-5146. Web address, http://www.mbta.com

Boston By Phone, (800) 374-7400. A web address for **Boston events** is http://www.boston.com For arts events the address is http://www.boston.com/home.htm

Boston Public Library, (617) 536-5400. Web address, http://www.bpl.org

Museum of Fine Arts, (617) 267-9300. Web address, http://www.mfa.org It can also be reached by clicking on *museums* after reaching the above **Boston events** address.

Harvard University, general information (617) 495-1000; **Cultural and Natural History Museum**, (617) 495-3045; **Art Museum,** (617) 495-9400. Harvard University web address, http://www.harvard.edu

MIT Arts Events, (617) 253-ARTS. Web address http://web.mit.edu

Rhode Island Department of Economic Development, (800) 556-2484. Web address, http://www.visitrhodeisland.com

RIPTA (Rhode Island Public Transit Authority), (401) 781-9400 or (800) 662-5088, or for the hearing impaired (TDD) 461-9400

Dear Readers,
        Your comments, suggestions, car free tips, etc. will always be appreciated. Please send letters to NEO Press, Box 32, Peaks Island, ME 04108.
        Sincerely,